POSTSECULARISM

The Hidden Challenge
to Extremism

Mike King

James Clarke & Co.

James Clarke & Co
P.O. Box 60
Cambridge
CB1 2NT

www.jamesclarke.co.uk
publishing@jamesclarke.co.uk

First Published in 2009

ISBN: 978 0 227 17247 6

British Library Cataloguing in Publication Data
A catalogue record is available from the British Library

Contents

For Osho, 1931-1990

Introduction

In the introduction to the *The Second Plane*, which he wrote after 9/11, Martin Amis asks:

> What has extremism ever done for *anyone*? Where are its gifts to humanity? Where are its works?[1]

This is a brief but powerful indictment of extreme religion. But Amis, and others who have recently been labelled as the 'new atheists' or 'militant atheists', appear to pursue an extremism of their own. The language is belligerent; for example, in the same introduction he says: 'The more general enemy, of course, is extremism.' It is perhaps only a literary flourish to describe an ideology such as religious extremism as an *enemy*, but it is put forward in a context where religious extremists are bombed, imprisoned and tortured. Amis prefaces these remarks with the more chilling: 'It is a mind with which we share no discourse.' The mind he identifies is the mind of the religious extremist, and for some individuals on the extreme of religion there may be no discourse because they are beyond reason. But to identify a 'mind' with which there cannot be any discourse is in itself an extremism, because all 'minds' – understood as a cultural grouping – can enter into a conversation, if there is sufficient good will. The concept of 'postsecularism' pursued in this book is such a conversation. It does not accept that reason must rule out religion.

This book begins with the observation that the 'mutual ignorance pact' between secular culture and faith tradition has broken down – particularly after 9/11 – and asks the question: can the term 'postsecularism' be given to the resulting phenomenon of a renewed openness to questions of the spirit? To what extent was such a renewed openness gathering momentum prior to 9/11? Furthermore: what might be the nature of an emerging postsecular sensibility that distinguishes itself from old religion, secularism, and the New Age, as a fourth way? Can postsecularism frame questions of the spirit in the mood of critical enquiry? And finally: in what way does postsecularism represent a hidden challenge to both religious extremism and the extremism of some atheistic response to religion?

It is not right, however, to suggest a moral symmetry between religious extremism and extreme atheism, as the latter has in itself no history of violence. It is also the case that where religious extremism has been confronted with major violence – by the American-led forces in Afghanistan and Iraq, for example – the intellectual background for it is hardly atheism. The argument here is quite different: it is to say that the laudable goal of eradicating religious extremism is unlikely to be achieved by force, particularly as most religious extremism has its roots in thwarted political aspirations rather than religious dogma. The visible intellectual challenge to extreme religion of extreme atheism is less likely to be successful than a quieter route, a hidden challenge perhaps, one that might come from the sensibility explored here as postsecularism.

How the book leads on from *Secularism*
This book is intended as the companion volume to *Secularism: The Hidden Origins of Disbelief*, which will be referred to throughout simply as *Secularism*. Although the concept of postsecularism developed here stands alone, it does draw on some key concepts from *Secularism*, in particular the 'Two-Fold Model of Spiritual Difference' and the analysis of the origins of the secular mind that flows from this model. These ideas are briefly recapitulated in this volume, so it is not essential to read *Secularism* first. Here it is useful just to mention some terminology from *Secularism* that may be unfamiliar. Firstly, 'God' is placed in quotation marks throughout to flag up that this is perhaps the most contested term in language generally, and in particular in the debates discussed here. Secondly, the term 'old religion' is used to denote religions which have their origins prior to the modern period: it helps to begin a disaggregation of the term 'religion' which is used by atheists to mean mostly Christianity, or perhaps all three monotheisms. 'Religionist' will be used here to denote someone who pursues the spiritual life, though not necessarily through old religion.

The work undertaken in *Secularism* was partly to achieve a much more thorough disaggregation of the term 'religion', based on the observation that monotheism had denied or elided the spiritual difference that was a feature of earlier and other pluralistic cultures, and that the secular world has inherited this monolithic understanding of religion. At the end of the book it was shown that the secular mind arose partly out of the failure of a different kind of religion to emerge from the Enlightenment period: it was hinted that postsecularism might be a term for such a religious sensibility, and that it might now have conditions more favourable for its development.

Book structure

This book is divided into three parts. Part One provides the background to the following discussions, providing some definitions of terms, a delineation of the fields of study, and a recapitulation of the origins of secularism. Part Two explores how the new debate between atheists and religionists shapes up and to what extent it has a postsecular quality. Part Three then turns to a variety of cultural contexts within which we can observe a renewed openness to questions of the spirit.

Part One:
Towards a Postsecular Sensibility

Chapter 1:
Some Establishing Principles

The twentieth century saw, in the post-war period at least, a Western world divided between a broadly secular culture – as portrayed in novels, film, television, theatre and so on – and a society in which religion lingered on in varying strengths across different Western nations. The de facto result was the broad establishment of a détente between secular culture and old religion in which there was a mutual ignorance pact allowing old religion to continue unmolested – but the price it paid was to fly below the cultural radar of the West.[1] Since the late 1960s, roughly speaking, with secular values established in what had seemed to be an unassailable position, signs of a renewed interest in questions of the spirit began to emerge – and will be examined in detail in Part Three. But whatever trajectory this renewal of interest in the spiritual life may have taken, the events of 9/11 were to dramatically disturb the religious-secular détente. It suddenly became obvious that not only was Islam as a religion going to make itself noisily visible to the secular mind, but that evangelical Christianity had been growing apace for a while. Suddenly, secular values seemed less unassailable.

So, in the period post 9/11, a new debate has impinged on the public sphere: religion no longer flies below the cultural radar of the West. As Martin Amis notes, it is the 'second plane' that was significant in the attacks on the World Trade Centre, and, whatever the contested account might be of how the planes disappeared from air traffic control radar that day, the metaphor stands: religion has created that blip on the screen of culture that has returned it, if not centre-stage, then at least as a legitimate topic within popular culture. But the phenomenon asserts itself as, to some degree, a recapitulation of the angriest exchanges during the Enlightenment between atheism and old religion. On one side are marshalled the 'new atheists' – Roy Abraham Varghese suggests that the term was first used by *Wired* magazine in November 2006[2] – while on the other side queue up what are called here the 'new defenders of faith'.

Many have noted that the new atheists appear as militant as the religious extremists they oppose. Michel Onfray, recognised as one of the new atheists, puts it colourfully:

> In this devastated landscape of a howling Western world, the tactics of some secular figures seem contaminated by the enemy's ideology: many militants in the secular cause look astonishingly like clergy. Worse: like caricatures of clergy. Unfortunately, contemporary freethinking often carries a waft of incense; it sprinkles itself shamelessly with holy water. As clergymen of a church of atheist bigots, the players in this not unimportant movement seem to have missed the postmodern boat.

Onfray's position will be considered later, but for now it is interesting to note that both sides in the debate make various assertions about postmodernism and its relevance to religion. The purpose of this book is not however to take positions in the atheism debate, but to examine the various positions for signs of a postsecular sensibility. Does such a sensibility offer a way out from what was a détente but is now rapidly becoming a more polarised impasse; a way out from a futile struggle for dominance between religion and secularism?

What is not being argued against here is the very important condemnation of extreme religion, and its detailed analysis. It is as absurd to make a moral equivalence between specific acts of indiscriminate slaughter and the entire sensibility of secularism as it is to attack the entire sensibility of religion as culpable for those attacks. When Dawkins talks of religion as the 'root of all evil' and 'the elephant in the room', this is an extremism of thought alone, not of act. Likewise, to ignore religious violence is to do a disservice to religion itself.

The British tradition of Locke and Mill, along with the genius of the British people for muddled compromise, permits the extremism of the new atheists, but doesn't really buy it wholesale. The 'ordinary person' will gradually assert a middle ground, though this may also merely bring superficial harmony and anodyne thoughtlessness. Interestingly, the writer who occupies this middle ground in the best kind of way is perhaps television and radio presenter John Humphrys, and his book *In God We Doubt: Confessions of a Failed Atheist* is a wake-up call to avoid the extremism pursued on both sides. He is the least academic of the writers we will consider in the debate, but perhaps the most attuned to the emerging zeitgeist. He was prompted by the debate on atheism to consider the whole issue for himself again, and to propose a radio series in which he interviewed religious leaders on the subject of 'God'. *Humphrys in Search of God* was broadcast on BBC Radio 4 in the autumn of 2006, and prompted a volume of letters, the contents of which persuaded Humphrys not that 'God' existed or didn't exist, but that the *issue itself* was alive again. His conclusion about religion was 'to judge by my own experience, the old reticence on the part of most people in this country is disappearing.'[3] And *reticence* is exactly what British secularism has been about for nearly a century, a retreat of the question of religion into the privacy of the home and theological college. To say that this reticence is disappearing is to say a great deal, but we also need to acknowledge that things are different in America, in what is known amongst the sociologists of religion as the 'American exception'.

We will consider more of Humphrys' position later on, but it can be summed up here as a positive agnosticism: the perception of the 'ordinary person' that they cannot claim to believe in God – not, at least, in the terms laid out in old religion – but that atheism simply *feels* wrong, or inadequate, or too hasty. Humphrys is not an atheist like Dawkins, but is also too fiercely independent to unquestioningly sign up to the faith of his culture, Christianity. His questions are quintessentially secular, but his openness to the question of faith itself is not secular. It could be called postsecular instead.

Provisional Definition of Postsecularism

With these opening remarks in mind, an initial definition of postsecularism can be ventured, one which will be refined as we progress. To be properly 'post' anything, the new sensibility usually incorporates something of what it goes beyond, even if it transcends many of the defining features of its precursor. In this vein postsecularism can be defined as a renewed openness to questions of the spirit, but one that retains the habits of critical thought which partially define secularism. 'Questions of the spirit' is just one way to put it; one may prefer 'a renewed engagement with religion' or 'questions of faith' or any of a number of such formulations. However, a defining feature of secularism through the twentieth century was its certainty that such questions were irrelevant. Secularism meant a dismissal of such questions, while extending a rather patronising toleration towards those for whom these questions – or the various 'answers' – were still important. To open up those questions, to engage with an open mind in these debates, yet to retain the specifically secular critical stance towards unsupported metaphysical assertions – this juxtaposition can broadly be called postsecular.

Naturally, it is a move that can be unpopular both with secularism and old religion. Secularism says: haven't we settled those questions long ago? Old religion says: do we have to suffer another Enlightenment? But, as we shall see in our brief recapitulation of *Secularism*, if we understand the Enlightenment as a failed attempt to update religion, rather than a successful attempt to marginalise it, then postsecularism may be the truer completion of the Enlightenment project.

Why Mysticism as a Foundation?

'Questions of spirit'. The phrase has an odd ring to the secular ear, associating 'spirit' perhaps with Hegel, and 'spirituality' with the New Age, or even worse, succumbing to the popular confusion of usage between 'spirituality' and 'spiritualism'. This should not come as a surprise, or be seen as a handicap in this debate; after all, the impact of secularism on culture and language has been almost unmitigated by old religion. Its 'God slot' on Sunday evening television or its tiny weekly outing in the broadsheets made no defining impact on culture. The term 'mysticism' has even more of a muddled currency than the term 'spirit', yet a hundred years ago this was not the case: scholars had a consensus on what the term should mean, and a tradition of scholarship ran from the late-nineteenth century until the 1970s which progressively refined the term. More on this later, but for now it is suggested that the mystic is at the heart of the world's religions; the mystic is the *specialist* in religion, not the priest, theologian, or philosopher of religion.

Few agree. Humphrys states what is obvious to most entering the atheism/theism debate from the outside: 'It seems logical that if you have questions about God the obvious person to put them to is a cleric and, ideally, the man at the top of his particular tree.'[4] (Sadly, one notes the assumption of 'man' here.) Hence he chose Dr Rowan Williams (the Archbishop of Canterbury), Professor Tariq Ramadan (Muslim academic and author) and Sir Jonathan Sacks (Chief Rabbi in the UK) to put his questions to. He was not 'converted' by what they had to say, and might well find the writings of the mystics no greater help. For different reasons most of the new atheists and the new defenders of faith either ignore the mystics, or consider them suspect.

Instead, the mystics are assumed here to provide crucial insights into the search for what lies at the core of religion and its fate in the

West. These insights will rely to some extent on the assumption of this proposed hierarchy within religion: the specialists of religion are the mystics, the functionaries of religion are the priests, and the scholars of religion are the theologians. A further category is provided in the philosophers of religion, who may approach the subject from a non-confessional basis, or are professional philosophers with a personal adherence to a major faith tradition. Theologians and philosophers of religion are divided as to the importance they attribute to the mystic: some ignore them altogether.

The philosopher and religionist Charles Taylor represents perhaps a middle ground on this issue. His magisterial *A Secular Age* will be discussed later, but some of its ideas can be anticipated by commenting on his approach to the mystics. He notes at one point that 'The hostility to mystery on the part of the defenders of religion is rather strange . . .'[5] while later commenting on the highest good in the spiritual life, whether eternal life or nirvana: 'This latter is usually sought more single-mindedly by elites, what Weber called religious "virtuosi": monks, sanyassi, Bhikhus'.[6] In the discipline of religious studies – rather than the sociology of religion – such 'virtuosi' are usually the mystics. Taylor generally downplays the scholarship of mysticism in favour of the sociology of religion, and draws on more mainstream cultural sources than is done in *Secularism* and in this book. But he is deeply open to 'eternity' for example as a core preoccupation of religious thinkers, which is a central term for a certain type of (non-devotional) mystic. And in his later chapter on 'conversions' he notes that while those drawn to religion may not have had a mystical experience themselves, or lived so deeply the religious life of the saints, 'the language one adheres to is given force by the conviction that others have lived it in a more complete, direct and powerful manner. This is part of what it means to belong to a church.'[7] He calls a person drawn in this way to religion a person in the 'middle condition', meaning one who is not a virtuoso but who responds to their language, particularly as a language of love.

It may be possible to draw a crude analogy with science. The great scientists such as Newton and Einstein are comparable with the mystics: they are the specialists in that the sheer time and human mental energy devoted to their pursuit makes them experts in their field. The 'ordinary' scientist is analogous with the priest in that he or she makes very minor contributions, but keeps the field alive, while the writer of popular science and the philosopher of science live on the fringes and don't actually practice science. This is a key idea: the mystic pursues a spiritual practice with extraordinary intensity;

likewise the great scientist pursues a scientific practice with great intensity (whether or not they work in a lab). But the analogy is not intended to suggest as some do that science is a 'religion'. It is to make the point that the real experts in both fields are rare, hard to understand, and that by the time their discoveries appear in popular culture they are almost completely adulterated.

Why did Heraclitus call himself 'obscure'? Why does the Buddha insist that his teachings are 'abstruse, subtle, deep, and difficult to see'?[8] (Note: as in *Secularism*, all references to the Buddha in this book are to the Buddha of the Pali Canon.) Why does Jesus speak so often in parables? Because the subject matter of mysticism, that is the profound unity of existence, is at the same time extremely difficult *and* extremely simple. Relativity and quantum mechanics, for example, are *just* extremely difficult. Full stop. But both science and mysticism take effort of study, and more than that: an act of faith in the first instance that the deeply counter-intuitive propositions of both fields can, with persistence, become comprehensible and coherent with experience.

Defining Spirituality and Religion

Religion is a massively varied phenomenon, but a large part of the new atheists' secular strategy involves defining religion in the narrowest of terms in order to discredit it. Despite their efforts, however, truly accurate definitions are elusive. Here spirituality will be initially defined as a *profound connectedness*. Religion in turn can be defined as a pursuit of this profound connectedness in a social context, though this should not be too limiting an idea: a solitary person may pursue a spirituality that looks just like a religion, or a conventional-seeming religionist may pursue a very solitary kind of inward spirituality.

Clearly, these definitions are not those of most commentators, but when worked out in detail through this volume they will converge somewhat on mainstream thought. The principal difference in this starting point is to omit the element of the supernatural. This is, however, essential, because deeply religious traditions such as the core of Buddhism, the Advaita, and Zen, to give some examples, exclude the supernatural from their doctrines and training (though not necessarily from their worldview). In terms of mysticism, most scholarship has noted that mystics, as opposed to occultists, make little reliance on the supernatural, whether in the form of variegated 'spirits' or even a single supernatural 'God'.

Charles Taylor, despite being a Christian, also avoids the supernatural in his initial definition of religion, drawing instead on the

Christian distinction between 'transcendent' and 'immanent'.[9] Broadly speaking, for Taylor, religion is the domain of the former and secularism the domain of the latter. Paul Tillich on the other hand says: 'Faith is the state of being ultimately concerned: the dynamics of faith are the dynamics of man's ultimate concern.'[10]

'Profound connectedness', 'transcendence', and 'ultimate concern' may all *sound* very different as starting points for the definition of religion, but they point to the same thing, something subtle and hard to pin down, but something of ultimate profundity. Initially each definition avoids reference to the supernatural, but does not rule it out either.

NOMA and the Cartesian Cut

Descartes can be understood as a deeply religious man, even a mystic.[11] Yet clearly his religiosity was not mainstream, and his movement from Catholic France to Holland and then to Denmark was partly to escape the vigilance of religious authorities. He was perhaps the first to see that the emergence of science (or to be more precise, physics) would require some way of distinguishing it from religion, because it appeared also to deal with profound questions about our universe; we can see his famous distinction between mind and matter in this light.

Many new atheists draw on science, including Darwinism, as an argument against religion on the basis that science provides better explanations of our experience, of life and how it got here, and of our place in the universe. To show that science and religion are not in fact in conflict is the cumulative work of much of this book, but it is worth establishing the basic argument here.

Scientific explanation, once the discovery is made and proven, is always only part of our lives as *recapitulation*. We see a tree and rehearse evolutionary theory in front of it. Or we don't. One can't make science part of everyday experience, or one becomes merely the absent-minded professor: absent because the mind is busy with the rehearsal of a chain of explanatory elaboration, and oblivious to the experience. One walks through local woods by the gasworks in a big city (made possible only by the status of the land as a disused cemetery) and one encounters a fox. The sun picks out its orange fur through the branches; it runs to denser cover, turns – all its limbs participating in the low fluid motion – and looks. Two sentient beings briefly rest in each other's gaze. It is an experience that lingers in one's mind as a call of the beyond, an experience of infinity. Science can attempt to retrospectively 'unweave' this experience, but it may also prevent it happening in the first place if we were to capitulate to the demands of the Darwinists to interpret life as a gene-machine. How impious – as Susan Sontag would say – to stand in the deep gaze of the animal and mentally rehearse its Darwinian lineage back to the first eukaryotic cells. The human mind cannot do both in that fraction of a second: rehearse the workings of a cause-and-effect biological evolutionary machine, and *be* there with the animal. And nothing in science can explain *why* we would want to be there with the animal in the first place, other than the pseudo-science of another long and rather implausible chain of reductionist reasoning about memes in the style of Daniel Dennett (whose work we examine below). But to feel that *connectedness* with other beings, whether a fox or a person, is what transforms the world as a machine into something unbounded. This is the domain of the mystic.

What, then, is the actual appeal of science? The desire to be Sherlock Holmes. A smartarse. And what cultural sanction and reinforcement is provided for this! Sherlock Holmes, Hercule Poirot, Dr Who, *House* (US TV hospital drama), *CSI* (US TV crime drama), *Numbers* (US TV intelligence drama) – it's endless. Where is the cultural counter-weight, other than the discredited Romantic? Where is the counter-weight that would point out the sheer geekishness of this desiccated obsession? Here should be the domain, for example, of the novelist, but their counterblast is too often mired in their admiration for the virility of science and their distrust of religion.

The admiration for science is endemic, whether it is naïve wonderment for or grudging acknowledgement of the technologies that flow from it. And what this brings, without any real resistance, is the acceptance of the materialist stance: that matter is as described in physics, chemistry and biology, and that the older values that aligned themselves with 'spirit' are either non-existent, an emergent phenomenon, or somehow an embarrassment for civilised conversation. If Humphrys detects that this embarrassment is waning in British society, then there is all the more need for a new articulation of the objections to materialism.

Stephen Jay Gould's concept of 'Non-Overlapping Magisteria' (NOMA) will be developed here as a possible basis from which to assert the independence of religion from science. (An alternative strategy, that of hierarchical forms of knowledge, will be introduced later.) NOMA, like mysticism, is unpopular on both sides of the atheism / theism debate. For those who base their atheism in Darwinism or other sciences, particularly Richard Dawkins and Daniel Dennett, NOMA is unacceptable because it posits a non-material aspect to reality, or at the very least a domain in which science has no remit. But this objection is not scientific: no domain of human thought can justify from within itself the status of sole arbiter of truth, with the possible exception of philosophy (most of which, in fact, proves that it can do no such thing). The findings of science, impressive as they may be, contain within them nothing upon which to build a claim of universality. It is philosophy, since Descartes' crucial distinction between *res cogitans* and *res extensans* – thinking stuff and extended stuff – which has slowly rejected his dualism and broadly given the nod to science and its domain of extended stuff *as all there is*. Of course, philosophers are not universal in their agreement on this, but NOMA is too close to the Cartesian divide to garner much support. Philosophers want a single overarching system in philosophy, just as physicists want their 'grand unified theory' in physics. The human mind wants it simple.

Tina Beattie, one of the new defenders of faith, writes in her book on the new atheists:

> In its war on religion, scientific rationalism constitutes the latest phase in the West's long history of domination by which it has sought to defeat every form of difference, including religious difference.[12]

Beattie is right that it is the Western mind that has continually sought a single system, a 'totalising' system of thought, as Levinas says, first in religion, then in science, and now to deny that there is anything valid called 'religion', or if it does exist that it must be investigated as part of extended stuff (using MRI scanners, or evolutionary theory, or whatever). A large part of *Secularism* was devoted to the concept of spiritual difference as a counterweight to the denial of difference in Western religious history.[13] And Gould's concept of NOMA, once elaborated upon, will be shown to be a possible and credible basis on which to resist the encroachment of science into religion. But, it will be shown here that the new defenders of faith are mostly so in awe of science as to barely reach escape velocity from its gravitational pull.

Some writers have no difficulty in accepting the Cartesian division as a better starting point than the extremes of either materialism or idealism. The 'man in the street' knows better, as Owen Chadwick points out:

> We have sharply to distinguish, it seems, between the theory of a philosopher and the axioms of society. Bishop Berkeley reasons with conviction, and is convincing in his argument, that all the world exists only in the human mind. And nobody

believes him, because men like Samuel Johnson stub their toes against walls and live happy under an illusion that the bishop needs no further refutation. D'Holbach tells us in the eighteenth century that all the world is matter, that nothing is which is not matter. The theory has no influence because nobody believes him. The common sense of the human race finds it as obvious that everything is not matter as it is obvious that everything is not in the mind.[14]

John Humphrys would find Berkeley's idealism bizarre, but equally finds the reductionist atheists – inheritors of Holbach's radicalism – unbelievable, as the majority in the eighteenth century felt towards Holbach. But Holbach's legacy has a long reach: it is the idea of existence as machinery. To rejoice in the conception of 'man a machine' – La Mettrie's coinage – or, in different terms, Nature and all creatures within it, including humans, as interacting machines is to participate in what was described in *Secularism*, and will be elaborated on here, as 'cultural autism'.[15] Dawkins and Dennett lead the field in this reductionist rejoicing, and it is these two new atheists who are also united in their condemnation of Gould's NOMA. Dawkins says, for example: 'Gould carried the art of bending over backwards to positively supine lengths in one of his less admired books, *Rocks of Ages*.'[16] Dennett calls NOMA a 'political hypothesis', adding that Gould's proposal 'found little favour on either side' and that 'few readers were persuaded.'[17]

The new defenders of faith, to the extent that they are not comfortable with NOMA, leave themselves perpetually open to attacks on religion from science. Of course, Gould was never suggesting that he had the expertise in religion that he did in science, and so it falls to others to pick up on NOMA and expand on it. This is what is pursued here, but in stages, as the objections to it from both sides of the 'God' debate are examined.

Science and Religion, Meta-Science and New Age Science

To build on Gould's conception of NOMA requires a careful definition of both science and religion, such definitions being of course extremely hard to come by. This is mostly apparent in the attempts by the new atheists – largely comfortable with science – to define religion, which we will see as we explore them one by one. Indeed, Dennett almost plaintively complains:

If theists would be so kind as to make a short list of all the concepts of God they renounce as balderdash before proceeding further, we atheists would know just which topics were still on the table, but, out of a mixture of caution, loyalty, and unwillingness to offend anyone 'on their side', theists typically decline to do this.[18]

A.C. Grayling also wades in to note how loosely terms are defined on the religious side of the debate:

> We understand that the faithful live in an inspissated gloaming of incense and obfuscation, through the swirls of which it is hard to see anything clearly, so a simple lesson in semantics might help to clear the air for them on the meanings of the 'secular', 'humanist' and 'atheist'.[19]

It turns out that 'inspissated' means thickened or dried by evaporation. Such terms, along with 'gloaming' and 'obfuscation' are part of the lexicon which seeks to deride religion, and which some, but not all, of the new atheists cannot resist resorting to, probably without any real intention to insult. But the point of these two quotes is to show that atheists believe that they have the virtue of precision on their side. It is not hard to see why: consider, for example, the common terms 'stress' and 'strain' in ordinary language. In general usage they are interchangeable, even if poets and linguists may argue over nuance of interpretation, but in physics they are defined with absolute precision: stress is the applied force per unit area, and strain is the resulting fractional deformation. The definition is precise and for all time. A misuse of the terms in a science context does not suggest that the user has a poetic ear for language and wants to avoid cliché – rather it suggests a howler, or someone untrained in physics. Attempts by atheists to define the least definable word in any language – 'God' – with the precision that scientific terms have are unhelpful.

Here we have an early difference between the magisteria of science and religion: the former requires and permits of the precise definition of terms, while the latter does not require and is hamstrung by comparable attempts. Even then, biology allows for much vaguer definitions than physics; for example the vexed question of what 'species' means exactly. But first a point usefully made by Dennett on the very term 'science' itself. He almost permits of a small move in the NOMA direction when he says: 'There is a good case to be made that the social sciences and humanities – the *Geisteswissenschaften*, or mind sciences – have their own "autonomous" methodologies and subject matters independent of the natural sciences.'[20] By using scare-quotes around 'autonomous' he shows how nervous he is of the idea that different branches of science might have different methodologies. NOMA requires not just different methodologies, but different epistemologies, an 'epistemological pluralism', as raised – and then quashed – by Ken Wilber.[21] But Dennett's remark usefully leads us to the problem of the German word 'Wissenschaft', broadly meaning knowledge or discipline, and its division, mentioned several times by Dennett in *Breaking the Spell*, between *Geisteswissenschaften* – mind sciences, humanities – and *Naturwissenschaften* – the natural sciences. In so many German texts, the term 'Wissenschaft' is loosely translated into English as 'science' without consideration as to which branch the author intended, or whether they more broadly meant just 'knowledge'. When reading translations of Hegel, for example, the term 'science' often crops up in a quite baffling way if one is not attuned to these distinctions.

Peter Watson, in his comprehensive survey of the ideas that shaped the twentieth century, suggests that knowledge embodied in the humanities around 1900 had a higher cultural status than knowledge embodied in the hard sciences at that time, but that by the year 2000 the situation had completely reversed.[22] Even in 1959 C.P. Snow could argue that progress in Britain was impeded by ignorance of science in the political establishment, 'most of whom had been educated exclusively in the humanities.'[23] More than this, one could argue, reductionists like Dawkins and Dennett are apparently winning support for the idea that the humanities embody no knowledge at all, and certainly not in the case of religion. Instead, by applying evolutionary theory to the arts and religion, as we will see, they appear to be attempting an epistemological reframing of the very bases of those disciplines.

But if we look at the hard sciences themselves we begin to discover quite different methodologies and epistemologies even between physics, chemistry and biology. When Lord Kelvin remarked that 'in science there is physics and there is stamp-collecting' he was not committing one of the errors for which he later apologised, or for which the history of science has apologised (for example his objections to Darwinism). He was simply suggesting that chemistry and biology have more of a taxonomical basis to their disciplines than physics. The same point was made rather piquantly to Dawkins by John Barrow, as recorded by Roy Abraham Varghese:

> With regard to Dawkins's approach to the rationality underlying the universe, the physicist John Barrow observed in a discussion: 'you have a problem with these ideas, Richard, because you're not really a scientist. You're a biologist.' ... 'Biologists', says

Barrow, 'have a limited, intuitive understanding of complexity. They're stuck with an inherited conflict from the nineteenth century, and are only interested in outcomes, in what wins out over others. But outcomes tell you almost nothing about the laws that govern the universe.'[24]

Barrow couldn't resist the chance to tease Dawkins, but he had a serious point to make: physics discovers laws whereas biology, to the extent it relies on laws, draws on physics. Biology is altogether a vaguer, more taxonomic and discursive science than physics.

Hence, when some of the new atheists insist that the methods of science should apply to religion, or even the issue of whether 'God' exists or not, they forget that methodologies vary, even across the hard sciences, never mind across the other 'sciences' (which may or may not be bad translations of the German 'Wissenschaften'). But who is to arbitrate as to which discipline can be called a 'proper' science? Language is elastic, particularly in translation.

We turn now to a few more issues that need staking out in these introductory remarks: that of meta-science, and that of 'New Age' science. The first is a term that is needed instead of 'metaphysics' to denote speculations arising from science, for example the concept of 'memes' with which Dennett and Dawkins are much preoccupied. Meta-science as a term would usefully distinguish such speculations which have a good chance of never gaining a physical explanation, from theories that are 'hypotheses-in-waiting' such as much of string theory. These are a class of theories in the ante-room of science, much as relativity was until its first experimental verification. They have the 'nod' as it were from the scientific community as likely to succeed, though of course, as with relativity, there may be many authoritatively dissenting voices until the experimental verification comes in loud and clear. 'Meta-science' as a term is not intended here to cover such hypotheses, but to cover theories at one remove from science, particularly attempts to theorise about *meaning* based on science. These are theories more likely to use metaphor, in the way that memes are metaphorically similar to genes, but with, as yet, no physical basis. Alternatively, they may involve speculation on entities never before regarded as physical such as ghosts or 'God'.

'New Age' science is a term that might usefully be applied to a subset of meta-science: those theories favoured by New Age thinkers that are inspired by science, such as the physics-proves-mysticism theory, or the belief that zero-point energy will provide free power to the human race in the near future. The former uses quantum theory to apparently support a number of assertions about human consciousness (to be discussed later), while the latter, promoted by New Age thinkers such as Erwin Laszlo and Lynne McTaggart, seems to overlook the fact that energy itself is boundlessly already present in the human environment, but that it is *extracting* it that is expensive (more on these thinkers later).

Contra Postmodernism: Towards a Hermeneutics of Trust

These remarks on science are not to be confused with the position largely adopted within postmodernism. Where the scientism of Dawkins and Dennett flattens out all domains or magisteria to conform to their imagined singular conception of science, postmodernism flattens out these domains as merely arbitrary social constructs or language games. The 'texts' of physics and religion are merely examples of metanarratives which compete within a social space, and have no intrinsic 'truths' of any kind within them, so they say. This is to exaggerate, perhaps, or to characterise postmodernism through only its most extreme assertions, but the point is that at the very least the various strands of postmodern thought, while hostile enough to science, are not likely to provide an argument for NOMA. This is because they either would want to tear down anything as grand sounding as a 'magisterium' or they secretly still want a 'unified theory of everything'. This may manifest itself, for example, in attempting to unify the thought of Marx and Freud, a quintessentially postmodern project found in the Frankfurt school or in Ricoeur.

The issue of postmodernism will crop up at times in the pursuit of a postsecular sensibility, and the question will have to be settled: is there a fundamental difference? Why advocate the relatively unheard of coinage 'postsecularism' when 'postmodernism' might capture a similar set of stances? Two initial reasons will be stated in advance here: firstly that it is false to claim that we live in a postmodern era, and secondly that it is true to say that postmodernism contains within it a pessimism largely incongruent with faith. To briefly deal with the first point: however considerable the literature of postmodernism and however numerous its adherents, it remains the domain of a subset of the educationally privileged. Whereas the modernists such as Freud and Marx have a huge presence in the popular mind – and whereas Darwinism has equal reach through promotion by the likes of Dawkins and Dennett, never minding its use to attack religion – the postmodern adumbrations of Freud and Marx are largely confined to the academy. Only in the arts, particularly in architecture, might the term 'postmodern' have some popular currency and understanding, but the contemporary world largely remains stubbornly modern. With some interesting exceptions, which we shall examine later, the 'God' debate plays out as modernism vs. premodernism, or rather as secularism vs. old religion.

The pessimism within postmodernism is usefully summed up in Ricoeur's phrase 'the hermeneutics of suspicion'.[25] Modernism is characterised by its progressive optimism, the earliest proponent of which amongst Enlightenment thinkers might be Condorcet,[26] but this optimism is a key target of the postmodernists. Ricoeur regarded Nietzsche, Marx and Freud to be the 'masters of suspicion', who undermined the progressivism of the Enlightenment project. One might suggest that Ricoeur himself is amongst the many pupils of the masters of suspicion within the broadly defined postmodern canon. Another obvious pupil might be Foucault, whose method of interrogating society in terms of structures of power lacking all benevolence is a form of 'deconstruction'. Where modernism opposes faith tradition as superstition, postmodernism opposes faith tradition as structures of power.

Having said this, one has to also concede that postmodernism is a complex tradition, if it can be identified as a single tradition at all. To the extent that it offers 'incredulity' towards faith tradition, and its stance is 'suspicion', then it will fail to engage with faith, but this is not the whole story, as we shall see. What would be a mistake is to suggest, along with Dawkins, that postmodernism has nothing useful to say, or to concede to Dawkins in any way that his appellation 'haute francophonyism'[27] – amusing as it might be – is valid. What is pursued in this book, and might well be considered as a hallmark of postsecularism, is what could be called a 'hermeneutics of trust' – that is, a way of reading religion as a phenomenon, and the texts of religion, in a more empathetic way. This is not a license for naivety, but a recognition that religion as a magisterium requires a stance towards life that is at some level a thankfulness. To 'give praise' to whatever ultimate principle one is inspired by – whether 'God' or even science – is a movement of the soul, a movement of the mind and heart, that is at the core of religion; to cling to a hermeneutics of suspicion, a method of analysis founded on mistrust, is to stifle that movement.

Of course we can find distrust, nihilism and despair within religious texts just as we can in any literature (Ecclesiastes for example), but this is simply a record of the human context wherever disaster, natural or otherwise, overwhelms an individual or group. Judaism may even be understood as the 'struggle' with 'God' but this does not undermine the conception of 'God' as providential. Buddhism as a religion of renunciation is badly understood as a nihilist creed; on the contrary it is concerned with ending the habits of thought that lead to suffering, and requires the placing of trust in the 'three jewels': the Buddha, his teachings, and the community of Buddhists.

Recapitulation of Opening Remarks

In this set of opening remarks positions have been set out on various issues relating to the contemporary 'God' debate. The term 'postsecularism' has been set out to mean a certain sensibility that permits of a reopening to questions of the spirit while retaining the secular habit of critical thinking. The observation has been made that the new atheists to some extent hold an extremity of position comparable with the fundamentalist religionists they attack, though to assert any straightforward symmetry would be incorrect. The contribution to the debate in this book also requires two more controversial core assumptions that will be argued in more detail later on: that the mystics are the 'experts' of religion and thus should be consulted to understand the essence of religion; and that Gould's non-overlapping magisteria provides a possible framework from which to consider the science/religion debate. The terms 'meta-science' to cover such speculations as meme theory, and 'New Age' science to cover a subset of meta-science favoured by New Age thinkers have also been introduced. Finally, the relevance of postmodernism should not be dismissed in the debate, but to the extent that it offers a 'hermeneutics of suspicion', it fails to tune itself to an essential aspect of religion, which is a stance of trust and thankfulness towards existence.

Chapter 2:

Recapitulating the Origins of Secularism

The current atheism/theism debate, which is also partly a science / religion debate, contains within it some genuine engagement across the divide and some considerable dialogue of deafness. This deafness is partly a 'tone'-deafness – that is a lack of empathy due to lack of direct experience of religion or science or specific cultural spaces – and partly a related issue of setting up straw men to knock down. The 'straw man' syndrome arises from undue haste to pin down or define what is foreign in simplistic terms, and in this debate it is religion that usually suffers from this treatment. Mostly, the definitions of religion and of 'God' put forward by the new atheists are definitions that the thoughtful religionist would not want to own. This would be like attacking science on the basis of the understanding that the lay person has of it, whether of Newtonian mechanics, quantum theory, relativity, or Darwinism. Lewis Wolpert, one of the new atheists, while more or less of the 'straw man' school of atheism, does usefully contribute a detailed account of how counter-intuitive all of science is.[28] After all, if the core discipline within physics, mechanics, was amenable to an appeal to intuition, Aristotle would have got it right and saved the world from the 2,000-year wait for Newton.

John Humphrys assumed, rather naturally, that the equivalent to the expert in science should be the cleric in religion 'at the top of his tree' and therefore invited the Chief Rabbi, the Archbishop of Canterbury and a leading Islamic scholar to participate in his radio programme. But this assumption is open to question once the role of the mystic within religion is seen more sympathetically. And to really understand the role of the mystic in religion it is necessary to have a better idea of what the term 'mystic' denotes in religious studies, rather than in popular thought. We will look shortly at the history of the study of mysticism, but first we need to briefly recapitulate the Two-Fold Model of Spiritual Difference presented in *Secularism.*[29]

The idea of 'spiritual difference' is the necessary missing element in the Western understanding of religion, which as Beattie pointed out, has followed an absolutist model of eliminating difference in the pursuit of various kinds of imperialism, whether of territory or of the mind. Fig. 1 sums up the Two-Fold Model, comprising a quasi-historical developmental model juxtaposed against a set of personal spiritual impulses.

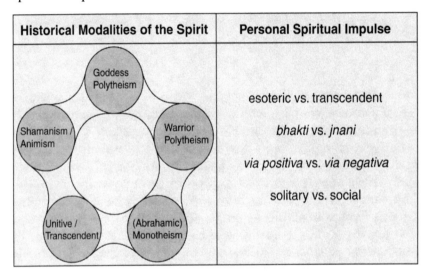

Historical Modalities of the Spirit	Personal Spiritual Impulse
Goddess Polytheism / Shamanism / Animism / Warrior Polytheism / Unitive / Transcendent / (Abrahamic) Monotheism	esoteric vs. transcendent *bhakti* vs. *jnani* *via positiva* vs. *via negativa* solitary vs. social

Fig.1 The Two-Fold Model of Spiritual Difference

The historical modalities of the spirit are less interesting here than the personal spiritual impulses, because the latter helps us define what a mystic is, and leads us to some insights regarding the nature of Western religion as it entered the isolation of the cultural ghetto it mostly occupied during the secular era. Nevertheless the diagram of the historical modalities is important in suggesting that monotheism be understood as one religious form amongst many. In this scheme monotheism takes its place at the table as one amongst five, the other four being shamanism / animism, Goddess polytheism, warrior polytheism, and the unitive / transcendent.

The key distinctions of personal spiritual impulse are between *bhakti* and *jnani* and between the *via positiva* and *via negativa*, and these distinctions provide for the radical analysis of the origins of the secular mind put forward in *Secularism*. Briefly, *bhakti* is the devotional spiritual impulse, familiar to us in its Western flowering in such mystics as Teresa of Avila and Richard Rolle, while *jnani* is the non-devotional spiritual impulse, a generally unfamiliar concept, but exemplified in the West in such mystics as Plotinus and Meister Eckhart. This idea leads to the rather Feuerbachian suggestion that the Western 'God' can be understood as having two very different constructions arising out of these two impulses: a 'God' of the devotional *bhakti*, and a 'God' of the non-devotional *jnani*.

Although Sanskrit terms such as *bhakti* and *jnani* are foreign to the West – and have been introduced only because no Western terms do them justice – what they refer to are often instinctively recognised by other commentators. Charles Taylor, for example, says: 'the movement to Deism involved some exclusion of practices which were previously seen as central to the love of / devotion to God, and their condemnation as excessive, extravagant, harmful, or "enthusiastic." ' He adds that 'What had got lost was the sense that devotion to God, for its own sake, was the centre of religious life.'[30] Further, he cites Count Zinzendorf (an eighteenth century bishop of the Moravian Church): 'Whosoever wishes to grasp God with his intellect becomes an atheist.'[31] These and many other examples show that Taylor understands the difference between a devotional religion on the one hand and one which Pascal characterised as arising from the 'God of the philosophers' on the other, and the historical tension that plays out between them. In *Secularism* the terms *bhakti* and *jnani* were used to pursue this crucial historical division within Western religion, which more normally only receives oblique references such as Taylor's.

The *via positiva* and *via negativa* impulses are defined as those which instinctively pursue mystical or religious goals in the context of either a turning towards the world, or away from it, respectively. This usage differs a little from that in theology, where *via positiva* is synonymous with cataphatic, and *via negativa* is synonymous with apophatic, or the negative theology. The so-called 'Dark Ages' represented a collective religious turn away from the *via positiva* to the *via negativa*, and the Renaissance and Enlightenment represented a turn again to the *via positiva*. At the same time, the Renaissance, Reformation and Enlightenment collectively privileged the *jnani* impulse over the *bhakti* impulse, the latter being at the heart of the new Christian experiment in religiosity, over and above the more *jnani* orientation of its parent religion, Judaism. Thus religion moves from prioritising one constellation of spiritual impulses to another over time. In *Secularism* it was suggested that the move from a *bhakti via negativa* religion of the Middle Ages, to a *jnani via positiva* religion in the Enlightenment almost succeeded, but failed in the end, resulting in a retreat of religion to a compromised position that ceased to hold the cultural imagination of the West and hence secularism arose by default.

In all of this, it is suggested that the mystics, though they are not always the prime engine of change, nevertheless hold the keys to understanding such changes. They both capture and push forward the religious zeitgeist, in the same way as artists and writers of the avant-garde capture and push forward the cultural zeitgeist. Amongst 'mystics' it is largely those of a transcendent rather than esoteric orientation that are important here, this idea resting on another key juxtaposition of spiritual impulses between *transcendent*, with its emphasis on the infinite and eternal, and the *esoteric*, with its emphasis on non-material beings and energies. (In *Secularism* the figures of Jiddu Krishnamurti and Rudolf Steiner are used to illustrate this distinction.)[32]

The Failure of Deism

In *Secularism*, it was concluded that the Enlightenment period represented the failure of a religious revolution – the completion of the journey from *bhakti via negativa* to *jnani via positiva* – rather than the success of secular revolution – the completion of a project to destroy religion. This failed religious, or spiritual, revolution is largely unrecognised other than through its rather limited characterisation as *Deism*. Those with only a passing acquaintance with the spirituality of the Enlightenment thinkers assume that Deism was no more than a contracted Christian vision of 'God' as the maker of the universe and its laws – a conception of 'God' that shrank as science grew, limiting him to the 'gaps' in explanation. At least, this is the conventional account of Deism, which for example Charles Taylor puts forward. It is this apparent shrinkage of 'God' that allows for a particular attack on religion that simply carries through this progression and abandons 'God' altogether – as Taylor acknowledges. The mystic who follows the *jnani* path has already conceived of 'God' in a non-anthropomorphic way, however, though in no way as a shrunken 'God', and it is this apparent paradox that dogs much of the atheism debate.

The contemporary view of Feuerbach as an atheist, for example, is part of this legacy of the failure of Deism. Most of the Enlightenment thinkers are better understood as making arguments within religion rather than against religion, and their arguments, broadly inspired by *jnani via positiva* temperaments, as behind the movement we now call Deism. As we saw, no less than Engels spotted this move in Feuerbach, when he said 'He by no means wishes to abolish religion;

he wants to perfect it.' Marx is equally sure that Feuerbach's thought is in no way consistent with the total atheism required for the abolition of 'false consciousnesses'. Instead, Feuerbach can be seen as amongst the last of the failed revolutionaries of deist religion, understanding the central *jnani* perception that consciousness, religion, and infinity are inextricably tied together.[33]

The trinity of secularism: Marxism, Darwinism, Freudianism
With the failure of Deism, or any other kind of popular religion that could properly capture the move in the Western mind towards a non-devotional world-curious religion, the great détente set in: official religion retreated to its cloistered concepts of 'God', constructing its own awkward and half-hearted accommodation with the 'God of Aristotle' and a non-renunciative orientation towards life, while secular culture accelerated away, taking with it the great minds and their innovations in the arts, sciences, and politics. Religion, confined to the private sphere and relegated to a cultural ghetto, avoided what it most feared: real critical debate, while culture in the form of radically new arts and media, including film and television, avoided what *it* most feared: interference from reactionary religion.

The independence of twentieth-century culture from religion, even if large numbers privately continued in the faith of their forbears, has three great architects: Marx (wittingly), Darwin (unwittingly), and Freud (wittingly). Each contributed a language of rejection which held sway in different sectors of culture, but which as a combined force appeared irresistible. What they have in common, and what marks the secular mind out from what went before, is the reductionism at the heart of each. They were inheritors of Galileo and his move to isolate 'primary qualities' that are measurable, and which became the basis of physics and in a more adumbrated way the other natural sciences. Each of the fathers of secular reductionism provided a different reduction: Marxism gave us historical materialism, which reduces everything to the means of production; Darwinism gave us genetic determinism, which reduces living things to genes; and Freudianism gave us eros (and, grudgingly, thanatos), which reduce us to a handful of psychological complexes. The status in some cultural contexts of Marxism and Freudianism as 'sciences' is controversial, but that flags up little more than the contested usage of the term 'science', rather than any cultural move to independence from these reductions.

Marx dismissed religion as part of an oppressive power structure that enabled dominant classes to find various justifications to retain their status. Freud's dismissal of religion was more detailed and comprehensive, and therefore perhaps the more devastating. When Freud's friend, Romain Rolland, wrote to him, largely in agreement with Marx's work, but reserving the term 'oceanic' to indicate precisely what the mystics become experts in, and as the very source of the religious impulse, Freud took this crucial term and made it ridiculous for a century.[34] He patiently considers the issue and concludes that 'oceanic' is a regression to a pre-oedipal state. In other words he provides for the sceptics of the twentieth century the best weapon anyone needs to dismiss an opponent: call their highest concept and aspiration *infantile*. Darwin, in contrast to Marx and Freud, had no program to ridicule religion, but Darwinism, or to be more precise the modern evolutionary synthesis, has become the tool of choice of the new atheists.

What the great architects of secular thought completed was the 'Copernican revolution' of the mind that Kant initiated, meaning the confinement of humanity to its own horizon: what Taylor and others also call the 'anthropocentric turn'. In *Secularism* this move was termed the 'narcissism of self-sufficiency' – a false but much-paraded belief that the human spirit can be adequately described in terms of human knowledge acquired through the sciences and humanities, stripped of any religious substratum. The phrase was adapted from Freud's 'narcissism of minor difference' which he used to characterise religious intolerance (though this is mostly a feature of monotheism). In turn we described the New Age as prone to the 'narcissism of difference denied', in order to highlight its reluctance to make meaningful distinctions within the spiritual life. Postsecularism is almost defined by the absence of these three narcissisms.

Most accounts of the origins of secularism are put forward by sceptics of religion, often sociologists, whose intellectual world is framed by the three reductions of Marx, Darwin and Freud. As both Tina Beattie and Alister McGrath point out, for example, the new atheists, in attempting to understand religion by peering in from the outside, often start with early works by anthropologists such as Sir James Frazer. Beattie comments that 'no serious scholar would cite Frazer as an authoritative source on religion',[35] while McGrath calls Frazer's *Golden Bough* 'a highly impressionistic early work of anthropology . . . now largely discredited'.[36] Frazer was a Victorian scholar immensely impressed by Darwin's theories before the genetic basis of them was discovered. The assumption of many early anthropologists was that religion was a primitive superstition, and hence the implication barely needed stating that secularism was the endpoint of a rationalising process, a freedom from the 'infamy', as Voltaire put it, of superstition.

Scholarship in the social sciences has produced more sophisticated and extensive accounts of secularism, generally referred to as a cluster of theories under the banner of 'secularization theory'. These and other accounts of the origins of the secular mind are all valuable and form an important backdrop to both the new atheism and the historical context for postsecularism.

Steve Bruce

Steve Bruce offers a useful survey of secularization theory in his book *God is Dead*, stating at the outset that the core of the theory is that 'modernization creates problems for religion.'[37] Elsewhere he says 'There is no secularization theory. There is a cluster of testable explanations that cohere as well as anything in the social sciences.'[38] The social science tradition of the analysis of religion has its origins in Durkheim and Weber, and is an account that begins with the Protestant Reformation. Bruce makes clear that his analysis does not defend the views of Freud and Marx, but Marx at least is at the heart of the intellectual framework that Bruce and secularization theory broadly follow: an historical materialism in which changing modes of production and their resulting changes in social structure give rise to the background for secularization.

Bruce was writing just prior to 9/11, so some of his assertions now seem more unfounded than would perhaps otherwise be the case. He sets out to describe three features of secularization: firstly a declining importance of religious institutions in public life; secondly a decline in the social standing of religion; and thirdly a decline in the extent to which people are religious.[39] His universalising claims for the secularization paradigm gradually become clear: ultimately he believes in its predictive power. He says for example 'I expect the proportion of people who are largely indifferent to religious ideas to increase and the seriously religious to become a small minority.'[40] He shows that the paradigm is under attack from those, such as Rodney Stark, who might suggest that firstly religion did not hold such sway in the past as is generally supposed, and that secondly new forms of religion, such as New Age beliefs, will increase as traditional forms decline. Bruce makes a good argument that both these assumptions are wrong. He is confident enough in secularization theory to even make a specific prediction: that without radical change the Methodist Church will be finished by around 2031. By then the Church of

England will be 'reduced to a trivial voluntary association with a large portfolio of heritage property.' He adds: 'Perhaps then the critics of the secularization paradigm will recognize that . . . decline is not a sociological myth.'[41] He ends his book: 'I see no grounds to expect secularization to be reversed.'

But futurology is a mug's game, to put it bluntly. The social sciences have much to offer to this debate, but one can detect 'physics envy' at work here as it has been across much of Western thought since Newton: Bruce wants the sociology of religion to have the status of a real 'science'. To claim that it would need the predictive power of physics, but, as we saw in Barrow's remark to Dawkins, outside of physics – and perhaps those elements of chemistry and biology which are based in physics – no *laws* can be asserted. Secularization cannot be a law like the inverse square law in gravitation. It cannot have predictive power, only a set of discursive insights into a complex phenomenon. This is because there is no underlying mechanism at work; instead there is the infinitely complex arena of human culture. Mechanics has predictive power because momentum is quantifiable, in amount and direction, but social momentum has a direction as irregular as the weather, perhaps more so: who foresaw the storm of 9/11?

Bruce admits that his account is mostly confined to the British scene, and acknowledges that America is rather different, but doesn't go as far as to term it the 'American exception' as Taylor does. Bruce believes that the difference, as far as it goes, is down to immigrants attempting to integrate via existing church communities in America.[42] Taylor thinks that the difference is great enough to be almost a refutation of the secularization paradigm, though he is not sure in the end why America is so different.[43] Perhaps it is a matter of 'enthusiasm': France had too much of it, and its atheism was a revulsion against it; Britain instinctively avoided it; but America is arguably a country where enthusiasm of all kinds, including religious, has a natural home.

While much of Bruce's work is a useful contribution to the current debate – and that wouldn't change if the secularization paradigm were to be overturned – some of the characteristics of social science need to be open to critical scrutiny in order to rescue what is truly useful. For example, Bruce says of the sociology of religion: 'That science and religion may clash over specific propositions about the nature of the world should not cause us to miss the similarities of cognitive style and epistemology.'[44] Yes, if the same method of investigation is applied to the social *communities* of scientists and religionists, no doubt similarities will appear, and may be of considerable interest. But those who participate in either or both science and religion ought to be wary of the assumption that there are any significant similarities of 'cognitive style and epistemology'. Few on either side of the new atheism debate believe such a thing.

Given all this, is it possible that Bruce's picture of religion, even when applied to just Britain, seems to have been overturned by Humphrys' experience only a few years later? Time will tell, but in the meantime, it is worth pointing out that this book is not a sociological exploration of the question of religion, but an *invitation* to engage with it in a certain way.

David Martin

Another key proponent of secularization theory is David Martin, whose *A General Theory of Secularization* was published in 1978, and which was revised in his *On Secularization: Towards a Revised General Theory* in 2005. The later work revises the earlier tenor of secularization, which had, as in Bruce, an air of inevitability about it – its extreme critics would say just another naïve historicism. Instead Martin suggests we 'rather think in terms of successive Christianisations followed or accompanied by recoils.'[45] This is a useful point: perhaps what Humphrys has detected is merely the aftermath of the last recoil. Martin also offers a centre-periphery theory suggesting that secularism is the privilege of an educated elite, who happen also to control cultural production, whereas less educated and rural populations may continue with faith traditions. This may be useful to some degree, but it could not explain the presence of vigorous atheism in some working-class populations, or why cultural production, with sophisticated market-response mechanisms, does not cater better for the religious.

What does emerge from Martin's work is a regret for the march of secularization. A telling statement from him, and a key idea in the formulation of NOMA is: 'Religious language is *sui generis*.'[46] It is exactly this that the new atheists deny, that religion is a magisterium in its own right. Martin goes further and suggests that religion is a 'gold standard' in danger of devaluation as Christianity is secularized, adding later on: 'the priority of faith, hope and love, above all love, cannot be translated in civic and constitutional terms.'[47] As we will see, Humphrys also turns to St. Paul and his formulation of religious love as the simple core of religion, and which represents for him the most important of human values. In terms of the Two-Fold Model, it is love that makes Christianity at core a *bhakti* religion.

Martin's thought is wide-ranging, examining secularization across the globe in a search for common factors and interesting difference, making his writings more dissipated and considerably less certain of the secularization paradigm than Bruce. For example, he says of secularization in his earlier work: 'And then I suggested it was in part an ideological projection on history based on an apotheosis of reason, on an existentialist anticipation of autonomous man, and on a Marxist leap into freedom and into reality with the conclusion of the historical dialectic in class society.'[48] Martin is now critical of these core modernist assumptions. He is also less sure than Bruce about the history of ideas and its relevance to the sociology of religion. Bruce asserts: 'sociological explanations rarely rest on the direct competition of ideas . . .',[49] and says, in the context of postmodernism: 'I do not want to dismiss the work of intellectuals as being of no account, but, if social science has taught us anything , it is there is often a huge gulf between what the "chattering classes" think and do and the lives and worldviews of ordinary people.'[50] Martin does admit that 'I found it very difficult to absorb approaches to secularization based on the history of ideas.'[51] But he also wonders: 'One wants to know whether the notion of the avant-garde is just a conceit, more particularly a French intellectual conceit, and whether there are key strata promoting secularization, such as teachers or scientists or engineers.'[52] What is not much commented upon by either Bruce or Martin is the way in which mainstream cultural production promotes secular values. This ambient culture is likely to be a more pervasive force for secularization than the efforts of the kind of professionals that he cites.

Charles Taylor

While Bruce and Martin work from the field of sociology, Charles Taylor is a philosopher whose *A Secular Age*, introduced earlier, has been published contemporaneously with the recent atheism/theism debate. Taylor, a Roman Catholic, received the 2007 Templeton Prize (worth over $1.5 million), which is an indicator of his importance in the contemporary debate (we will see however that the new atheists, especially Dawkins, are dismissive of the Templeton Foundation and its aims).

Unlike Bruce and Martin, Taylor is not sceptical of the importance of the history of ideas, but his book also draws considerably on the sociological. Like Bruce, he does not believe that science in itself had a simple role in secularization. But it is almost impossible to sum up a work as big and as sophisticated as *A Secular Age* in a short space, partly because Taylor pursues familiar themes with a sharp eye for a fresh phrasing, providing terms that inject great vigour into the current debate.

Taylor identifies three facets of secularity: the common institutions and practices (the domain of the sociological); the practices and beliefs themselves, which are falling away; and what he calls the 'conditions of belief'. It is the latter category, secularism three, which he is most interested in, quite naturally, as a believer and a philosopher. In considering pre-Reformation religion he introduces the notion of 'fullness' as central to the vision of a good human life, and which requires 'God'. He then defines religion, as we saw earlier, in the terms that seem most appropriate to him from the Western tradition – and in considerable awareness of other traditions – as what is 'transcendent' over what is 'immanent'. This allows him to describe a key concept – 'human flourishing' – as that which is defined in terms of the immanent, or material world, against which religion demands a level of self-sacrifice which entails a curtailing of that flourishing. He is then able to make a key definition: 'a secular age is one in which the eclipse of all goals beyond human flourishing becomes conceivable . . .'[53]

Of course, 'human flourishing' here is a secularized version of what people have taken flourishing to mean, so the definition is a little circular, but it does not matter: it captures something essential about the secular mind. Taylor can then go on to say that modernity is about a 'shift in the understanding of what I called "fullness"'. The new understanding progressively does without 'God', and is well-characterised in Weber's term 'disenchantment'. Taylor explains the loss of enchantment through the shift from the 'porous' sense of self in the Middle Ages to the 'buffered' and atomised sense of self in modernity. For example, the porous self is prone to influence from all kinds of spirit entities, some of which could be malign, and hence our peasant ancestors would have thought us insane in our attempts to capture a frisson of this by watching movies of the uncanny.[54] (Indeed, it is an interesting thesis that horror films of the supernatural, such as *Carrie* and *The Exorcist*, allow for an encounter with a certain kind of spirituality that is otherwise denied in secular cultural production.)

Taylor then provides us with another of his telling phrases, this time by which to understand science – that is the Newtonian form discovered in the seventeenth century – as the 'domain of the exceptionless natural law'.[55] He contrasts this to what had been an enduring social reality, that of codes that contained within them the anti-codes, in a way that the laws of natural science could not do. The more ancient codes provided for the 'ludic interval', that is a brief period of play, jest, or overturning of the natural order in carnivals, feasts of misrule, and the like. (Some survive into modernity, such as festivals in Europe where quantities of ripe oranges or tomatoes are hurled at and by participants in a day of celebration.) For a brief period society experiences 'the world turned upside down' not as a negative and regrettable state, but as energising. Drawing on the work of anthropologist Victor Turner, Taylor says that more than just letting off steam, we understand that 'the code relentlessly applied would drain us of all energy; that the code needs to recapture some of the untamed force of the contrary principle.'[56]

Taylor's contrast between the domain of exceptionless natural law, and that of the ancient ludic intervals – structures which contained within them their antistructure – seems to go to the heart of disenchantment. When he says in passing that the arts in modernity now seem the main source of such antistructure, the image is compelling. But he then makes clear what the ludic intervals do in a religious sense: they are irruptions of *eternity* into mundane time. Indeed, to discover that Taylor uses the term 'eternity' as he does is to grasp that he is open to what is core to religion. If we compare his early broad-brush definition of religion (as transcendent over immanent) and include in that his recognition of eternity as a religious term, to Steve Bruce's definition of religion as 'beliefs, actions and institutions that assume the existence of supernatural entities with powers of action or impersonal powers or processes possessed of moral purpose', then we see a radical difference. Bruce offers the more common definition of religion as *intrinsically* bound up with supernatural entities, a definition which almost all of the new atheists we will examine share. If we go to the mystics of the religions as the experts as to what religion is, then supernatural entities are not the common factor at all: they speak more like Taylor does. He also helps us understand why the mystics have disappeared from the contemporary debate, though they are also absent in his account in any direct form. He does so by highlighting the role of the Reformation as ending the ludic spaces of earlier religion.

Firstly, according to Taylor, 'radical Protestantism utterly rejected the multi-speed system.' By this he means that the religious world was stratified into a laity who depended on the clergy, and a clergy likewise distinguished between various callings, broadly divided between the contemplative and the active. In the new order the same religious standard now applied to all without exception. This is laudable in its egalitarianism, but what was lost was the idea of the 'specialist' in religion, and the notion, as Bruce puts it, of the transfer of religious merit.[57] In the pre-Reformation world, and for example in Buddhist countries, the general population participate in religion to a limited degree, but central to that was support for the specialists, the clergy or monks, who, on behalf of the community, maintained the relationship with the sacred, with eternity. But Protestantism created a single category of person in the religious life, even if clergy were retained (though in extreme cases like the Quakers they were not). Secondly, the Reformation becomes the 'engine of disenchantment' by eradicating the old festivals, and pronouncing a new code, a new structure that did not contain within it its anti-structure. Carnivals, feasts of misrule, and all similar events were now seen only as an invitation to license and sin.

Taylor sums it up: 'The energy of disenchantment is double. First negative, we must reject everything which smacks of idolatry ... the second energy was positive. ... A great energy is released to re-order affairs in secular time.'[58] We will return to this idea later on, but here it is worth commenting upon the points of departure between Taylor's account of the emergence of the secular age, and that in *Secularism*. What both have in common is the shared belief that the spiritual or religious impulse is natural to humanity and won't disappear, even if it takes new forms unrecognisable to earlier epochs. As a committed Christian and Western philosopher Taylor presents a more mainstream account, drawing both on more conventional histories of religion and more conventional cultural sources. His much more detailed account of the Reformation and its role in secularization provides some further context that is missing in *Secularism*, but it fails to show that this was in many ways a *regression* to a more Old Testament sensibility. Hence when he assumes that disenchantment was partly a theological move, he is right, but doesn't spot its Old Testament source in the horror of nature religions. Likewise in his account of the proliferation of alternative manifestations of the religious impulse in modernity, he regards this as a 'nova' – something new and expanding, instead of a restoration of the spiritual pluralism found prior to monotheism, and in the far East where monotheism never took hold.

Yet Taylor's immense thoughtfulness and acceptance of what is good in secularism, combined with his quiet certainty of the centrality of the spiritual life, gives his work a subtly postsecular feel. Hence we will later examine his thought again amongst the new defenders of faith.

Graeme Smith

If Taylor's thought occupies the middle ground: reflective, subtle, fully aware of the nature of the secular mind, yet able to retain the sympathy for the religious mind, then Graeme Smith offers an account of secularization that could be a genuine target for the new atheists: he simply denies it. He says that secularization, as usually understood, has not happened. Where Taylor's thought is subtle, Smith's is clumsy, but nonetheless his work is interesting, and provides the counter-argument against which Bruce and other sociologists of secularization have to hone their theories.

In Graeme Smith's *A Short History of Secularism* he states his position early on, and then elaborates with not a great deal more supporting evidence. He believes that 'a majority of people believe in God and call themselves Christians.'[59] Further, he states that 'secularism is the latest expression of Christian thought' as proved in the persistence of ethics; that low church attendance today is just the reversion to the norm of the medieval period after exceptionally high attendance rates in the Victorian era; and that the only difference between the so-called secular era and previous times is that science now provides the medical technology that Christianity used to provide. For his thesis to work, he has to show that Christianity in the medieval period held no greater adherence than today, which he argues on the basis of the notion of 'vicarious religion' (a term owing to British sociologist Grace Davie). This is actually an interesting point, and relates to the issue discussed above in both Taylor's and Bruce's accounts of the transfer of religious merit.

Smith's point is that the medieval peasant did not attend church that assiduously, and that even many priests, being not that well educated, didn't grasp some key basics of the faith, citing as evidence for this the complaints in church records of the time. Bruce pays considerable attention to this argument, noting that whatever the apathy of the laity might have been, they were universally superstitious – a fact complained of in the literature of the day.[60] Bruce's evidence seems stronger than Smith's, but it is Taylor who makes clear the shift that the Reformation brings about: an end to the 'transfer of merit', by which the religious vocation benefits the laity who financially support it. Vicarious religion today – by which Smith means the vague distant approval of the existence of the Church, and the use of it for ceremonies of birth, marriage and death – if it really exists, has a completely different character than in medieval times. It does not assume that the specialists in religion are at all times performing an important intercessionary role for the whole of society.

Smith appears in his outlook to be a theologian of the type that is wedded to his tradition but has no particular interest in the mystics. Where his account is unfortunately parochial is in his insistence that 'Christianity' is coterminous with religion. Nevertheless his broader challenge to secularization theory is of interest, as when he says 'liberalism is the ethical guidance by which most people in the West give substance to their belief in God.'[61] Most secularists might dismiss this, but the secular humanist, when pressed hard on the origins and fundamental source of their prized humanist ethics, is reduced to mumblings or laboured recourse to evolutionary theory (as Dawkins and Dennett attempt). Smith's version has the advantage of brevity: ethics comes out of the religious impulse. It is here that our definition of this impulse – as a profound connectedness – gives purchase: the moral law is the ramification of a reluctance to harm the extended articulation of self discovered in such a profound connectedness. One *naturally* avoids self-harm. An image of this stance can certainly be a 'belief in God', but it can be equally expressed through many other compelling images.

Varieties of Secularization

In the pursuit of an articulation of postsecularism it is important to have a thorough perception of what secularism has come to mean. In this brief examination of the positions of Martin, Bruce, Taylor and Smith we have encountered many of the strands that make up contemporary understandings of secularism and its origins. What must be emphasised alongside these accounts, however, is the thought of the mystics. Thinkers such as Descartes, Spinoza and Leibniz can be interpreted *as* mystics, which quite reframes their contribution to the revolutions of thought leading to the secular world.[62] Hence a further discussion of mysticism now becomes important.

The Negative Theology and the Fate of Mysticism

A hundred years ago the public perception of the 'mystic' and the respect accorded to this person was dramatically different to today. The mystic presented a problem to mainstream religion, and, over the last hundred years, any deference from secularists towards mystics as a thorn in the side of clericalism has been mostly forgotten through the decreasing acquaintance with and sympathy for their writings. From around 1900 to the 1980s a distinguished tradition of scholarship on mysticism produced a religious studies literature that was fairly consistent both in its definition of the mystic, and in the recognition of the mystic as core to religion. The scholars in this tradition include:

Richard Maurice Bucke, Rudolf Otto, William James, Evelyn Underhill, R.C. Zaehner, W.T. Stace, F.C. Happold, and Robert Forman.

William James' seminal work *The Varieties of Religious Experience* was written after Richard Maurice Bucke's *Cosmic Consciousness* and was undoubtedly influenced by it, but Bucke placed the emphasis on transformation rather than experience. He gives the following criteria for the 'cosmic sense' of the mystic which is a state or continuum, rather than an experience:

1. The subjective light
2. The moral elevation
3. The intellectual illumination
4. The sense of immortality
5. The loss of the fear of death
6. The loss of the sense of sin
7. The suddenness, instantaneousness of the awakening
8. The previous character of the man intellectual, moral and physical
9. The age of illumination
10. The added charm to the personality so that men and women are always strongly attracted to the person
11. The transfiguration of the subject of change as seen by others when the cosmic sense is actually present[63]

Later scholars, from Underhill to Happold, have all adopted some variation of Bucke's scheme. Agreement on who is or is not a mystic is not universal, naturally, because of the different backgrounds of each scholar and their confessional alignment, if any. Nevertheless, the common set is large enough, and the literature consistent enough to provide considerable consensus on the nature and status of the mystic. An example of how an early version of this consensus permeated into more general thought can be found in Bertrand Russell's essay *Mysticism and Logic*, first published in 1914, some thirteen years before the text better known to atheists: *Why I Am Not a Christian*. In the essay he seriously considers what he calls 'mystical philosophy', and finds in it four characteristics:

1. Sudden, penetrating, coercive wisdom
2. Unity
3. Denial of the reality of time
4. Evil as mere appearance[64]

These could easily be a condensed version of Bucke's list, and in Russell's elaboration of his four characteristics he writes as one who has an honest and open respect for the possibilities of this 'intuitive' form of knowing. He simply adds: 'Of the reality or unreality of the mystic's world I know nothing',[65] and then goes on to say that he seeks the knowledge given by science instead as a better guarantee of truth. Russell expresses his position as a *preference*, but later in the century no such balanced view of the relative merits of mysticism and science was really open to the serious thinker. Roy Abraham Varghese, who does defend mysticism, suggests that 'Dawkins's intellectual father seems to be Bertrand Russell', on the basis of Dawkins's autobiographical notes, and then goes on to cite Russell: 'Nothing can penetrate the loneliness of the human heart except the highest intensity of the sort of love the religious teachers have preached.'[66] Varghese adds: 'You would be hard put to find any passage that remotely resembles this in Dawkins.'[67] This illustrates that the period between Russell's thought and that of Dawkins represents a hardening of secularism, a move to an extremity. But we will see that mysticism is an issue with a complex response amongst both the new atheists and the new defenders of faith. While the avowed atheist Sam Harris believes in mystical experience,[68] the Roman Catholic Tina Beattie rejects it and find Harris to be a 'heretic' amongst the atheists.[69]

So what happened then to the reputation of mysticism over the last hundred years? The answer, at least in part, is the linguistic turn.[70] The late 1980s and early 1990s saw a debate between religious studies scholars which staked out two positions regarding the undeniable difference in the reportage of the mystics on their experience, a difference that was locatable in the difference in cultural backgrounds. According to the 'perennialist' position this is due to the reaching for the closest metaphors to hand in the prevailing religious (or even secular) culture, while according to the 'contextualists' mystical experience itself is programmed by language and the reportage is merely the documenting of a construct previously encountered in language. As we saw, this culminated in Don Cupitt's assertion that 'mysticism is surfing language.' These two positions are almost impossible to arbitrate between, as it would take the unravelling of the entire linguistic turn in philosophy, its total refutation, to enable a return to the position of Russell in 1914. Of course this is only a question of debate with those who 'buy' the linguistic turn in the first place, which in itself requires one to have some exposure to postmodern thought, or to be a disciple of Cupitt (which by implication members of the *Sea of Faith* organisation are). To put it another way: to take the mystics seriously, in their own terms, is to reject some key strands of modern and postmodern philosophy.

Another issue which has clouded the reputation of 'mysticism' is its conflation – understandable to some degree – with occultism. What is interesting is that the scholars of mysticism listed above are again fairly unanimous that the occultist belongs in a different category, and may meet few or none of the criteria for identifying the mystic. A key occultist of the late-nineteenth and early-twentieth century, with a fairly untarnished reputation to this day, is Rudolf Steiner, and he made it clear why he was not a mystic.[71] Steven Bruce also helps us understand why the mystic, particularly if of the Eastern variety, has been bowdlerized in recent times: this is largely due to naïve New Age adoptions of the principles of mysticism.[72] Mysticism for many contemporaries means only crystals, Tarot cards, dream-catchers, astrology and the like.

For those who are not adherents of the linguistic turn, the question remains: to what degree can one ascertain the 'reality or unreality of the mystic's world'? It seems to be a confused issue if religionists are so often dismissive of or hostile towards the mystic, while some atheists seem to have a real feel for it. And this is what it comes down to, as in Weber's comment about being 'unmusical' to religion. Mysticism is like music: an otherwise apparently homogeneous social grouping will show amongst its members an unpredictable affinity and capacity for either music or mysticism. No amount of logical argument can bridge the gulf between the musical and unmusical. What can be retained, as Russell does, is *respect*.

If Christian theologians seem as divided as the rest of the population in their response to mysticism, they do have a way into the subject via the term 'apophatic' or the negative theology, as mentioned earlier. The negative theology involves a language of 'God' that denies him all attributes, and is hence a powerful force in de-anthropomorphising 'God'. It is mentioned again here because many of the new atheists are aware of this category, while some commentators even conflate mysticism in general with the specific tradition of the negative theology.

But how can the earlier assertion be justified, that mystics are the 'experts' in religion, the 'virtuosi', behind which trail the clergy, the theologians and the philosophers of religion? Clearly at the very least we are asking for a retreat from the linguistic turn. But much more than this, the assertion also implies that the founders of religion, such as Krishna, the Buddha, Lao Tse, Jesus, Muhammad, and so on, are mystics, and that other mystics continue to fructify and give impetus for change within religion. Otherwise the founders of religion would require yet another category. This proposition is usually more abhorrent to religionists than non-religionists, because it removes the special status of the founder of their religion. It is also more abhorrent to Westerners than those from east of Iran, though it is a familiar idea in New Age thought. Little more will be said about this idea at this stage, other than to point out that a postsecular sensibility is open to this possibility.

Scientism and Cultural Autism

The mystical is a category of experience and worldview that relates to Taylor's concept of the 'porous' self of medieval and earlier times. If the mystic is the expert of religion, it is because they have placed themselves at that porous boundary – a move fraught with danger – and have partaken directly of the eternal. Taylor is keen to show that religion provides the irruption of the eternal into secular time, through 'ludic intervals', but does not make it clear that it is the mystic who stands as the advocate for eternity and becomes the engine for its transmission through religion. Otherwise, a football match, or getting drunk, or both, would be ludic intervals sufficient to be religious. Of course, the very value of such secular activities is that they have a family relation, as does drug-taking, with mystical experience: all of this is to do with the suspension of linear mechanical time, the feeling-tone of which is of captivity (Weber's image of the 'iron cage'). But a family relation is not identity, as Huxley made clear with regret at the end of his life: he knew that his drug experiences were a cheap relation to the mystical state of mind of his friend Krishnamurti.[73]

Taylor contrasts the 'porous' self of old with the 'buffered' self of modernity, the latter being isolated and atomised. This self may be sanguine, even joyously separate from the cosmos, as Taylor describes in a variety of memorable images.[74] It is invulnerable, full of macho independence that is perhaps self-consciously hubristic, but proud of it, and if not, Prozac will help.[75] If secular remedies fail there looms anomie, disenchantment, angst, depression, iron in the soul, and so on, a thousand terms made necessary for the 'century of alienation' that is secularism. We will see that the positive image of this buffered self is everywhere in contemporary literature – and will use Ian McEwan's character Henry Perowne in *Saturday* to explore this later. At the same time the negative image of the buffered self, those whose secularist wings inconveniently melt and pitch them into the sea of horrific nihilism, are also well represented, for example by Sartre's Roquentin in *Nausea*.

Secularism introduced a concept by which to flag up the cultural support given to the buffered self: 'cultural autism'. It is now recognised that genius is often accompanied by an emotional impairment, recognized in the terms 'Asperger's syndrome' or 'high-functioning autism'. The joint acronym AS/HFA can be used for this condition. The literature on AS/HFA shows an on-going debate about whether, for example, there can be a clear distinction between Asperger's syndrome and high-functioning autism, but often acknowledges that the film *Rain Man* was a watershed in public awareness of the issue.[76] There is general agreement that autism involves a triad of impairments: social difficulties, communication difficulties, and restricted or repetitive activity.[77] Within AS/HFA there will be normal or above normal intelligence and language skills which may mask social difficulties; the repetitive behaviour which is so limiting in the ordinarily autistic may be part of artistic or scientific activity in the high-functioning version. One account suggests that 'many higher-functioning autistic individuals have particular islands of ability such as unusual memory . . .'[78] and goes on to list the kind of skills exhibited by the autistic character Raymond Babbitt in *Rain Man*. The term 'islands of ability' is useful here, indicating the possibility of genius within a personality that is not rounded, specifically being poorly developed in the emotional and empathetic domains. The autistic protagonist Christopher in the novel *The Curious Incident of the Dog in the Night-Time* perfectly illustrates AS/HFA and how those suffering from the condition gravitate towards the safety of the regular patterns of maths and science.[79]

Individuals such as physicist Albert Einstein and artist Andy Warhol have been considered as suffering from Asperger's syndrome on the basis of impairment of social interaction. Obsessive behaviour is another symptom – Warhol, for example, famously insisted on always wearing the same make of green cotton underpants. However, since *Rain Man*, it is possible that the term 'Asperger's' has gained a popular currency beyond its clinical definition. British popular singer and electronic music pioneer Gary Numan – known for his dystopian lyrics – was asked in an interview about Asperger's syndrome. He replied 'It was suggested I had it when I was younger but no one knew much about it then. I've read a lot about it since and I fulfil some of the diagnostic criteria but not others. I probably only have a mild form.'[80] It is also commonly reported on the Internet that director Stephen Spielberg has been diagnosed as an adult with Asperger's syndrome. In a well-meaning book called *Different Like Me: My book of autism heroes*, a series of well-known and successful public figures are cited as suffering from 'autism' (though better as AS/HFA), including Einstein, Andy Warhol, Wassily Kandinsky, Piet Mondrian, Alan Turing, Lewis Carroll, Isaac Newton, and Immanuel Kant.[81] The issue is now publicly debated, and may even have reached the point where celebrity cachet attaches itself to the term beyond the world of careful clinical research and deliberation.

This is by way of leading to the definition of 'cultural autism' as a stance in the modern mind which *doesn't notice* emotional impairment, or dissonant or inappropriate feeling-responses to events. 'Cultural autism' does not imply actual autism, or even AS/HFA. Instead it is a stance that doesn't notice alienation; indeed, it provides much cultural support for strategic behaviour likely to increase alienation rather than decrease it. It is the milieu of the 'buffered' mind. A key component of this cultural ambience is scientism, the broad philosophy which eliminates vertical time, eliminates the irruption of the eternal, and confines us to the 'domain of the exceptionless natural law'. Scientism completes what the Reformation began. The concept of cultural autism will be useful in considering the stance of some of the new atheists whose argument is based in science.

Defining a Postsecular Sensibility

Having recapitulated the account of the origins of the secular mind as explored in *Secularism*, and considered different accounts that highlight other aspects of the same trajectory and its supposed end-point, we are in a position to refine a little more the concept of postsecularism. So far it has been proposed as a renewed openness to questions of the spirit, while retaining the secular habit of critical thought. To this can be added that such spiritual searching, and the religious or spiritual practices that accompany that searching, are typically *pluralist*, cognisant of mysticism, and reject the cultural milieu identified here as cultural autism.

One can discern the beginning of a postsecular sensibility in the 1970s, but whatever trajectory it was following was altered by the collective cultural response to 9/11. This cultural response includes that of the new atheists and what are called here the new defenders of faith. 9/11 ushered in the end of the 'mutual ignorance pact' or cultural détente that had come into being at the end of the Enlightenment period, where culture and politics became energised, as Taylor comments, while the domain of the sacred became a cultural ghetto, immune to serious debate. An example of this would be the significance of what is known as 'higher criticism' in theology, a form of literary criticism applied to the Bible. Figures such as

Coleridge and George Eliot were involved in the controversy, and it reached a peak around the time of Albert Schweitzer's *The Quest of the Historical Jesus* of 1906. This tradition held within it the possibility of applying all the emerging secular rigour of new disciplines such as literature, history, textual analysis, anthropology and so on, in order to clarify the significance of the Gospels. But the interest in this project faded on both sides: on the religious side because of the failure of the evidence to support anything like the conventional account of Jesus, and on the secular side as interest in religion faded in general. Religion was let off the hook as it were, and subsided thankfully into its enclave.

But since 9/11 secularists are studying religion – though often with the single-minded aim of discrediting it – while religionists are studying science – though often with the single-minded aim of finding gaps into which 'God' can be inserted. Despite these caveats there is a new engagement across the old divide, and, as an example of this, the issue of the historical basis for Jesus is now emerging again into daylight.

Three Eras

Charles Taylor uses the term 'post-secular' just once in his *A Secular Age*, saying of the term:

> I use this term not as designating an age in which the declines in belief and practice of the last century would have been reversed, because this doesn't seem likely, at least for the moment; I rather mean a time in which the hegemony of the mainstream master narrative of secularization will be more and more challenged. . . . In any case, we are just at the beginning of a new age of religious searching, whose outcome no one can foresee.[82]

If postsecularism is emerging it will not look like old religion: modernity is too massive a fact for that. What the term 'postsecular' in juxtaposition to 'secular' also invites is a third term: 'presecular'. The latter might be roughly the same as premodern, but this three-way division of history allows for a different analysis than the more common premodern-modern-postmodern division. Another useful term that is unfamiliar to many is that of the 'religious left'. Some of the anger, or anxiety, of the new atheists is directed at the religious right in America. But what of the spectrum of religious adherents in the West who can broadly be described as liberal or left-wing? Who are anti-war, religiously tolerant, and have adopted many of the basic tenets of modernity? Could postsecularism be better subsumed under the umbrella of the religious left?

Two concerns raise themselves here: firstly that the religious left is – as its proponents bemoan – far more dissipated as a movement than the religious right. Its foundational principles of ecumenism and toleration almost guarantee that. Secondly, that the religious left already holds within it a tension that may be more destructive than creative: the legacy of Marxist scepticism towards religion. How can one truly hold to both socialist principles and faith tradition, when the history of socialism is so predicated on a rejection of faith?

Alternatively, why not subsume postsecularism under the New Age? This is answered in the characterisation of the New Age as prone to the narcissism of difference denied: it does not readily engage in critical thinking. However, even if the religious left is more able to question its own assumptions than the religious right, it is still broadly Christian, and is hence circumscribed in a way that the New Age is not. If a movement really does emerge that can call itself postsecularism, then it will have confluences of thought from both the religious left and from the New Age. But can *any* religious movement really pursue critical thinking, the acuity of which has given Western thought its great heritage of the arts, science and politics? To answer this in the next two sections of the book we examine firstly how a postsecular sensibility appears in some of the new atheism debate, and secondly in a range of other cultural contexts.

Part Two:
Postsecularism and
the New Atheism Debate

Chapter 3:
The New Atheists and Extreme Positions

The new debate between atheists and religionists is no doubt fuelled by anger on one side about the perceived role of religion in terrorist violence and more widespread human rights abuses, and on the other by the intensity of the new onslaught against religion. On both sides extreme positions are taken. The extremes of behaviour which receive religion's sanction in some form or another do make the role of religion in such behaviour a crucial issue. In many ways the new atheists are performing an essential task in bringing to public debate that which might otherwise be swept under the carpet. If one chronicles a majority of the excesses of violence in Western religious history, then their collective root can be identified without qualification: monotheism. We saw that comparable violence, which was and is a universal of human behaviour, gained little sanction or impetus from non-monotheist religions originating east of Iran.

In the following discussion the issue of religious violence and human rights abuses pursued in the name of religion will not be foregrounded, however, because it is assumed as read that these are to be condemned. Neither is there scope here to distinguish between the religious and political elements in the motivations for such acts as Muslim suicide bombings. Such distinctions are vital to make, of course, but to properly explore them requires a very different framework of concepts and historical background to what is provided here or in *Secularism*. All that can be said is that the 'new atheism' clearly has arisen out of revulsion for what *appears* to be religious violence, in particular the attacks of 9/11.

When examining the range of writings that broadly pursue the rubric of the new atheism, one can argue for a ranking that puts the work of Richard Dawkins, Sam Harris and Christopher Hitchens as the most extreme. Dawkins is Professor for the Public Understanding of Science at Oxford University; Harris is an American non-fiction writer and philosopher; and Hitchens is British-American author, journalist and literary critic. Their backgrounds are hence very different, and at times their politics too – particularly on the issue of the Iraq war. What unites them is the certainty that religion is wrong.

Richard Dawkins

Richard Dawkins was introduced in *Secularism* as the 'most truly vituperative of the scientific atheists today'.[1] This is not necessarily a bad thing: the vituperative has the energy of anger, often the anger of moral outrage. Indeed, perhaps the first observation one might make about the new atheists is that they have injected energy into a debate that last had any passion in the nineteenth century. An unattributed witticism holds that the job of the Church of England vicar is to inoculate his parishioners against religion, perhaps making a jest out of an old English distaste for 'enthusiasm' in religion. Energy for religion is a good thing, if there is some genuine engagement, but on the surface at least it appears that Dawkins's energy for religion is purely antagonistic.

His position, spelled out in *The God Delusion*, can be briefly summed up as follows: he defines 'God' as the Old Testament supernatural creator, and this is the 'God' that is a delusion; NOMA is wrong; 'God' is a hypothesis that can be proved or disproved scientifically; moderate religion is bad because it provides the ground for extreme religion – it corrupts the minds of the young; and, finally, though 'Einstein's God' is *not* a delusion, this 'God' is not the subject of Dawkins' attack, but can be trivially believed in, and has a proven capacity to confuse.

The starting point for all the new atheists in their attack on religion is to define religion as a belief in 'God', and to define 'God' in the above terms. Dawkins cites physicist Steven Weinberg (discussed below) who objects to the breadth of use that the term 'God' is put to: 'Weinberg is surely right that, if the word God is not to become completely useless, it should be used the way people have generally understood it: to denote a supernatural creator that is "appropriate for us to worship." '[2] This is stated fairly early on in *The God Delusion*, because Dawkins needs to pin down the 'God' he is sure doesn't exist before stating his main arguments. He goes on to compare the creator 'God' of the Old Testament, who is appropriate to worship, with what he usefully terms 'Einstein's God' – a principle, essence, or whatever we wish to call it, but not a Supreme Being. Dawkins says:

The metaphorical or pantheist God of the physicists is light years away from the interventionist, miracle-wreaking, thought-reading, sin-punishing, prayer-answering God of the Bible, of priests, mullahs and rabbis, and of ordinary language. Deliberately to confuse the two is, in my opinion, an act of intellectual high treason. . . . My title, *The God Delusion*, does not refer to the God of Einstein and the other enlightened scientists of the previous section. That is why I needed to get Einsteinian religion out of the way to begin with: it has a proven capacity to confuse.[3]

This extract is crucial to the whole atheism debate, because the atheists, both now and historically are against a specific under-standing of 'God'. What the new atheists insist on is that the 'God' of 'ordinary language', as Dawkins says, is the Old Testament 'God' – and that he doesn't exist. Scientists such as Dawkins attempt to use science to show that the alleged characteristics of a 'God' so defined are provably untrue. This will not be much under discussion here, other than to point out for the time being that this 'God' is a straw man, and will hence always be an easy target. What is more interesting is Dawkins's genuine admiration for what he calls 'Einstein's God'. Later in *The God Delusion*, in passing, he suggests that 'God' in the Einsteinian sense is something 'we can all trivially subscribe to'.[4]

Dawkins can be described as a nascent *jnani*, meaning that his spiritual impulse – as far as one can discern from his writings – is of a transcendent, non-devotional, *via positiva* type, though perhaps undeveloped. The 'God' of Einstein is the 'God' of the *jnani* impulse, and that to subscribe trivially to it may be easy, but to approach a deep facility with it, the vocation of a certain type of mystic, is arduous.

We saw earlier that Dawkins is quite against Gould's concept of NOMA, saying: 'I simply do not believe that Gould could possibly have meant much of what he wrote in *Rocks of Ages*.'[5] John Humphrys takes Dawkins to task for this: 'How can Dawkins or anyone else presume to know whether someone *means* what they write?'[6] But once NOMA is disposed of it allows Dawkins to pursue his own professional expertise, evolutionary biology, of which he is a fascinating and skilful expositor. The argument against 'God' then becomes an argument against 'God-the-creator' – because Darwin-ism in biology (and cosmogony in physics) gives a more plausible account of the origins of the world and life. This argument is based on the false assumption that, firstly, explanation is paramount to people in general as opposed to just scientists, and, secondly, that religion is primarily about explanation.

What is interesting in Dawkins's work is that he implicitly extends his opposition to NOMA to include the domain of the arts – another vast field of human endeavour that could be dignified with the term magisterium. To put it another way, he believes that the arts are as much amenable to the scientific approach as religion, and perhaps takes this stance in the first instance because artists and poets are often religious, and because the heights of, for example, music, are often cited by the defenders of faith as something close to religious feeling, even ecstasy. The book in which Dawkins explores this in depth is *Unweaving the Rainbow*, which we will look at in Part Three.

Dawkins's stance on moderate religion is crucial. He says:

> Fundamentalist religion is hell-bent on ruining the scientific education of countless thousands of innocent, well-meaning eager young minds. Non-fundamentalist, 'sensible' religion may not be doing that. But it is making the world safe for fundamentalism by teaching children, from their earliest years, that unquestioning faith is a virtue.[7]

Christianity, since its early days, has held faith to be a higher virtue than mere learning, mere science, mere explanation of natural events and phenomena, and this was forcibly expressed by one of Christianity's great intellectuals: St. Augustine. It is also sadly true that Augustine helped cement the association of the word 'unquestioning' with the word 'faith' despite the fact that his faith was the end result of half a lifetime of questioning. Returning to moderate religion briefly, another indicator of Dawkin's dismissal of moderate religion is his dismissal of the work of the Templeton Foundation. He was invited speaker (a 'token atheist') at a Templeton conference in Cambridge where he ascertained that the journalist audience was paid to attend, which prompted this remark: 'My long experience of academic conferences included no instances where the audience (as opposed to the speakers) were paid to attend. If I had known, my suspicions would immediately have been aroused. Was Templeton using his money to suborn science journalists and subvert their scientific integrity?'[8] Yet perhaps a defining feature of moderate religion is that it accepts the findings of science: Templeton does more, in that he funds genuine scientific research.

Nonetheless, Dawkins leaves us with a good question to pursue: what truth might there be in his assertion that 'even mild and moderate religion helps to provide the climate of faith in which extremism naturally flourishes'?[9] And we cannot leave Dawkins without introducing one of his more unique contributions to the religion debate: the idea of the 'meme'. Initially introduced in the book that brought Dawkins to fame – *The Selfish Gene* – 'as a noun that conveys the idea of a unit of cultural transmission or a unit of imitation',[10] it has been developed since then by Dawkins and other writers including Daniel Dennett. It is interesting that one of the earliest uses he puts the idea to is that of the idea of 'God' as 'a meme of high survival value, or infective power, in the environment provided by human culture.' We will explore the role of the meme in the current debate when looking at the thought of Dennett.

Sam Harris

Sam Harris has no difficulty in answering the question, raised by Dawkins, of moderate religion. In *The End of Faith: Religion, Terror, and the Future of Reason*, he says: 'One of the themes of this book, however, is that religious moderates are themselves the bearers of a terrible dogma: they imagine that the path to peace will be paved once each of us has learned to respect the unjustified beliefs of others.'[11] He goes on: 'I hope to show that the very ideal of religious tolerance – born of the notion that every human being should be free to believe whatever he wants about God – is one of the principal forces driving us toward the abyss.' Harris is not trained in science as Dawkins is, and it seems that his readings in religion are more of a life's habit than a venture into the enemy's territory to learn of their alien beliefs. What is alien to Harris, it seems, is monotheism, while Buddhism and what Dawkins refers to as 'Einstein's God' are not. Harris is comfortable with mysticism and spirituality, but clearly does not hold that monotheism as a religion has a source in mysticism: presumably he would deny the proposition that the mystics are the experts or virtuosi in religion. He says: 'Many of the results of spiritual practice are genuinely desirable, and we owe it to ourselves to seek them out.' He adds:

> Such experiences are 'spiritual' or 'mystical', for want of better words, in that they are relatively rare (unnecessarily so), significant (in that they uncover genuine facts about the world), and personally transformative. They also reveal a far deeper connection between ourselves and the rest of the universe than is suggested by the ordinary confines of our subjectivity.[12]

The idea that mystical experience could uncover 'genuine facts about the world' would find strong disagreement from most other new atheists who happen to draw on science to attack religion. This suggests already a divergence of opinion between the new atheists, and hope that the new atheism is more interesting than the old.

Harris sharply divides religion and spirituality and is able to do it by positing brain science as the foundation for the proper understanding of spirituality and mystical experience. He says: 'Science will not remain mute on spiritual and ethical questions for long. . . . [It] will bring even the most rarefied mystical experience within the purview of open, scientific inquiry.'[13] Possibly. But there is nothing ever in science in the present that can make safe a prediction about what will or will not enter science in the future. Just as secularization theory must be bad science to the extent that it predicts the end of religion, so is any assertion that science must necessarily pronounce definitively on spiritual and ethical questions. However, this has become one of the issues thrown up by the new debate, and it is an important one.

Harris agrees with Dawkins that NOMA is not an option, though he does not mention it by name. He says: 'And yet, intellectuals as diverse as H.G. Wells, Albert Einstein, Carl Jung, Max Planck, Freeman Dyson, and Stephen Jay Gould have declared the war between reason and faith to be long over. On this view there is no need to have all of our beliefs about the universe cohere.'[14] He talks about the kind of mentality that can maintain disparate systems of knowledge as 'partitioned'.

But let us return to the key issue that Harris has contributed to the debate: the issue of moderate religion. Nobody on either side of the debate justifies the atrocities of extreme religion, but what Harris emphasises more than most of the new atheists is the proposition that moderate religion, as the background milieu for extreme religion, is fully culpable. Here he is at his most extreme, but also offers some penetrating observations that the defenders of faith have to answer. Firstly, he says, in various ways, that *moderate religion can only exist through the ignorance of its own scriptures*. He maintains that: 'This is a problem for "moderation" in religion: it has nothing underwriting it other than the unacknowledged neglect of the letter of divine law',[15] and that 'Religious moderation is the product of *secular* knowledge and *scriptural* ignorance – and it has no bona fides, in religious terms, to put it on par with fundamentalism. . . . religious moderates betray faith and reason equally.'[16] We will see that Keith Ward, amongst the new defenders of faith, gives the best answer yet to this issue. But it is a good question: how can the religions of the Book update themselves – as Ward would claim they can – when they regard their written scriptures as 'gospel'? This is one of the most useful challenges collectively laid down by the new atheists as they analyse the texts of the religions of the Book, and show how truly ghastly much of it is. How is the moderate believer to answer that? Clearly, as Harris suggests, a strategy deployed up to now has been ignorance. This ignorance, or rather a quiet sweeping of inconvenient textual passages under the carpet, was made possible through the secular era because of the 'mutual ignorance pact'. In this détente Dawkins- and Harris-type objectors were largely absent. Now the issue is in the open again. How is the moderate going to respond to Harris's statement that the 'Bible and the Koran both contain mountains of life-destroying gibberish'?[17] Particularly when the same man says that we owe it to ourselves to seek the genuinely positive results of spiritual practice?

Christopher Hitchens

Christopher Hitchens was an ardent Communist when young, having joined a post-Trotskyite Luxemburgist 'sect'. He makes it clear in *God is Not Great* that he gave up Marxism as the true extent of its excesses became known, but this background still gives his atheism a different edge to that of Dawkins and Harris. He appears still to believe, for example, that Trotsky's materialist critique enabled him 'to be prescient' to an impressive degree.[18] The subtitle to *God is Not Great* is 'How Religion Poisons Everything', which suggests already a fairly extreme position on religion. When discussing car bombs in London he says: 'In one of the most secular and multicultural capitals in human history, the lives of everyone are being poisoned by hatred and violence.'[19] This is a gross exaggeration: a city as vast as London absorbs such events with almost no perceptible change. Even the continued campaign of the IRA only left markers like concrete barriers around the City and the absence of waste bins on the Underground: such things hardly poison lives. He is a clumsier thinker than either Dawkins or Harris, and his scholarship at times is faulty, but his verbal pugilism means that he lands some telling blows. He can do this because of the extent of his acquaintance with religion, acquired through long, and it seems curious contact with people of many different faiths. He even jokes that if this goes on much longer he will be able to update William James's *The Varieties of Religious Experience*.[20] But his engagement with religion is hostile. He states early in his book:

> There still remain four irreducible objections to religious faith: that it wholly misrepresents the origins of man and the cosmos, that because of this original error it manages to combine the

maximum of servility with the maximum of solipsism, that it is
both the result and the cause of sexual repression, and that it is
ultimately grounded on wish-thinking.[21]

These four objections are not systematically explored, but they
are common objections within the atheist canon. They can also be
disposed of quickly, before looking at the more interesting detail of
Hitchens's challenge. 'The origins of man and the cosmos' are not at
all central to religion, merely an accidental and cultural accretion.
The Buddha's insistence on the irrelevance of these questions didn't
mean that Buddhism didn't later acquire certain cosmogonies, but it
is a good indicator that the issue *shouldn't* be central to religion. Why
Hitchens thinks that this 'original error' is the source of 'servility' and
'solipsism' is not spelled out. What he understands as servility is, in
the devotional or *bhakti* traditions, an expression of spiritual love, not
a necessary outcome of a particular cosmogony. And Hitchens's use
of the term 'solipsism' is throughout his work an oddity: he means
by it that the human race thinks of itself as important or central.
Presumably when Alexander Pope says that the 'proper study of
mankind is man' Hitchens doesn't object? In any case, any deeper
acquaintance with religion will show that the *apparent* conceit of the
centrality of man is the opposite. 'Servility' implies – though with
admittedly unfortunate connotations – that the religious aspirant
seeks to come into a proportionate relationship with what is sacred,
however conceived. This proportionality requires a very specific,
though easily misunderstood, self-effacement requiring, in theistic
traditions, the placing of 'God' first in all things. The *bhakti*, however,
does this through love and surrender, while the *jnani* does it through
the purification of the will. As to religion being both the cause and
result of sexual repression, this is mere regurgitated Freudianism.
The issue of celibacy is a purely practical one in religion, in the
first instance, because a real depth of religious feeling demands
the devotion of the majority of one's energies, just as in art and
science. Newton was celibate because he jealously and passionately
guarded his time; a similar motivation has been observed in
Leonardo da Vinci.[22] Of course, every true thing in religion can be
misunderstood and even perverted, hence celibacy can become a
culturally misconceived issue. Finally, when Hitchens says that
religion is grounded on wish-thinking, he is once more repeating
Freud. Again, the perversion, bowdlerisation, popularisation, and
trivialisation of religion takes place much as it does of any serious
endeavour. It is not at all hard to find those who, as in some Christ-

ian or Buddhist cults, pursue religious practice in order to achieve, for example, a brand-new sports car. This isn't religion.

Let us turn to the more interesting points Hitchens makes. As with most of the new atheists he quite rightly catalogues the crimes committed in the name of religion, including various abuses of children such as circumcision, clitoridectomy, the offered filicide of Abraham, denial of medicine on religious grounds, whipping out of the devil, and the teaching of creationism.[23] There is no need to repeat his entire listing; these are mostly incontrovertible evils associated with backward cultures everywhere. The use of religion to justify any of the wrongs listed by the new atheists is a crime both against the victims and against religion, and the new atheists are performing a valuable role in pointing out the former. Hitchens is also consistent with most of the other new atheists in insisting that ethics is and should be independent of religion. His approach to the Bible and Koran is amongst the most extreme, but also perhaps quixotic: while his rejection of much of the Old Testament can be justified, his argument that 'The "New" Testament Exceeds the Evil of the "Old" One' – as his chapter heading has it – is very weak. Certainly it is valuable to note that Christians need to answer the challenge that some of the Gospel account appears to have been constructed in order to retrospectively fulfil Old Testament prophecy. Certainly it is worth pointing out that the contradictions in the externals of the Jesus story across the four gospels make a literal historical interpretation impossible. But to then suggest that fraud is the only alternative is absurd, as it is to condemn Jesus for demonstrating in his parables a 'primitive attitude to agriculture (this extends to all mentions of ploughing and sowing, and all allusions to mustard or fig trees)'.[24] If Jesus is a mystic, then to communicate the 'abstruse, subtle, deep, and difficult to see' teachings – as the Buddha characterises them – requires metaphor, analogy, allusion, in short all the literary devices ever constructed to convey the intangibles of human life. The Buddha, despite growing up a courtier, likewise constructed metaphor out of the ordinary facts of rural life in India. And the failure of mustard seeds to sprout on stony ground hardly flies in the face of modern horticultural theory.

But where, in all of this, does Hitchens find an 'evil' that exceeds for example the widespread exhortations in the Old Testament to the murder of idolaters? Apparently, it is enough for Hitchens that Jesus would not initially tend to the Canaanite woman in Matthew 15:21-28. Jesus tells her that he has been sent only to the lost sheep of Israel. When pressed again he tells her that one should not take the bread from children and give it to dogs, which, it is true, is rather insulting. But when she fails to take offence, and adds that the dogs eat the crumbs from the master's table, he relents, because he sees her faith is great. But what is it she wants? An exorcism. A religious act that Hitchens presumably believes to be only superstition. And what is the evil in all of this for Hitchens? That Jesus racially discriminates. But he only does so to the extent of refusing a free service, and relents when the woman show great faith, indicating that for him, faith is more important than race. Elsewhere in the gospels he shows again that race is not important to him. Perhaps he was tired, or having a bad day, who knows? But this brings us to another crucial point that Hitchens wants to make: it is unacceptable for him that Jesus could be a flesh-and-blood man, a religious teacher. Either he is a supernatural being or he is a madman, to be locked up. Hitchens quotes C.S. Lewis (whose opinion he appears to respect): 'But let us not come with any patronizing nonsense about His being a great human teacher.'[25] Of course, the idea of Jesus as 'merely' a teacher is difficult for Christians, whether they have a rather presecular outlook such as Lewis, or even in the more postsecular sensibility of Charles Taylor, who says: 'The Crucifixion cannot be sidelined as merely a regrettable by-product of a valuable career of teaching.'[26] Hitchens concludes: 'Either the Gospels are in some sense literal truth, or the whole thing is essentially a fraud and perhaps an immoral one at that.'[27] Both Lewis and Taylor stumble here in what could be a true postsecularism; Lewis at the first hurdle, Taylor at the last.

Hitchens's views can be taken as a microcosm of the new atheist stance. Either religion is literally true, as its believers claim, or it is a fraud. Based on the evidence, it is not literally true, ergo it is a fraud. The possibility that religion uses a language of metaphor is ruled out, apparently, because the faithful don't understand it as metaphor. Yet, what on earth are the parables, if not some of the most beautiful religious metaphors ever constructed? Hitchens, as a writer himself, concedes that the Old Testament is replete with 'lapidary phrases' and 'fine verses',[28] so presumably he has heard of allusion, poetics, metaphor, imagery and so on? In which case why is the use of the mustard seed in a parable an example merely of a primitive understanding of agriculture? The issue here is one of reading sympathetically. By all means let us look at the Gospels with critical awareness regarding contradictions surrounding the historical exterior details of Jesus' life, and for good measure let us hold open the very question of his status as a historical figure. But when his teachings are examined with an empathetic attention to the complete oeuvre, as it were, of direct exhortations and indirect instruction through parable, something of palpable goodness and beauty emerges. But Hitchens is too impatient, as is shown when he dismisses as 'pointless pseudoprofundity' Jesus' injunction 'let not thy left hand know what thy right hand is doing'.[29] Hitchens leaves out the contextualising first part of the injunction: 'But when thou doest alms' and the explanation that such charitable acts are to be done in secret, rather than for show (Matthew 6:3-4). Who could argue with the exquisite humanity of this dictum, even if the further explanation in terms of the 'Father' holds no resonance for the modern mind? (Even then, it is not so hard to understand 'Father', as Jesus uses the term, as a metaphor for existence itself.)

What enables Hitchens and the other new atheists to pursue the strategy of insisting on the literalness of religion rather than accepting its statements as metaphorical, is the unfortunate insistence of many religionists on this very point. This is partly an outcome of the Reformation, which renewed the emphasis on the text of the Bible, on both sides, and partly the tendency of Western religion to be a tradition of texts, in contrast to the East where religion is more a tradition of teachers. Hence, also, C.S. Lewis's indignation at the idea of Jesus as a teacher: it isn't a Western idea at all.

Hitchens is also against Eastern religion, and is somewhat remarkable in apparently believing that the Dalai Lama is as culpable a promoter of bad religion as any Old Testament prophet. This may be partly due to his Marxist background, shown perhaps in the remark that Tibetan Buddhism 'kept the population in permanent serfdom to a parasitic monastic elite.'[30] He also suggests, as do many of the new atheists, that it 'can even be argued that Buddhism is not, in our sense of the word, a "religion" at all.'[31] This is an interesting issue. Atheists, in setting up a Western-style anthropomorphic 'God' to knock down, generally want to knock down all of religion, but notice that the death of 'God' is no death-blow at all to non-theistic religions like Buddhism. Hence the frequent avowal that Buddhism is not a 'religion'. In this there is collusion from some monotheists, from many of whom emanates a long-standing hostility to Eastern religion. What is also notable is that atheists in an inverted way collude with the cultural assumption that Christianity is the natural heritage of the West, and is superior to other religions. This is noticeable, for example, in Steve Bruce's account of Eastern religion in *God is Dead*: there is an undercurrent of Western chauvinism in it. Taylor notes: 'Even French atheists are a trifle horrified when religion doesn't take the standard Catholic form that they love to hate.'[32] Clearly British and American atheists show similar tendencies.

Finally, two more elements in Hitchens's thesis must be addressed: that the excesses of Nazism and Communism are somehow religiously inspired, and that Gould's NOMA is implausible. The issue of the horrors of totalitarian regimes, such as those of Hitler, Stalin, Mao Zedong and Pol Pot, crops up regularly in the new atheism debate. The defenders of faith generally cite these regimes to argue that secular ideologies are in fact more dangerous than religious ones, if one goes by body-count at least. The new atheists on the other hand have come to regard the ideologies behind the Nazi and Communist slaughters as a *form of religion*. It is perhaps John Gray in his book *Black Mass* who has pushed this thesis the hardest. Hitchens neatly demonstrates the mileage in this idea when he says 'To begin with a slightly inexpensive observation, it is interesting to find that people of faith now seek defensively to say that they are no worse than fascists or Nazis or Stalinists. One might hope that religion had retained more sense of its dignity than that.'[33] This issue will be examined in further depth later, but it remains to complete these notes on Hitchens with his particular take on NOMA. He does agree that science and religion are separate magisteria, but disagrees with Gould in that he believes them to be antagonistic.[34]

Richard Dawkins, unlike Sam Harris and Christopher Hitchens, is a scientist who draws on his own expertise to make the case against 'God'. He is joined by a number of other scientists, including Francis Crick, Victor J. Stenger and Steven Weinberg. Crick was a vituperative enough atheist, but died in 2004, and left no major written contribution to the new atheism debate. Dennett himself is not a scientist, but draws heavily on science, while Stenger and Weinberg add different scientific arguments that bulk out Dawkins's position. We now look at the work of Dennett, Stenger and Weinberg, and then move on to examine two philosophers, Michel Onfray and A.C. Grayling.

Daniel Dennett

Dennett is a philosopher who has adopted evolutionary theory and artificial intelligence as scientific domains from which to pursue philosophy, making him perhaps more important as an expositor of science than as a philosopher. His position on religion in *Breaking the Spell* can be summed up as follows: 'God' is an anthropomorphic agent who can intervene in real time, while a religion without 'God' is like a 'vertebrate without a backbone';[35] religion can be investigated scientifically (with the emphasis on Darwinism); and what he calls 'folk religion' (shamanism etc) developed into organised religion by analogy with the domestication of animals. As an outsider peering into the domain of religion he is often generous towards it, saying for example: 'There is much for religion lovers to be proud of in their traditions, and much for all of us to be grateful for.'[36] He also advocates a modest non-supernatural spirituality, and so is in good company with Harris, though he makes no claims to personal experience as Harris does.

Dennett's approach starts from this belief: 'The spell that I say *must* be broken is the taboo against a forthright, scientific, no-holds-barred investigation of religion as one natural phenomenon among many.'[37] He wants the 'most intensive multidisciplinary research' we can muster to investigate the global phenomenon of religion, adding that up to now, 'there has been a largely unexamined mutual agreement that scientists and other researchers will leave religion alone.' This observation could lend support to the idea that NOMA has been a de facto position amongst scientists up to now, and to the idea that the 'mutual ignorance pact' is now breaking down. As with other new atheists however, he rejects NOMA. He disagrees with Émile Durkheim and Mircea Eliade that to properly study religion one must bring to it something of a religious sentiment, and that it must be grasped at its own level. Dennett usefully labels their stance as 'pre-emptive disqualification' meaning that those who do not have a religious sensibility are regarded by the defenders of faith as unqualified to research religion.[38] Quite obviously religion has been studied from the external vantage points of philosophy, anthropology, psychology and so on, and it would be foolish to argue that this should not take place. What can be demonstrated is that the picture of religion so constructed will contain within it the assumptions of that external, secular discipline, rather than its own. Hence such studies often represent a *disengagement* with religion, rather than the possibility of a deeper understanding.

Dennett is adamant that religion has to have a 'God' and that this 'God' is anthropomorphic. If Dennett *really* wants a global research programme into religion, then both of these stances have to be abandoned (because of the existence, spread historically and geo-graphically, of non-theistic religions), but he makes them central. Even the three monotheisms have made strenuous efforts to rid their 'God' of the accretions of anthropomorphism, though it is true that these efforts are not widely known to the ordinarily faithful. Dennett is aware of such moves within monotheism however, and considers them a 'pious fog of modest incomprehension.'[39] He goes on:

> If what they call God is really *not* an agent in their eyes, a being that can *answer* prayers, *approve* and *disapprove*, *receive* sacrifices, and *mete* out punishment or forgiveness, then, although they may call this Being God, and stand in awe of *it* (not *Him*), their creed, whatever it is, is not really a religion according to my definition.

He adds that, while it is not a religion, it might be a wonderful (or terrible) surrogate for religion, or a *former* religion, or an offspring of religion that bears a family resemblance, but is another species altogether. But 'species' of what?, one might ask Dennett. All that Dennett is achieving here is to conform to the Western religious cultural assumptions of which he is the unquestioning inheritor, and allowing himself, as with the other new atheists, to create the straw man (or straw 'God') that takes no effort at all to knock down.

He draws on the sociologists Rodney Stark and Roger Finke who suggest that there are 'godless' religions all over the world which include, in their characterisation, 'elite forms of Buddhism, Taoism, and Confucianism.'[40] But 'elite' means 'expert' in science, so why not accept that 'elite' in religion likewise implies a truer religion? Dennett returns to the theme when he declares of the efforts over time to de-anthropomorphise 'God': 'I can think of no other concept that has undergone so dramatic a deformation.'[41] In *Secularism*, it was pointed out that the move to de-anthropomorphise 'God' is simply that taken by any religious person with a *jnani* as opposed to a *bhakti* temperament.[42] It is not a deformation, but a different conceiving.

NOMA as a theory is not much developed, because, as its detractors remark, it has not (so far) had much support from either side. While NOMA regards religion as *sui generis*, it does not suggest that religion cannot be studied from other disciplines, merely that the results of such study may not be attuned to the essence of religion. Much may still be learned, however, so what is it that we might learn from Dennett's and Dawkins's application of meme theory to religion? As Dennett says of NOMA: 'the disciplinary isolation it creates has become a major obstacle to good scientific practice'[43] – so what is the good practice revealed as he breaks down the 'isolation'? Is it in fact good *scientific* practice to apply the methods of science to religion at all? Descartes was sure that the methods of science apply to extended stuff only, to material things, which can be repeatably and consensually observed. In psychology this approach leads to behaviourism, and in human affairs more generally it leads to the social sciences. The social science approach to religion is well represented in the work of Steven Bruce, as we saw earlier, and to the extent that Bruce strays from the observational basis of his discipline, the more of a speculative futurology it becomes. So how does meme theory as an approach to religion stand up against the more established 'sciences'?

The theory of memes arose with Dawkins's introduction of the term in 1976, as an analogy with 'gene'. Dennett has been an enthusiastic promoter of the idea and wrote the entry on memes for *The Encyclopaedia of Evolution*. He begins by saying that natural selection is substrate neutral, meaning that it can be observed in a number of systems beyond the biological one, and then defines three conditions for evolution: replication, variation (mutation), and differential fitness (competition).[44] There is of course an immediate problem with this, in that to convincingly claim that evolution is substrate neutral would be to have observed evolution in a variety of material substrates – after all, science deals with material stuff. But 'evolution' outside of the biological substrate has only been 'observed' in the non-material field of human ideas, or in human artefacts such as tools or aeroplanes, which are the product of human thought. Of course, there is a suggestion that memes will one day be found to have a physical basis in synaptic configurations in the brain. But this is like saying that an idea has a physical basis in the storage of data in the bistable devices of computer memory and the algorithms operating on that data. But it is not possible to reverse engineer computer hardware and find 'ideas' in it, any more than ideas reside in the ink of printed books. Robert Pirsig, in his second philosophical novel *Lila*, is adamant on this: such an attempt is the error of hierarchical category mistake (more on this later).[45]

The selfish gene survives because it lends to its organism a feature that helps the organism survive, which means that it can extract energy from its ecological niche long enough to reproduce. This is called the 'fitness function' – the context external to the organism that provides the selection pressures on the genes. Meme theory as an analogy with gene theory has no difficulty in the parallel: ideas are seen as replicable, and subject to variation or mutation. But where is the equivalent between the iron economics of energy exchange between organism and environment that provides the fitness function for the gene, and that for the meme? One example suggested by Dennett is that by acting as host to the 'God' meme, the human who does so will become more attractive to a mate, and therefore reproduce. Those without the 'God' meme have to continue with the precarious task of extracting energy from the environment with less guarantee of mating. Hence their competing meme, perhaps the atheism meme, will die out. But, given that the 'God' meme also carries within its 'memeplex' a sub-meme that in many cases calls for sexual restraint or even celibacy, it is hard to see how this particular meme theory of 'God' takes us anywhere. Also, we note that atheists breed quite successfully. Dawkins has made the 'atheism' meme attractive to millions, based on the energy and imagination of his writings. How then do these two memes slug it out in the ecology of human culture? Perhaps the fitness function for memes is their truth-value: how closely do they correspond to real-world facts? Which brings us back to the proofs for and against the existence of 'God'. If 'God' is proven to exist then the meme for it will survive, on this theory, and if not, it will be replaced by the atheism meme. Which is to say nothing at all. One doesn't need meme theory to know that proven ideas are likely to succeed. What is very hard in the religion debate is to know what stands as 'proof'. For most committed religionists it is *feeling* that proves religion, not intellectual proof – and certainly not scientific proof.

Victor J. Stenger

Victor Stenger's work is interesting precisely because he believes that the existence of 'God' is open to scientific proof, or rather that, because scientific proof is absent, so is 'God'. This part of his book *God: The Failed Hypothesis* is the least interesting, though entirely consistent with the mainstream of new atheism. He says: 'My analysis will be based an the contention that God should be detectable by scientific means simply by virtue of the fact that he is supposed to play such a central role in the operation of the universe and the lives of humans.' He adds later: 'The existence of a God will be taken as a scientific hypothesis.'[46] Stenger is emeritus professor of physics and astronomy at the University of Hawaii, and also has a post in philosophy, so his stance here is interesting. What, normally, constitutes a 'scientific hypothesis', and, more specifically, for a physicist? Is Stenger speaking here as a physicist or a philosopher? The issue is that physics, when constructing scientific hypotheses, does so in terms of matter, defined as substances capable of energetic exchange. But, even according to the literalist and extremely narrow definition of 'God' common to the new atheists, 'God' isn't material. This means that hypotheses about 'God' *cannot* be scientific:

there are no energetic exchanges possible between a non-material object and material objects, as there can be between material objects alone.

Stenger does not address this problem, instead defining his 'God' through a list of his alleged acts and attributes, including creator of the universe and its laws, interest in humans to the point of intervening in their lives and providing morality, and so on. By ignoring 'God's' universally-agreed on status as non-material, Stenger provides a portrait of his 'God' which is even more literal than that of extreme Protestants. What Stenger proposes, then, is to consider all the accounts of 'God's' alleged involvement in the physical universe, and see if evidence exists for that involvement. He does this under two main categories: Intelligent Design (ID), and 'fine tuning'. Intelligent design is the theory that, while evolution is true, it only holds *within* species as they adapt to environments, and so cannot account for the origin of species; neither can evolution account for the origins of the first life forms, or biogenesis. The fine tuning argument holds that various values of dimensionless scientific constants, ratios and other features are fine-tuned for life, because the slightest variation in them would produce, for example, no stable planets, or even no stable atoms. Fine tuning is sometimes used interchangeably with the 'anthropic principle', but is in fact a subset of it. The anthropic principle includes fine tuning and also elements of quantum theory (and *ought* to include aspects of relativity).

What is really valuable in Stenger's contribution is to show what is at stake when the defenders of faith draw on either Intelligent Design or the anthropic principle to support their outlook. In other words, what is at stake when religionists attempt to use science as an argument *for* 'God' rather than against 'God'. As a physicist, it is perhaps natural that his arguments against the anthropic principle are the more important part of his contribution, whereas his arguments against intelligent design are duplicated elsewhere. Stenger says 'One of the many major flaws with most studies of the anthropic coincidences is that the investigators vary a single parameter while assuming all the others remain fixed.'[47] The importance he places on this shows at the very least that, firstly, caution is needed when clinging to the anthropic principle as evidence that the universe was designed for human life, and, secondly, that a considerable grasp of physics is needed. Stenger also appeals to a sense of proportion: 'If God created matter with human life in mind, he did not use very much of it for his purpose. If God created order, he did not make much of that either.'[48]

One could call this an issue of 'cosmo-theophany', the question of whether manifest existence reveals the divine to us. The existence of beauty and order in Nature appears to the *via positiva* kind of religionist as the revelation of what is sacred, and, if they happen to be monotheists, they call this sacred quality 'God'. So it is interesting that Stenger points out that, if you add it up, there is not much order in the universe, and, if life is 'God's' key creation, that he breathed it into so little of the vast amount of matter he made.

Unlike Harris, Stenger has no sympathy for mystical experience (though the thinks meditation may have a therapeutic effect), saying 'we will see that no information supposedly gained during a mystical or religious experience, which could not have been otherwise known to the individual claiming the experience, has ever been confirmed.'[49] But he largely conforms to the new atheist view that those who believe in a non-literal 'God' are, variously, not playing by the rules, 'deforming' the concept, or, essentially, non-combatants in the debate. If a religionist chooses not to believe in Stenger's 'God' then he says: 'I have no quarrel with her. . . . This type of deist god . . . is functionally equivalent to nonexistent as far as humans are concerned.'[50]

Steven Weinberg

Steven Weinberg is an American physicist, and Nobel laureate for his contributions to the understanding of the forces between elementary particles. He is known for his atheism and for two aphorisms. The first of these is: 'Religion is an insult to human dignity. With or without it you would have good people doing good things and evil people doing evil things. But for good people to do evil things, that takes religion.'[51] This is memorably expressed, but open to the serious objection that Marxism and various forms of fascism also persuade good people to do evil things: more precisely it is extreme ideologies that do so. This point was raised earlier in connection with remarks from Hitchens, and will be returned to later as part of the discussion on the 'Black Mass Fallacy'. Weinberg's other 'much-quoted aphorism' according to *The New York Times* is 'The more the universe seems comprehensible, the more it also seems pointless.'[52] Weinberg tells us that this was a little rash; what he meant was that progress in science does not increasingly reveal a purpose to the universe.[53] But whatever his precise intention, the cat is out of the bag: science can reveal no meaning.

Weinberg keeps good company with the new atheists, sharing much common ground with them. He is against Gould's NOMA, and does not believe that the anthropic principle is any kind of evidence for 'God'. He considers religious liberals to be irrelevant. 'I happen to think that the religious conservatives are wrong in what they believe, but at least they have not forgotten what it means really to believe something. The religious liberals seem to me to be not even wrong.'[54] This is interesting because it crops up quite regularly: atheists almost nostalgically cling to a conservative vision of the religion they want to disprove. Putting it another way, Weinberg wants 'God' to have a certain character, so that he can deny him: 'Einstein's God' is not for Weinberg, this is too vague. He says: 'Some people have views of God that are so broad and flexible that it is inevitable that they will find God wherever they look for Him. . . . But if words are to have any value to us, we ought to respect the way that they have been used historically.' For Weinberg, as for the other new atheists, 'God' must be an interested 'God', the lawgiver and punisher. Spinoza's 'God', where the term is interchangeable with 'Nature' or perhaps order or harmony, is not good enough. Weinberg concludes: 'Of course, anyone is free to use the word "God" in that way, but it seems to me that it makes the concept of God not so much wrong as unimportant.'[55]

It is worth commenting a little further on the habit of the new atheists to demand that 'God' be defined in a certain way, protesting loudly at any broader usage. Historically the word has had a huge range of meanings, but what Weinberg and the others seem to be defending in order to knock it down is a central part of Western cultural heritage. The move by Hitchens and Dawkins, for example, to praise the Bible as an important part of Western cultural heritage is part of this mindset. It is hard to see anything more in this than a form of cultural conservatism, consistent with their general disinterest in the transgressional and anti-hegemonical basis of avant-garde art and cinema in the twentieth century. To the extent that the new atheists are broadly cultured – and are insistent that the arts no more introduce the 'spiritual' than religion – it appears that their interest tends to peter out in the early part of the nineteenth century.

Weinberg has, like most of the others, an aesthetic sense, and is keen that this is not evidence of 'God' or a reason to take religion seriously. Let us pursue the idea introduced above of a 'cosmo-theophany' as a response, necessarily intense to some degree, to the cosmos – that is, to the material world in the very small, from fundamental particles up to bacteria, the middle, the world of visible Nature, and the very large, the astronomical. It is has a family resemblance to what is normally called 'theophany', an experience of 'God', and indeed 'theophany' would be a perfectly adequate term if the 'theo' in it did

not limit its purview to 'God'-oriented discourse. Weinberg objects
to this passage in the Psalms: 'The heavens declare the glory of God;
and the firmament showeth his handiwork.' He says: 'The stars tell
us nothing more or less about the glory of God than do the stones on
the ground around us.'[56] But he also admits that 'nature seems more
beautiful than strictly necessary' (he has blue jays, yellow-throated
vireos and, 'loveliest of all', the red cardinal outside of his window)[57]
and that there is a beauty in the laws of nature. There is also beauty in
stones, as the great poet of the *via positiva*, Thomas Traherne, remarks.
Later on we will return to this issue: why do the new atheists, to the
extent that many of them find beauty in the world at a pitch that we
could call a cosmo-theophany, divide this so fiercely from religious
experience? When Einstein, their touchstone it seems for greatness in
all respects, wrote so movingly about the beauty of existence?

Michel Onfray

Michel Onfray is a postmodern French philosopher who considers
psychoanalysis essential to philosophy. It is significant that about
the only works of his so far translated into English are those that
propound his atheism, particularly *In Defence of Atheism: The Case
against Christianity, Judaism and Islam*. The book is useful as a French
take on atheism, though the cultural specificities are only hinted at
in it. Onfray proposes an 'atheology' to counter theology, and defines
his atheism as a 'total immanence' in which all transcendence is
denied. While it was argued in *Secularism* that the traditional Western
opposition in the terms 'immanence' and 'transcendence' made the
latter term more problematic than it need be, there is no doubt that
it is a useful shorthand in the atheism debate. Where Charles Taylor,
as a contemporary philosopher, holds the transcendent within this
dualism as credible, Onfray is certain from the outset that philosophy
must deny it. He argues for postmodernism as the proper framework
for the denial of the transcendent, and accuses other atheists of
missing the postmodern boat, as mentioned earlier.[58]

Onfray is generally scandalized that Enlightenment thinkers such
as Voltaire, Montesquieu, Rousseau, and d'Alembert 'strenuously
rejected atheism'.[59] Even worse is Kant, 'a monument of timid
audacity', whose epic works he dismisses because atheism is not the
destination of his thought: 'The Kantian mountain gives birth to the
Christian mouse.'[60] Likewise he asks: 'Where is Spinoza's atheism?
Nowhere. We could scour his life's work in vain for one sentence
asserting the nonexistence of God.'[61] Instead, Onfray praises the first
atheists, including Holbach and La Mettrie, and then Feuerbach,

Nietzsche, Marx and Freud as ushering in the 'age of suspicion' which both separate faith and reason and provide the basis for postmodern thought. Darwinism does not feature in Onfray's system, which omission is consistent with postmodern scepticism towards science as just another grand narrative.

But Onfray is a little conflicted: firstly in a wonderful story he tells of time spent in the Mauritanian desert with a Muslim, and secondly when he finds that the extreme relativism of the postmodernism he broadly adheres to is crushing. Onfray travelled in Africa with a local driver called Abduramane, and initially attempted a dialogue regarding the parts of the Koran that justify terrorism. The new atheists are united in this: they hold up parts of the 'holy' books to the believers in an attempt to show them how unholy they are – because, as Harris points out, the faithful largely remain so through *ignorance* of their own scriptures. But Abduramane is offended, and they lapse into silence. Later on Onfray returns to what he regards as a key fraud perpetrated on the monotheist believer: the rewards of the afterlife. But instead of convincing Abduramane of the deception in it Onfray was himself confronted with a moral issue that clearly affects him. Abduramane confessed to him of a crime that he would have to answer to when the time of reckoning came: he had run over and killed a jackal on a desert road while breaking the speed limit. Had he obeyed the law, he was convinced, the animal would have lived. 'Abdou had failed to respect the law, and would have to account for his crime on the day he died. In the meantime, he must strive in his smallest actions to atone as best he could. The jackal would be waiting at the gates of paradise.'[62] For Onfray the creature becomes the 'ontological jackal' and symbolises for him the contradiction: how could the same religion lead both to the saintliness of Abduramane and to the actions of the 9/11 perpetrators? Onfray cannot accept that the guilt of Abduramane is willingly borne and in any way beneficial, or perhaps he is simply responding with a generosity of feeling when he adds: 'I would have given anything for the animal to disappear and liberate the soul of this honest man.' But a religionist would say that the animal, in its continual presence, *is* Abdu's liberation: it is the image of his conscience, the organ by which he feels his profound connectedness to all things.

A.C. Grayling

A.C. Grayling is one of the few other philosophers to have waded into the recent debate as a new atheist. His is perhaps the typical stance of a philosopher against religion, regarding it as a sophistry which would be easily exposed by the rationality of Aristotle and Kant, were the faithful only to study them. In his *Against All Gods: Six Polemics on Religion and an Essay on Kindliness* he several times asserts that religion is in its death-throes,[63] though he does not draw on the sociology of religion, as does Steven Bruce, in order to support the assertion. What Grayling does do is insist that the terms of the new atheism debate are highly charged: 'And if the tone of the polemics here seems combative, it is because the contest between religious and non-religious outlooks is such an important one, a matter literally of life and death, and there can be no more temporising.'[64] However conventional Grayling's take is on religion as a philosopher, he marks his entry into the new debate with this remark by stepping out of the decorum that had marked it through most of the twentieth century. He is also very much a philosopher when he wants to lecture the faithful on the precise meaning of terms, in the belief that this will sort out the confusion.

As with the other new atheists, and a world away from the thought of a philosopher like Charles Taylor, he thinks the faithful ruin things by being vague about 'God'.

> Apologists for faith are an evasive community, who seek to avoid or deflect criticism by slipping behind the abstractions of higher theology, a mist-shrouded domain of long words, superfine distinctions and vague subtleties, in which God is nothing ('no-thing, not-a-thing') and does not even exist ('but is still the condition of the possibility of existence' – one could go on) – in short, sophistry, as it would be called by those who have attempted a study of the real masterworks of philosophy, for example the writings of Aristotle and Kant.[65]

One might conclude from this that Grayling cannot see the distinction between philosophy and theology, and, unlike Onfray, has not spotted that Kant leaves behind just such an indeterminate 'God' of which he complains. Neither does he take note of Tertullian's sharp complaint, echoing through the early Christian centuries: 'what has Athens to do with Jerusalem; what has the Academy got to do with the Church; what has the heretic got to do with the Christian?' It seems that philosophers and even many of the faithful – perhaps most of them – have forgotten that Aristotle was a heretic until the time of Aquinas. At the core of Christianity is the stance that to *read* philosophy is to *do* heresy, or at the very least philosophy and the like just 'puffeth up' as St Paul puts it (I Corinthians 8:1).

So far we have mainly looked at new atheists drawing on science or philosophy to argue against religion. Hitchens, while he also argues from these fields, is a journalist and critic by trade, and it is interesting to consider the broad field of criticism to see what other new atheists emerge from it. Obviously, the new atheists are mostly long-standing atheists who have been galvanised since 9/11; what is new is the energy of their objections. Amongst journalists in the UK one might include *Guardian* writers Polly Toynbee and Johann Hari amongst the new atheists: Hari wrote positive reviews of Hitchens's *God is not Great* and Harris's *The End of Faith*. Also worth pointing out is the phenomenon of atheist scientists such as Dawkins and Atkins publishing either articles or letters in the press just after 9/11, ranting about the evils of religion, in addition to novelists like Martin Amis. Amis comments: 'An unusual number of novelists chose to write some journalism about September 11 – as many journalists more or less tolerantly noted.'[66]

But what about the wider world of contemporary culture: novels, film, TV, plays, music, and poetry? Here it seems that some novelists, who had prior to 9/11 pursued a strongly secular agenda in their fiction, have been galvanised into more direct protest against religion. At first glance it seems that this is a phenomenon that takes different shape in the US compared to the UK and Europe. The British novelists Martin Amis and Ian McEwan appear much more strident than, for example, American novelist John Updike, in their approach to terrorism. (Updike is not an atheist, but his brand of contemporary secularism makes his work an interesting comparison.) Fantasy novelist Philip Pullman, in his long-standing hostility to Christianity, also seems to have no direct counterpart in America.

Martin Amis

Martin Amis is the most vituperative British novelist amongst the new atheists, almost spittingly so. His anthology *The Second Plane* includes essays published in *The Guardian*, *The Observer*, *The Times*, and *The New York Times*, and a short fiction piece imagining the last moments of one of the 9/11 hijackers, published in *The New Yorker*. There is a note of hysteria in his new atheist writings, despite his cool prose: his British parochialism is punctured; his importance as a 'writer' undermined by *world events* – how *rude* – hideously indifferent to the small round and certainties of his cocooned literary existence. He acknowledges with great honestly that he felt a couple of hours after the 9/11 attacks that 'all the writers on earth were considering . . . a change of occupation.' His published books – a 'staccato biography' – now seemed so unimportant, and, as an additional belittlement, his own oeuvre ended with a book called *The War Against Cliché.*[67] He ruefully notes: 'I thought: actually we can live with "bitter cold" and "searing heat" and the rest of them. We can live with cliché. What we have to do now, more testingly, is live with war.'

Amis, of course, does not have to live with war: it is the Iraqis and Afghanis who live with war as a result of 9/11. But he has pursued what is open to him as a writer, to turn journalist to some degree, and, more appropriately as a writer of fiction, has engaged in what fiction is largely for: envisioning the *what-it-is-like-to-be* of the object of current attention, the terrorist. His short story 'The Last Days of Muhammad Atta' will be compared later with John Updike's novel-length venture into the same field, *Terrorist*. But first, let us consider him as a new atheist. Although, as we shall see, he conforms to most of the tenets of new atheism, he has written at one point that he had 'reclassified' himself as an agnostic.[68] A bible-burning atheist at the age of twelve, he later recognised that the 'soul had legitimate needs' and that spiritual needs can be met by contemplation of the 'bizarre, prodigious, and chillingly grand' universe (a recognition of what is hinted at with the clumsy coinage 'cosmo-theophany'). Amis is a writer, after all, and perhaps can't sign up to a totally immanent universe, à la Onfray. But he is a functional atheist in terms of religion, saying for example that 'Since it is no longer permissible to disparage any single faith or creed, let us start disparaging all of them.'[69] He adds: 'Religious belief is without reason and without dignity, and its record is near-universally dreadful.' When comparing George W. Bush with Saddam Hussein, he calls Bush more 'psychologically primitive' for being more religious,[70] an interesting assumption. This is compounded when he declares that 'Opposition to religion already occupies the high ground, intellectually and morally.'[71] It is often just this claiming of the moral high ground for atheism that the new defenders of faith react against.

Amis perhaps best represents the outrage of middle-class 'middle-England' which has little experience of or interest in other cultures, including the working class in its midst. Hence Amis opposes any move to establish some kind of moral symmetry – what he calls the 'fetishisation of balance'[72] – between Islamism and the West; he downplays the role that legitimate grievance may have, and laments the political correctness that requires temperate language regarding Islam.

Ian McEwan

The novelist Ian McEwan contributed an essay titled 'End of World Blues' to Christopher Hitchens's compilation, *The Portable Atheist*. It focuses on the apocalyptic element of extreme monotheism – a topic not yet elaborated on in our survey of the new atheists, but which will be considered in more detail when exploring the 'Black Mass Fallacy'. McEwan concludes his discussion of apocalypticism with: 'end-time faith is probably as immune to the lessons of history as it is to fundamental decency.'[73] His atheism is summed up in the rather staid middle-England formulation 'it is highly improbable that there is anyone up there at all.'[74] Of more interest is seeing how his atheism stretches its legs in his novels; we will briefly consider *Saturday* and *Enduring Love*. McEwan writes for the British middle-classes, and in these two novels the anxiety caused by the intrusion of coarse 'working class chappies' as the main 'other' (along with burkha-clad women), is in the end assuaged by healthy doses of British all-round public-school competence.

Saturday follows one day in the life of neurosurgeon Henry Perowne, a day which happens to be that of the culmination of antiwar protest in London: 15 February 2003, when perhaps a million marchers made known to the Government their objection to the imminent invasion of Iraq. Perowne can stand for us as the left-leaning secular middle-class Englishman whose world since 9/11 has shifted on its granite foundations. Its discrete middle-class atheism – refined under the mutual ignorance pact as a polite but secretly disdainful tolerance of 'enthusiastic' religion – has been rudely confronted with the world of religion that had under the same pact agreed to an equally middle-class silence. The soporific reticence of both sides is gone: how will the Perownes of the world cope? He lives near the Post Office Tower – a symbol, he thinks, of more optimistic days. 'And now, what days are these? Baffled and fearful, he mostly thinks when he takes time from his weekly round to consider.'[75] Perowne is a modern man, however, his worldview shaped by science and his profession: he thinks the supernaturally inclined show a primitive inability to contemplate their own unimportance, their reasonings belonging on 'a spectrum at whose far end, rearing like an abandoned temple, lies psychosis.'[76] 'Self-importance' here stands for the religious belief that there is a Creator that cares; Hitchens, as we saw, uses the term 'solipsism' for this. But strangely, Perowne's assumed self-*un*importance, by the end of the book, seems deeply rooted in his lavish upper-middle-class lifestyle and in his God-like ability as a neurosurgeon to bestow life upon the

dying, granted thanks to a science of biological determinism, and
not superstition. It is very British to assume unimportance when
you have everything: refined goods and a Georgian home, a loving
family, professional respect, social status. His very British heroes
are Newton, Boyle, Hook and Wren.

Perowne's distaste for the emergence of religion into his ordered
world is perhaps symbolised by the march taking place that day – a
direct outcome of 9/11. Elsewhere it has specifics, as when he has
to rationalise his irritation with three burkha-clad women in Harley
Street,[77] or his observation that the followers of the Falun Gong
religion now outnumber the members of the Communist Party in
China. Perowne is a cultured man, a man who ranges across his
cultural heritage – though of course it is McEwan who does this
– including references to Schrödinger's cat and 'life's grandeur',
a phrase from Darwin and Steven Jay Gould.[78] He does like the
modern jazz greats, Evans, Davis and Coltrane, but doesn't like
'magical realism' in literature, a genre that his poetess daughter
wants to acquaint him with. But what really intrudes on him on the
day of the anti-war march is a working-class criminal who invades
his home and holds his family to ransom. Nearly approaching total
humiliation, he and his son eventually overpower their tormentor,
leaving him in a coma. With delicious generosity, Perowne gives
up the last hours of his twenty-four to save the brute's life, sparing
him from prison too. Although the intrusion of muscular working-
class brutality appears to undermine his entire lifestyle and even his
masculinity, Perowne – almost effortlessly – redeems himself and his
class. His social class is the deus ex machina.

In *Enduring Love*, another middle-class male, Joe Rose, has to endure
religion and a very working-class enthusiasm wrapped up in the
same antagonist, Jed Parry. The novel is pre-9/11 but pursues a more
intense anti-religious polemic than *Saturday*, delivered as a satire on
devotional religious love. As a bulwark to middle-class British atheism
the device might not invite much attention, but to those versed in the
devotional mystics the satire is disturbingly accurate in places. The
source of this accuracy is not empathy at all, however – merely the skill
of a sensitive and talented writer. Yet in many ways the elegant satire
does more harm to religion than all the rants of vituperative atheists
like Dawkins. Jed 'falls in love' with Joe after a ballooning accident,
and stalks him. Joe is a science journalist, whose career has taken a few
unexpected twists, but is a middle-class professional, whereas Joe,
an English-language teacher who now lives on his inheritance 'feels'
working-class, even if only for his religious evangelism.

Ostensibly, *Enduring Love* is about a man suffering obsessive love for another man, under the compulsion of a neurotic disorder called de Clérambault's syndrome. But McEwan has added a dimension that was not required by the overall story structure: this love is religious. Early in the novel Jed sets out his aims:

> To bring you to God, through love. You'll fight this like mad because you're a long way from your own feelings? But I know that the Christ is within you. At some level you know it too. That's why you fight it so hard with your education and reason and logic and this detached way you have of talking, as if you're not part of anything at all? You can pretend you don't know what I'm talking about, perhaps because you want to hurt me and dominate me, but the fact is I come bearing gifts. The purpose is to bring you to the Christ that is in you and that *is* you. That's what the gift of love is all about. It's really very simple?[79]

What is interesting about Jed's description of Joe's inner life is that it fits so closely to Taylor's account of the 'buffered self'. But McEwan wants to show that the religious critique of the secular scientific mind is naïve. As Taylor remarks of self-sufficient secularism 'what happens is that people are convinced that there is something more mature, more courageous, readier to face unvarnished reality in the scientific stance. The superiority is an ethical one . . .'[80] This is the moral high ground of the atheist.

Jed is a delusional obsessive stalker of his quarry, reading confirmation of Joe's love in each alternating exasperated rejection and attempt to reason with him. But a deranged homosexual stalker would be enough to cause a rift in Joe's heterosexual relationship, given that the other main plot element revolves around the ballooning accident which had resulted in the death of an onlooker, who, like Joe, had intervened to save a boy's life. Isn't the provocation to Joe's settled love-life and professional career from the twin disruptions of being drawn into a fatal accident and the delusional world of a sex-stalker enough? But as Joe has to draw on the resources of his middle-class rationality to cope with these, so perhaps McEwan wanted to further heighten its triumph in the novel by the even starker contrast with evangelical religion. What gets confused in the process is whether Jed wants to convert Joe or become his lover. What can be made out of it, however, is an analogy between the derangement which finds love in another man 'in the teeth of evidence' (as Dawkins likes to say), and the alleged derangement of those who find love in 'God', whose existence is again clung to 'in the teeth of evidence'.

What McEwan does throughout the novel is have Jed suggest to Joe that he is 'living in the desert' of his rationality. Jed finds all of Joe's research papers and reads them obsessively, sadly, on account of the lack of 'God' in them, and is determined to rectify this abysmal state of affairs. As in *Saturday*, it eventually gets physical, a demand on the masculinity of the middle-class protagonist to defend his loved one(s) against a deranged killer. Having passed this test – which is, of course, a deep anxiety in the middle class male who may never have been in a fistfight in his life – the protagonist also has to demonstrate that the rational middle-class order of life, built on humanistic science, can solve the deeply emotional. As lullabies for the middle-class conscience, McEwan's novels serve to cocoon their readers from both the poor and the religious.

John Updike

The American author John Updike's novel *Terrorist* couldn't stand in greater contrast to the works of Amis and McEwan in its lack of class basis. Instead of middle-class British establishment atheism, coupled with the model lifestyle of urban success, Updike takes us deep into American classless nihilism amongst the 'losers' of American society. When Allan Bloom, in *The Closing of the American Mind*, says: 'American nihilism is a mood, a mood of moodiness, a vague disquiet. It is nihilism without the abyss',[81] he was exaggerating, but nonetheless indicating some important transatlantic difference. The nihilism of Updike's characters is mostly uncultured, it is true, but at the same time it makes for a very different context in which to encounter religious fundamentalism. Where Amis and Updike have the surety and complacency of middle-classness honed over the centuries, Updike's Americans are not at all certain that hard-core religion is an affront to their values. They really are open to the possibility that the 'God'-freak might be on to something, might have found just what is so achingly absent in their own lives.

Updike isn't an atheist, as Christopher Hitchens acknowledges, but nevertheless Hitchens uses an extract from Updike's *Roger's Version* in his *Portable Atheist* to demolish the 'fine-tuning' argument for 'God', or anthropic principle. What the extract in fact shows is the extraordinary degree to which novelists such as Amis, McEwan, Updike, and David Lodge (discussed later) are now conversant in science, in contrast to the period in which C.P. Snow put forward his 'Two Cultures' thesis. Indeed, the research that these novelists pursue in the sciences is apparent not only in the acknowledgements that may appear at the end of their novels, but in the sometimes unlikely depth of knowledge that their characters display. In the *Roger's Version* extract, the anthropic principle is spelled out at length, and demolished in equal measure, by protagonists *at a drinks party*. The extract ends with 'God? Forget the old bluffer', after offering the 'clay' theory of Cairns-Smith (originally put forward in 1985).[82] For Hitchens, the arguments here are apparently convincing for atheism, but Updike himself, deeply influenced by Soren Kierkegaard and Karl Barth, says that 'Among the repulsions of atheism for me has been its drastic uninterestingness as an intellectual position. Where was the ingenuity, the ambiguity, the humanity (in the Harvard sense) of saying that the universe just happened to happen and that when we're dead we're dead?'[83]

In *Terrorist* Updike provides just that 'ingenuity, the ambiguity, and humanity' in a fictional exploration of the 'what-it-is-like-to-be' of the young male terrorist. Where McEwan presses into service the language of religious devotion in order to make it ridiculous, Updike presses the same language, and its underlying motivations, just as hard, but with an open mind. His jihadist protagonist is a young American with an absconded Egyptian father; his Islamism is partly a protest against the lax morals he perceives in his mother, and his gradual embrace of a suicide bombing mission has a convincing inevitability about it. But the genuine shallowness of youth and the possible shallowness of the religious indoctrination he receives are not contrasted with any equivalent to the British unquestioning complacency of an outraged middle class; instead what surrounds the young man is quite possibly more corrupt than the doctrines that lead him to his mission. At the same time, amidst the wasteland that is – in Updike's portrait – contemporary American suburbia, there does live a relic of the European certainty, of the secularised Judaeo-Christian belief in providence, and in a non-triumphalist way it wins the day.

We can profitably contrast this novel with Martin Amis's short story, 'The Last Days of Muhammad Atta'. While one is a novel and the other a short story, and one is entirely fictional and the other based on the real-life suicide bomber who piloted the plane into the North Tower of the World Trade Centre, it is the feeling-tone of the two that is the real contrast. Updike defends the imagined Western values of life over the perceived Islamic values of death in the most open-minded way possible. His research into Islam is almost overwhelming; perhaps his debt to Kierkegaard and Barth make it possible to pursue it with sympathy; perhaps his own sense of secularism as a wasteland allows for the fundamental insight necessary to make contact with the 'other' of Islam. But for Amis the 'other' is pure affront. His fictional re-creation is not based on extensive and sympathetic research into Islam, because for Amis religion is signed off in his mind as primitive. But he won't even allow Atta the cloak of religion, saying 'Muhammad Atta was not religious; he was not even especially political. He had allied himself with the militants because jihad was, by many magnitudes, the most charismatic idea of his generation.'[84] But how can Amis be so sure of this? And why does Amis adopt the narrative device of focussing on Atta's bodily functions, in particular on constipation? The polemic in the story – which is utterly understandable – is discredited by this. But worse, as a novelist, Amis fails in the 'what-it-is-like-to-be' potential of the story – we learn more about Amis than anything else, that he belongs to a cocooned culture of middle-class Britishness, determined to shut out uncomfortable new realities. Amis is sure that to take a *real* interest in Atta would be a 'fetishisation of balance'; Updike, in contrast, achieves balance without fetishisation because he is not class-bound.

Philip Pullman

Philip Pullman's atheism takes a quite different shape to that of Amis and McEwan, though Pullman agrees with McEwan that Marxist regimes and theocracies are identical in the pursuit of millennial historicist goals, and are equally antithetical to democracy. But Pullman's 'atheism' is better known from the *His Dark Materials* trilogy, a children's fantasy adventure with philosophical and theological overtones. The work is anti-clerical but in a subtle way, prompting Pullman to say in a 2003 interview:

> I've been surprised by how little criticism I've got. Harry Potter's been taking all the flak. I'm a great fan of J.K. Rowling, but the people – mainly from America's Bible Belt – who complain that Harry Potter promotes Satanism or witchcraft obviously haven't got enough in their lives. Meanwhile, I've been flying under the radar, saying things that are far more subversive than anything poor old Harry has said. My books are about killing God.[85]

On a closer investigation of his work, what emerges is an anti-clericalism that would have been at home in the late Enlightenment, but accompanying it is what can only be described as a Neoplatonist sensibility. In other words Pullman's atheism is not so much the blanket rejection of religion, but derives instead from an alternative religious sensibility that is offended by its persecution by monotheism. (Authors

Donna Freitas and Jason E. King suggest in their analysis *Killing the Imposter God: Philip Pullman's Spiritual Imagination in His Dark Materials* that Pullman's is a 'pantheistic' rather than an 'atheistic' position.)

Issues in the New Atheism

We will pause here briefly to list some of the arguments raised by the new atheists we have discussed before turning to examine the new defenders of faith. Broadly, one can divide the atheists' issues into those raised from science and those not. The scientific issues include the superordinate topic of NOMA – the new atheists generally reject this position. Those with a deeper commitment to science are also keen to discredit Intelligent Design – which is relatively easy – and the anthropic principle or 'fine-tuning' arguments – a little more difficult. Some are also keen to promote meme-theory as an explanation of religion. Issues with less reliance on science include the existence of 'God', though the denial of his existence may have a scientific basis. Crucial in the discussion of 'God' is the insistence by the new atheists on certain anthropomorphic characteristics, and the almost universal sense that to define 'God' otherwise is somehow cheating.

Other issues include the question of the inevitable relationship between religion and violence, and also the cluster of ideas that propose extreme ideologies such as Nazism and Communism to be 'religions'. Another issue lies with the respective natures of scripture and Jesus, and their historical bases – if any. Finally, there is considerable hostility to the concept of the religious moderate, based on the assumption that the moderates provide the context in which religious extremists flourish.

Chapter 4:
The New Defenders of Faith

The new defenders of faith and the new atheists pursue arguments that have, of course, a long history. What makes them new is the post-9/11 context, in which the argument has acquired a new intensity and a new level of engagement. 'Defenders of faith', where faith becomes plural, is a term owing to the provocative statement made by Prince Charles in 1994 that he wanted to be 'defender of faith' rather than 'Defender of *the* Faith', a centuries-old formulation. But another term for a defender of faith is an apologist, or most often in this context, a Christian apologist. What makes the new defender of faith different to the old Christian apologist is the rude awakening of the post-9/11 attack on religion, or perhaps a positive sense of opportunity to speak beyond the ghetto. What we will see, however, is that they are largely unaccustomed to it. The 'mutual ignorance pact' made Christian apologists a protected species as it were; their audience, as Harris points out, is the faithful who have a poor acquaintance with their own scriptures and are only too happy to have a contemporary Christian interpret it in ways they can relate to in the modern era. We now look at Alister McGrath, Keith Ward, Richard Swinburne, John C. Lennox, Francis Collins, Tina Beattie, Graeme Smith, Antony Flew, Charles Taylor and John Humphrys, with an eye as to who is 'new' and who is 'old' amongst the defenders of faith.

Alister McGrath
Perhaps the best-known new defender of faith is Alister McGrath. His writings on Dawkins made him the best placed authority to launch the immediate counter-attack to the key new atheist manifesto, Dawkins's *The God Delusion*. McGrath's answer was *The Dawkins Delusion?*, subtitled *Atheist fundamentalism and the denial of the divine*. One notes immediately the question mark in McGrath's title – why the hesitancy? Does McGrath want to say that Dawkins might *not* be

deluded? However, what makes McGrath such an interesting writer on this topic is his own history as a Marxist, a materialist atheist, who converted to Christianity. He says 'I too was an atheist, and was awoken from my dogmatic slumbers through reading books that challenged my rapidly petrifying world view.'[86] His conversion was intellectual, however, rather than based on religious experience, and reminiscent perhaps of C.S. Lewis. Updike, as we saw, thought that atheism was simply an uninteresting position; similarly McGrath finds Christianity more intellectually satisfying. For the new atheists this is hard to understand. How can an apparent contradiction be more intellectually satisfying?

But McGrath's stance is instructive of the field. In entering the debate with Dawkins he has to concede that some of what Dawkins says is unassailable. This in itself sets an asymmetric tone to the debate: the new atheists mostly rubbish all of religion, even if they have to do it by carefully excluding such things from their definition of religion as Buddhism or the negative theology. But how can the new defenders of faith begin without agreeing at least that violence carried out in the name of religion is utterly reprehensible? Or that much of religion outside seemingly modernised versions lives in a superstitious past? Let us look at how McGrath treads by first recapitulating the key points of Dawkins's attack. It's fairly simple: Dawkins defines 'God' in anthropomorphic terms, using the Old Testament; he then shows that the so-called 'proofs' of his existence from Aristotle to Descartes are bunkum, and that belief in 'God' is a delusion. The delusion is malign however, because it leads to violence and it 'actively debauches the scientific enterprise'.[87] And it is the 'scientific enterprise' that will ultimately decide on the existence of 'God' – though provisional conclusions are firmly against.

McGrath's obvious strategy would be some combination of the following: (a) disagree with Dawkins's definition of 'God', (b) recapitulate and update the 'proofs' of the existence of 'God' based on a more subtle definition, (c) demonstrate that the scientific enterprise is constitutionally unable to answer the question of 'God's existence, (d) argue that the historical negatives of religion are cultural accretions from feudal eras, and (e) note that the Bible is not to be taken literally. Interestingly, McGrath at no time disagrees with Dawkins's definition of 'God', and insists that the 'proofs' of his existence offer only 'persuasion, not proof'.[88] This is not very convincing when debating with a scientist: what might 'persuasion' mean, if it does not pursue a rational argument? Does it mean perhaps 'browbeat', or, alternatively, 'preach to the converted'? Nor does

McGrath's distinction between an *a posteriori* demonstration of the coherence of faith and an *a priori* proof of faith really wash either: if one could really demonstrate the *coherence* of faith through argument, then unbelievers would be converted en masse. What Dawkins *et al.* do very well is to show the incoherence of faith as a (merely) rational system. McGrath's next step is to agree with Dawkins that a 'God of the gaps' is not tenable, saying it was a foolish move in theology and was 'increasingly abandoned in the twentieth century'.[89] It might have been, but it is increasingly being taken up in the twenty-first century, by McGrath's fellow defenders of faith.

What McGrath does do, as he does more thoroughly in other books including *Dawkins' God*, is to argue that science cannot answer the question of the existence of 'God'. But McGrath's stand here is weak, because he won't fully commit to NOMA or an equivalent position, perhaps because of his background in molecular biophysics. Although McGrath has some sympathy for a modified form of NOMA, he appears hesitant about suggesting that science has limits, saying: 'let's be quite clear that suggesting that science may have its limits is in no way a criticism or defamation of the scientific method', and 'The question of whether science has limits is certainly not improper, nor does a positive answer to the question in any way represent a lapse into some kind of superstition'.[90] More specifically, McGrath thinks that Gould is wrong to consider that the magisteria of science and religion do not overlap, though he would accept a partial overlapping, as opposed to Dawkins for whom there is only one magisterium. McGrath suggests that 'science and religion offer possibilities of cross-fertilization on account of the interpenetration of their subjects and methods.'[91] Oddly, he then cites Francis Collins, head of the Human Genome Project, who believes that science and religion are complementary. 'Complementary' is precisely what Gould was arguing, but not 'interpenetrating'. They are radically different interpretations. Elsewhere McGrath talks of 'not warfare but a constructive synergy between science and religion'.[92] This variety of terms allows for a confusion of thought in which the legitimacy of science to answer the 'God' question is left open. Dawkins *et al.* can then claim victory, if not now, then in the future.

A feature of *The Dawkins Delusion?* is its *ad hominem* tone. It is true that Dawkins can be blunt in his statements, but he pursues a coherent argument against extreme manifestations of religion that none of the defenders of faith support either. The question is how valid his arguments are – a powerful case for NOMA, for example, would cut straight through them. But McGrath resorts to what often *feels* like the impatience of hallowed authority, the outrage at the affront to his long-sanctioned cultural tradition, the displeasure of the tribe against the one. For example, in connection with Dawkins' meme theory he says 'An already faltering argument is simply given the kiss of death by the recycling of these implausible notions, which fail to command assent within the mainline scientific community.'[93] While it is true that meme theory has yet no adequate basis in neuroscience, one cannot rule out the possibility. It is McGrath's language here that is the problem – it is the reader who will decide whether his objections so far cause Dawkins' arguments to falter. The 'kiss of death' is plainly premature; 'recycling' is a pejorative term; and 'implausible' has to be demonstrated. Or another example: 'Dawkins seems to view things from within a highly polarized worldview that is no less apocalyptic and warped than that of the religious fundamentalisms he wishes to eradicate.'[94] To say of one's intellectual opponent that their worldview is 'warped' is inconducive to critical debate.

These are perhaps the exceptions in McGrath's writings, much of which are thoughtful and interesting. His *Twilight of Atheism*, for example, gives a good account of the rise of secularism, but one might suspect that in his conversion to Christianity he is also eager to take on the mantle of its presumed earlier authority. His tone at times is reminiscent of that adopted by Malcolm Muggeridge and Mervyn Stockwood (then Bishop of Southwark) in the 1979 television debate with John Cleese and Michael Palin over their film *The Life of Brian*. Stockwood accused the Monty Python team of being 'being undergraduate and mentally unstable' and generally seemed to resort to his status as bishop instead of arguing the point. His tone was that of schoolmaster about to cane little boys, but in this case it was the boys who won the moral argument.

Keith Ward

In contrast to McGrath, Keith Ward's vocation as a Christian seems to have come from something more than intellectual persuasion. He has had many academic posts in philosophy and religion, and was ordained a priest in 1972. His book *Is Religion Dangerous?* is the most obvious contribution to the new debate, but is also part of a large oeuvre which predates 9/11. His strategy in this book, as the title makes obvious, is to target the issue that gives the new atheists their energy and moral purpose: the question of religious violence. If that can be disposed of, then the new atheists have a much reduced parish.

He begins with the issue that McGrath ducks: the literal interpretation of 'God'. He says:

> Ideas of God *are* imaginative projections. . . . It is a construct because it is trying to form some image of a reality that is beyond all images. . . . So in religion there may be an appropriate form of intellectual imagination that gives access to a reality that cannot be known by the senses.[95]

Ward says that religious believers should to some extent accept that 'God' is an imaginative projection. He is also adamant that no simple definition of religion will suffice; he says that when professor of the History and Philosophy of Religion at London University he was consulted by lawyers for a definition of religion, declaring: 'I confess that I was unable to come up with a definition, or at least with a definition that would satisfy a lawyer.'[96] The new atheists should take note of this because Ward's extensive background in both religion and philosophy makes such a confession significant. It is not a failing of either Ward or of religion; it is in the nature of the subtlety of religion. Ward gives justification for his position: 'if you have a short, snappy definition (such as the early anthropologist E.B. Tylor's minimum definition of religion as "belief in spiritual beings"), you eliminate things like Buddhism, which are pretty obviously religions.'[97] Ward is particularly critical of the early anthropologists of religion like Edward Tylor, Sir James Frazer and Émile Durkheim, saying of them: 'One rhetorical tactic of those who oppose religion is to take its most primitive or undeveloped forms and consider them as definitive of religion.'[98] As we have seen, Ward is not alone in criticising new atheists like Dennett and Dawkins for basing their definitions of religion on such anthropologists.

This brings us to the main argument that Ward presents, which is that religions *develop*, and to attack them on the basis of their manifestation in the ancient past is to attack what has disappeared. This position is rather promising because it contains within it a dynamic that could both answer the new atheists and promise further development of religion. At the same time, it could leave Ward under attack from both sides. Let us see how his argument develops. In the first instance he wants to reinforce the idea that the 'God' that the new atheists attack is not a correct understanding: 'Many contemporary Christians totally reject the idea of God as a superhuman controller. For theologian Paul Tillich, for example, God is not a particular being, but the power of Being itself, and the supreme moral ideal to be reverenced for its value, not its controlling power.'[99] The new atheists are, however, very aware of this move, and deny that it is representative of the bulk of the faithful, citing the Bible as source for the anthropomorphic, controlling 'God'.

Ward then has to bring forward his argument, developed in many books, that biblical scholarship is an evolving discipline which has sorted out early, primitive and undesirable descriptions of 'God' in the scriptures to produce a Biblical understanding far removed from what the new atheists attack. He says: 'If it is argued that religious texts breed intolerance, the question that must be asked is: what causes people to choose those texts, which according to the general scholarly consensus of religious scholars were for situations long in the past, and which have since been overridden both by other specific texts and by the general sense of scripture?'[100] To take his last point first, he argues that there is a 'general sense of scripture' which can be used to arbitrate over controversial passages in the Bible (which he is calling 'texts'). Secondly, he implies that there is a scholarly consensus amongst theologians that certain passages were for 'situations long in the past', perhaps, for example, when patriarchy was the norm. Thirdly, he suggests that those who use scriptural passages to justify violence should be questioned as to why they have chosen them, given that the scholars have refuted them. His claim is that all the world's major religions have within them the resources to correct their excesses or mistakes. Nazism, he suggests, did not.

But Ward has manoeuvred himself into a tricky position. He is attempting to refute Harris (though he does not name him) when Harris says 'Religious moderation is the product of *secular* knowledge and *scriptural* ignorance'. No, Ward is saying, the moderate position does not require scriptural ignorance (or secular knowledge), it requires an audit, as it were, of those passages deemed outdated and those that are not. So what kind of example does Ward give of this process? He chooses a particularly offensive passage from Deuteronomy 20:16 called the 'Ban'. This requires that the enemy, including all men, women and children, should be slaughtered for the crime of idolatry. Ward properly calls it a 'primitive moral idea', but even as he condemns it, he appears to attempt a partial justification. The 'Ban' applies to those cities that will not submit peacefully to conquest, and then only to those near enough to become part of Israel. For far away cities only every male should be slaughtered, but their women, children, cattle and other possessions should be taken as rightful spoil. Nearby cities should be utterly destroyed however: 'save alive nothing that breatheth'. While

admitting that it is 'a pretty horrific scenario', Ward gives the partial
justification that the injunction that 'no slaves or booty should be
taken for personal use' is an admirable moral stance.[101] Later he adds
'even the Ban expresses some perception of the divine will – in this
case, a will for total devotion to God, and for the renunciation of
all private gain from battle.'[102] But one searches in vain within these
passages in Deuteronomy for any injunction against taking spoil
in battle. It is *prescribed*, not *proscribed* in Deuteronomy 20:14, in the
case of distant cities, and in the case of nearby cities the taking of
living things, such as women, children, and presumably, livestock,
is forbidden only because they are to be slaughtered. No mention
of other spoil, and certainly no injunction to renounce private gain
from battle. Or does Ward mean to commend the *collective* taking of
spoil over the individual taking, for which again there is no support
in Deuteronomy?

Ward rather loses what argument he has here by defending the
'Ban' in this way, which is regrettable, because he continues in a
more rigorous vein. When he says 'So the Ban is a horrible rule, but
most scholars believe it was never put into practice, and was obsolete
even before it was written down',[103] we can hope that the scholars are
right. When he adds 'It would be slander to suggest that any Jew
has ever seriously considered massacre to be ordered by God in any
actual historical situation since the writing down of the Law', we
hope even more fervently that he is right. We want to agree with him
when he states 'The main lesson is that you must read the particular
rules of the Bible, especially of the Old Testament, in the light of later,
more developed moral views found within the Bible itself, which
often render them obsolete or transform their interpretation.' But we
might consider him just a touch parochial when he says 'We might
well say that the Bible shows a process of continuing moral reflection
that is far in advance of most other human societies of the time.'[104]
Any acquaintance with the Pali Canon or the Jain *Agam* literature,
for example, might suggest otherwise.

Ward inadvertently sets out a very significant challenge to the
religions of the Book. If they contain a mixture of reprehensible
injunctions like the 'Ban' and 'later more moral views', then why not
get rid of the former in the light of the latter? After all, the Protestant
tradition in particular is not so keen on having 'scholars' dictate
to them how to read their scriptures, so they may not have been
listening. Why not rewrite them now, and eliminate the grounds on
which extreme secularists rage against the scriptures and moderate
secularists just shake their heads and walk away in sorrow? Religions

are now, more than at any time in their recent history, called upon to demonstrate – as Ward claims – that they have the resources within them to correct their extreme interpretations.

Given all this, it is important to note the strengths in Ward's thesis, including the idea that all institutions are prone to corruption. Ward says simply: 'It is pointless to condemn politics or science because they are so widely misused; instead it is necessary to ensure that they are used for good.'[105] The same, he believes, holds true of religion.

Richard Swinburne

Where McGrath and Ward can be counted as 'new' defenders of faith, Richard Swinburne is more old school, and belongs more properly to the apologists for Christianity. The crucial difference here is not so much whether they have waded into the debate at this post-9/11 Dawkins-aware stage, but whether their work is really attempting to reach beyond the converted. Swinburne may think that he is, but Dawkins is not impressed:

> It is a virtue of clear writing that you can see what is wrong with a book as well as what is right. Richard Swinburne is clear. You can see where he is coming from. You can also see where he is going to, and there is something almost endearing in the way he lovingly stakes out his own banana skin and rings it about with converging arrows boldly labelled 'Step here'.[106]

The 'clarity' of Swinburne's writing lies in the adoption of pseudo-mathematical and pseudo-scientific language. What he deals with is familiar to any student of religion, and much of it – if one ignores the 'clarity' – is a valuable treatment of issues, for example that of theodicy. It is valuable, however, only if one is already in sympathy with religion in general, and with Christianity in particular. For Dawkins, Swinburne's arguments are simply circular – Swinburne has made up his mind that 'God' exists, and speaks lovingly of this entity to those who agree with him. But for those who don't, or who are looking for a good reason to believe, statements like the following are guaranteed to alienate: 'With e as the existence of human bodies, h as theism, and k as the evidence of a universe conforming to natural laws, $P(e \mid \sim h \,\&\, k)$ is very low.'[107] With friends of religion like this, who needs enemies? What Swinburne is saying in this pseudo-mathematical form is that to evolve human bodies from a lifeless universe with only natural laws and without 'God' is unlikely. But that is what a belief in a creator 'God' entails, and no amount of Boolean algebra will add to the likelihood of that belief. Swinburne would have to study Dawkins' *Climbing Mount Improbable*, or comparable arguments, and show that they are false in order to move an audience out of the circularity of his belief. 'Mount Improbable' is in fact a metaphor standing for both the problem and its proposed solution, as put forward with great imagination and skill by Dawkins. To ignore his thesis is to have backed out of the debate, to have consigned oneself to a presecular imaginary. What Swinburne does is to rehearse the very 'proofs' of the existence of 'God' that McGrath has downgraded to 'persuasion' and which have never seemed to either prove 'God' to the atheist nor persuade them.

John C. Lennox

Swinburne was introduced here to give an example of what might be required to be a 'new' defender of faith as opposed to an old one, i.e. a Christian apologist. John C. Lennox, in his book *God's Undertaker: Has Science Buried God?*, makes just that necessary step to be included amongst the new defenders of faith: he tackles the arguments of the new atheists head on, in the arena of science. Lennox's approach is interesting because he is a mathematician, and this colours his understanding of physics and biology as he pursues Intelligent Design and fine-tuning arguments. His stance on NOMA is not explicit, saying early on in his book that Atkins, Dawkins, and Dennett 'argue that there is strong scientific evidence for atheism. They are therefore happy to make a scientific case for what is, after all, a metaphysical question.'[108] To draw the distinction between science and metaphysics is what NOMA does, and so to adhere to NOMA is to disallow that science has anything to say about 'God'. But Lennox does the opposite; he argues that science leads to theism, not atheism.

Lennox introduces his argument on Intelligent Design in this statement: 'Why are scientists not prepared to draw the obvious inference, and say that living things look as if they are designed precisely because they are designed?'[109] This is provocative, and Lennox needs to rehearse in detail the work done by Intelligent Design theorists if he is to have any case at all. In fact, he usefully assembles the key issues for us, revolving around speciation and biogenesis. Speciation – how new species emerge – and biogenesis – the origins of life in the first place – are apparently the weak spots in evolutionary theory. Intelligent Design theory does not reject Darwinism outright, but pushes hard at these weaknesses – a valuable contribution if nothing else because it forces the Darwinists to work harder. On the subject of speciation Lennox can argue that, while 'microevolution' – adaptation within a species – does take place, 'macroevolution' – the origin of new species – does not.[110] On the subject of biogenesis, Intelligent Design theories are on less contentious ground as scientific theories here are still speculative (we encountered the 'clay' theory of biogenesis above in one of Updike's novels). Lennox is keen on the term 'irreducible complexity' as used by American biochemist Michael Behe, and so raises a useful debate, to which he contributes a mathematician's perspective. Lennox draws extensively on the thought of Behe, whose work is at the forefront of Intelligent Design. Victor Stenger has this to say about Behe:

Behe is a biochemist, not an evolutionary biologist, and was unaware when he wrote his book that the mechanisms for the evolution of 'irreducibly complex' systems were already discussed six decades earlier by the Nobel Prize winner Hermann Joseph Muller and have been common knowledge in the field since then.[111]

Behe's own department says

While we respect Prof. Behe's right to express his views, they are his alone and are in no way endorsed by the department. It is our collective position that intelligent design has no basis in science, has not been tested experimentally, and should not be regarded as scientific.[112]

Those who adhere to science as a worldview, such as Stenger, Dennett and Dawkins, believe that there is no such thing as irreducible complexity. Dawkins quotes Darwin on the subject of the human eye: 'To suppose that the eye, with all its inimitable contrivances for adjusting focus to different distances, for admitting different amounts of light, and for the correction of spherical and chromatic aberration, could have been formed by natural selection, seems, I freely confess, absurd in the highest degree.'[113] Dawkins adds that a Fellow of the Royal Society – a physicist – has recently confessed to the same doubt. Hence the evolution of sight becomes the subject of a whole chapter in Dawkins' *Climbing Mount Improbable*; all those who enter this debate should read it. What the argument of the Darwinists such as Dawkins always proposes is the development of organised complexity out of historically less complex systems, via very simple mechanisms, and without intervention by a 'designer'. It is the vast timescales involved that enable this, and which perhaps defeats the imagination of the objectors. The first point to make of this, and of

Lennox's insistence that 'living things look as if they are designed precisely because they are designed', is that the physical sciences are counter-intuitive. Lennox is appealing to intuition: if it looks like a duck and quacks like a duck then it is a duck. But science doesn't work that way, as Lewis Wolpert spells out in his book *The Unnatural Nature of Science*. The second point is that a considerable amount of scientific imagination is required to engage with the argument. Not to at least consider the 'Mount Improbable' argument seems like a failure of imagination.

What Lennox adds to this debate is an argument against 'Mount Improbable' from mathematics. Drawing on the analogy with the 'ex nihilo' argument – the idea that something cannot arise out of nothing (perhaps another failure of imagination?), Lennox argues that life and information are interchangeable, and so an 'information ex nihilo' argument is derived. How could the vast amount of information locked up in the complexity of life on earth derive from nothing? What if, he asks, 'there is something like an information-theoretic parallel to the law of energy conservation?'[114] Lennox tells us that Nobel Laureate Peter Medawar posits this law and points out that Euclid's famous geometric theorems are simply a 'spelling out, or bringing out into the open, of information already contained in the axioms and postulates'. This is an interesting question: does any physical system merely bring out into the open organisational information encoded in its primal state, or does such information grow, in quantity and perhaps quality, through natural laws? Or does the information get added along the way by an intelligent designer?

Dawkins' answer, often repeated, is simple: if the designer adds the information, then the designer must be complex, i.e. contain as much if not more information. You are back at the same problem, only you now *also* have to account for the mechanics of intervention. Why intervene on a macro scale (speciation), and not on a micro scale (local adaptation)? And so on. A whole new set of questions are raised. But Lennox's mathematical argument needs examination, because it is interesting. Are the results of mathematics really contained within the axioms? Is information really subject to a conservation law? Or is it not possible that a simple set of laws can produce information not contained within the laws? For example, music is constrained by physical laws such as acoustics and so on, so how is it that the general public are continuously entranced by *new* music, of whatever genre? Was 9/11 contained within the laws of economics and global political history? If so, why the stupendous impact of it, a television-watching world replaying it again and again and again?

Perhaps Lennox, as a mathematician, has a different kind of imagination to that of physicists and biologists. Even so, it would be interesting to know how he regards the mathematics of the Mandelbrot fractals: are the endless and astonishing images that can be generated from a couple of lines of software embodying the fractal equations already contained within the equations? Stenger uses a similar argument to show that comparable complexity arises within software programmes such as those that simulate cellular automata.[115] Lennox's argument would also dispose of the entire discipline of algorithmic computer art,[116] the public reception of which – according to Lennox – should be a demand to see the software, not the art.

When it comes to the fine-tuning argument, it seems again that there is no early resolution from within science itself, as Stenger's discussion of it shows. The early proponents of fine-tuning arguments such as Tipler and Barrow received little direct refutation, but as the 'new debate' gathers momentum, Stenger is able to marshal the work of a number of scientists who are examining the thesis piece by piece, and mount a serious challenge to it.

Lennox has raised some interesting issues, particularly the 'conservation of information' argument, but one cannot help noticing the Christian bias in his writings that suggests he has already made his mind up. Anyone attuned to the wider perspective of religious studies would be alarmed when he says: 'polytheism arguably constitutes a perversion of an original belief in One Creator God'.[117] This is a fond theory of some theologians who have avoided any contact with world religions or the history of religion, but it has no basis in fact. Wherever monotheism arises, it clearly does so out of a polytheistic or animist past, and to call polytheism a 'perversion' of anything is insulting.

The most contentious of issues raised by Lennox, of which he is well aware and attempts to deal with, is the criticism that his work argues for a 'God of the gaps'. When Newton completed the *Principia*, in which he found a solution to the near-two-thousand year old 'problem of the planets' based on the inverse-square law of gravitation, there was an outstanding anomaly: the precession of the perihelion of Mercury. Until Einstein's solution to this, it was possible to argue that, while 'God' had created the laws of nature, he subsequently intervened here and there, and that anomalies are cases of such interventions. A gap in our scientific knowledge becomes a place where 'God' is invoked, hence the term 'God of the gaps' – the principle accusation against Deism. When Lennox argues in favour of intelligent design, he is acutely aware of this accusation, saying: 'How can we, then, avoid the charge of intellectual laziness or "God or the gaps" thinking?'[118] He deals with it by dividing the 'gaps' into two sorts, good ones and bad ones: 'Good gaps will be revealed by science as not being within its explanatory powers. They will be those (few) places where science as such points beyond itself to explanations that are not within its purview.'[119] As an example of what he thinks is a 'bad' gap he says: 'we might think of Newton's suggestion that God occasionally had to tweak some of the orbits of the planets to bring them into line.' An example of a 'good' gap according to Lennox is the bacterial flagellum, and other 'irreducibly complex' biological structures that do not yet have a convincing explanation – and of course biogenesis and speciation. However, as we shall see now in the work of geneticist Francis Collins, science is making rapid inroads into these 'good' gaps, and Lennox's argument looks rather set to fail.

Francis Collins

Francis Collins has an extensive training in the sciences and has been leader of the Human Genome Project. He joined US President Bill Clinton in the announcement of the working draft of the human genome in June 2000, and was pleased to agree to the draft of the statement where Clinton announced: 'Today we are learning the language in which God created life. We are gaining ever more awe for the complexity, the beauty and the wonder of God's most divine and sacred gift.'[120] Collins used a phrase from this speech as the title of a book, *The Language of God*, in which he explains his personal synthesis of science and religion. He has made a similar journey from atheism to theism as C.S. Lewis, Alister McGrath, and Antony Flew, and it was in fact C.S. Lewis's small book *Mere Christianity* which helped him in the transition. His position as an eminent scientist who happens to believe in 'God' has made him a natural choice to enter debate with Dawkins, featured for example in the 13 November 2006 issue of *Time* magazine.

Where Collins parts company with Lennox is that he eschews Intelligent Design, on all its positions, including irreducible complexity, biogenesis and speciation. He makes the obvious point that 'Faith that places God in the gaps of current understanding about the natural world may be headed for a crisis if advances in science subsequently fill those gaps.'[121] He gives as an example what he calls the 'poster child' of ID, the bacterial flagellum, which has begun to yield to patient research. It has been discovered that a different part of the bacterium, the 'type III secretory apparatus', shares components with the flagellum, and it is not so hard to see an evolutionary path from one to the other.[122] (Dawkins also covers this in some detail in the *God Delusion*.)[123] Such discoveries leave ID proponents with 'smaller and smaller territory to stand on.' He adds: 'Ultimately a "God of the gaps" religion runs a huge risk of simply discrediting faith.'[124] For Collins, the great advances of biological science do not shrink 'God's' purview; instead he says: 'For those who believe in God, there are reasons now to be more in awe, not less.'[125]

So how does Collins reconcile his science and his faith, when he avoids the kind of strategies supported by Lennox? Does he support NOMA? In the first instance, apparently not. As an option he says of it: 'But this, too, is potentially unsatisfying. It inspires internal conflict, and deprives people of the chance to embrace either science or spirit in a fully realized way.'[126] But on the very next page Collins says:

> There is no conflict in being a rigorous scientist and a person who believes in a God who takes a personal interest in each one of us. Science's domain is to explore nature. God's domain is the spiritual world, a realm not possible to explore with the tools and language of science. It must be examined with the heart, the mind, and the soul – and the mind must find a way to embrace both realms.

Is this not a good summary of the NOMA position, using the terms 'domain' and 'realm' instead of 'magisteria'? Particularly when Collins adds that science is powerless to answer the questions that are truly important to us? And that later on he cites Gould: 'Science simply cannot by its legitimate methods adjudicate the issue of God's possible superintendence of nature'?[127] But as we progress through his book, it seems clear that he seeks a *synthesis* of science and religion, a harmonisation, not a separation, motivated perhaps by the awe he feels for the discovery of the human genome, and the feeling that it is 'God's' work.

Although Collins rejects Intelligent Design he does not reject fine tuning. He notes with some alarm that 'Young Earth Creationism' – the literal adherence to the Bible, and Bishop Ussher's dating of the Earth's age – is held by some 45 percent of Americans. But his source of hope for a synthesis lies with the example of the heliocentric theory, fiercely resisted by the Church in Galileo's time, but long since reconciled with doctrine. Why not the same with Darwinism? All that is needed is a somewhat looser interpretation of Genesis. His solution then is a form of 'theistic evolution' which he terms 'Biologos'. Its tenets include the creation of the Universe by 'God', including the natural laws that allow for evolution to produce humans from primate ancestors. Humans are special because of their 'spiritual nature' and, while 'God' does not intervene directly, he does so in effect, because 'God' is outside of time and space and 'In that context, God could in the moment of creation of the universe also know every detail of the future.'[128]

It is not surprising to find that Sam Harris has written an utterly scathing review of Collins's book, driven it seems by outrage that it is authored by a scientist at the cutting edge of the very science that seems most opposed to 'God'. While the attack seems intemperate even by the standards of the new atheists, it is worth drawing on a couple of Harris's points. Firstly, Collins has followed C.S. Lewis in arriving at 'God' through the 'Moral Law' that they both perceive in human altruism. Harris says: 'Collins performs a risible sprint past ideas in biology like "kin selection" that plausibly explain altruism and self-sacrifice in evolutionary terms.'[129] 'Risible' is unfair, but 'sprint' is not: the very success of Dawkins' work is to show in great detail how altruism can be explained, not by the selfish organism, but by the selfish gene. For Collins to offer a convincing justification of 'God' through human altruism requires that he exercises his professional expertise to counter Dawkins' theory: this is just where his status as geneticist would carry weight. A lost opportunity. But Harris finishes his review with: 'This is an American book, attesting to American ignorance, written for Americans who believe that ignorance is stronger than death. Reading it should provoke feelings of collective guilt in any sensitive secularist. We should be ashamed that this book was written in our own time.' This is to miss *another* opportunity: to seriously ask why renowned contemporary scientists can also be devout believers.

Graeme Smith

Another strategy open to the new defenders of faith is to assert that secularism is an insignificant challenge to religion. We saw that Graeme Smith pursues such an argument by claiming that church attendance has only dropped to a low today which was common in the Middle Ages, as compared to an historical high in the Victorian period. Certainly church attendance in America is much higher than in Britain, though Bruce points out that figures obtained through asking the population are higher than when asking the churches. Smith simply dismisses the arguments raised by Dawkins *et al.* by claiming that the number of atheists is still very low in society, and that significant numbers still attend church baptisms, weddings and funerals. Smith's arguments against the significance and scope of secularization look weak against that put forward by Charles Taylor, a believer with no less at stake than Smith. Nevertheless they are a useful corrective to the bland assumption of widespread atheism that Grayling *et al.* continually make. We have to work harder if we want a true picture in sociological terms.

Antony Flew

Another line of defence that religionists might put forward in favour of faith would be to find atheists who have been converted to the belief in 'God' by the various arguments, for example Intelligent Design and fine tuning. By chance they have a high-profile example in the philosopher Antony Flew. His book *There is a God* is subtitled 'How the world's most notorious atheist changed his mind', though it is hard to imagine in late-twentieth-century Britain how one could be notorious for being an atheist. The point is that Flew was perhaps the leading *philosopher* of atheism; his 1950 paper 'Theology and Falsification' became the 'most widely reprinted philosophical publication of the last century.'[130] Flew's book has a preface and appendix by Roy Abraham Varghese, and another appendix which is the transcript of a conversation between Flew and N.T. Wright, Bishop of Durham in the Church of England and a leading New Testament scholar. More on these shortly, but to start with we note that Flew begins his book by stating that his conversion was to *Deism*, not theism. Later he makes clear that his 'God' is the 'God' of Aristotle,[131] or, to use Pascal's phrase, the 'God of the philosophers'.

Flew, like Hitchens and many other intellectuals of his generation, had been a communist in his thinking, and had become an atheist due to the problem of evil. Unusually, given the mostly materialist basis for much atheism, Flew had an early interest in parapsychology, and his first published book was on that subject.[132] His conversion to Deism came late in life, but it appears to have been the result of exposure to the intelligent design argument. He says: 'What I think the DNA material has done is that it has shown, by the almost unbelievable complexity of the arrangements which are needed to produce life, that intelligence must have been involved in getting these extraordinarily diverse elements to work together.'[133] The issue for Flew is the statistical improbability of life. He says he was particularly impressed by the work of Gerry Schroeder who looked at the probabilities of monkeys at typewriters actually producing anything in English, let alone a sonnet from Shakespeare. Apparently, in a real project, six monkeys hammering away at a computer keyboard for a month had produced fifty typed pages, but not a single word (not even the word 'a' which requires a space either side to be a word). Schroeder points out that the probability of producing the correct 488 letters in one particular sonnet would be one in 26 to the power of 488, which is one in ten to the power of 690. The number of basic particles in the universe is only ten to the power of eighty by comparison; these are staggeringly huge numbers.[134] Lennox cites another study in which a computer simulation of monkeys typing did produce 24 consecutive letters from Shakespeare's *Henry IV* in about 10^{40} monkey years, where the age of the universe is only 10^{11} years.[135]

Intelligent Design, or the Argument from Design, often rests with such statistical reflections: the 'argument from improbability'. Fred Hoyle, as mentioned by several authors on both sides of this debate, apparently said that 'the probability of life originating on Earth is no greater than the chance that a hurricane, sweeping through a scrapyard, would have the luck to assemble a Boeing 747.'[136] The 'monkey-sonnet' scenario is based on the same thinking. But Flew doesn't seem willing to give Dawkins *et al.* a chance to explain why the phenomenon, 'correctly extolled to be statistically improbable', as Dawkins says, *has* an explanation in science. Surely one has to engage with the scientific explanation of the improbability before taking the improbability as persuasion of 'God' as designer. But conversions are not like that: Flew was anyway moving in the direction of ruling out Darwinism (he says for example: 'In my book *Darwinian Evolution*, I pointed out that natural selection does not positively produce anything. It only eliminates, or tends to eliminate, whatever is not competitive.'),[137] and perhaps the monkeys really were the turning point.

Even if Flew nominally characterises himself as 'deist' rather than 'theist', he otherwise seems to have relaxed into a very conventional Christian outlook. This is shown in his conversation with the Bishop of Durham in Appendix B. Flew tells the bishop:

> In point of fact, I think that the Christian religion is the one religion that most clearly deserves to be honoured and respected whether or not its claim to be a divine revelation is true. There is nothing like the combination of a charismatic figure like Jesus and a first-class intellectual like Paul. Virtually all the argument about the content of religion was produced by St. Paul, who had a brilliant philosophical mind and could both speak and write in all the relevant languages. If you're wanting Omnipotence to set up a religion, this is the one to beat.

There appears to be a schoolboy enthusiasm in the way he explains his feelings to the bishop, but beyond that one must seriously challenge

Flew's understanding of St. Paul as a 'first-class intellectual'. Is this really the same Paul who dismisses all things Greek and says that knowledge 'puffeth up'? Isn't Michel Onfray closer to the biblical St. Paul when he says of Paul that he 'transformed his lack of culture into a hatred of culture. He called on the Corinthians and Timothy to turn their backs on the "addled and foolish questionings" and "hollow frauds" of philosophy.'[138]

Flew adds to the bishop that 'Today, I would say the claim concerning the resurrection is more impressive than any by the religious competition.' The bishop must have been pleased. But Wright contributes his own measure of Christian chauvinism when he says: 'actually the evidence for Jesus is so massive that, as a historian, I want to say that we have got almost as much good evidence for Jesus as for anyone in the ancient world.'[139] He continues: 'in fact I don't know of any historians today, who doubt the existence of Jesus. There are one or two.[140] [G.A. Wells]. . . . It is quite clear that in fact Jesus is a very, very well documented character of real history. So I think that question can be put to rest.' Francis Collins is also keen to assert the historical status of Jesus, suggesting that it is comparable with Julius Caesar.[141] Wright also says, obviously aware of the many theories that the Jesus story was constructed out of other myths concerning dying and resurrected god-kings, '"resurrection" doesn't feature in the Greco-Roman world'.[142] But both these points are in fact widely disputed. When Collins says that it is risky to pin faith on Intelligent Design, because science is eroding its ground, one could say the same about the historicity of Jesus.

Tina Beattie

Tina Beattie is interesting as the only woman writer in our survey of the new defenders of faith. One could argue that Karen Armstrong was an important defender of faith writing from a fairly rigorous perspective, but she rarely seems to have the tenets of the new atheism in her sights. Beattie's book *The New Atheists: The Twilight of Reason & The War on Religion* is perhaps even the first to have the term 'New Atheists' in the title. The book's cover shows Harris, Hitchens, Toynbee, Dawkins, Dennett and Amis as the new atheists. Beattie is a Roman Catholic whose position is influenced by feminism and postmodernism, and is receptive to *culture* as a crucial space representing the strongest rebuttal of atheism. To the extent that her position is postmodernist she has common ground with Michel Onfray, and so one may note that postmodernism seems grist to both mills. But she distances herself from most of the new defenders of faith, saying 'those who have sought to present a more positive view of religion so far have tended to come from a fairly conservative Christian perspective. As a result, the debate is too narrowly focused on questions of rationality and belief. . . .'[143] She is critical of many of the new atheists for not having sufficient background in religion, but says of Keith Ward and Alister McGrath: 'However, although they are considerably more knowledgeable about their subject than the new atheists, they still tend to focus on the preoccupations of a minority of predominantly male Western thinkers.'[144]

Dawkins, who as we saw is scathing of postmodernism, writes insultingly of those whose work is at the 'ditzily unreal intersection of theology and feminism'.[145] 'Ditzy' means silly or scatterbrained which Beattie is certainly not: she represents a constituency Dawkins has little awareness of or sympathy for. But Beattie is not a proponent of 'Goddess' spiritualities, she is simply a modern Christian whose religion in her view has moved on from the nineteenth-century (or earlier) version of Christianity that Dawkins is attacking. From a woman's perspective she offers this: 'There is something a little comic, if not a little wearisome, about this perennial stag-fight between men of Big Ideas, with male theologians rushing to defend the same pitch that they have fought over for centuries, which is now being colonised by men of Science rather than men of God.'[146]

Beattie quotes from Terry Eagleton's scathing review of Dawkins' *The God Delusion*, in which Eagleton identifies a 'North Oxford' tendency at work, a specific cultural context for Dawkins' atheism.[147] An article in *Wired* also confirms Oxford as the heartland of the new atheism,[148] but it is also the home of McGrath and Ward and other new defenders of faith. What emerges from this is perhaps the sheer parochialism of the debate. As one walks up St. Giles in Oxford, past the Eagle and Child pub where C.S. Lewis, J.R.R. Tolkien and other 'Inklings' would 'drink Beer and read books', as the plaque has it, the road to North Oxford forks, just around the faculties of maths, computing and engineering. Antony Flew would have known the two branches, the Banbury and Woodstock roads, as the North Oxford of two philosophers he mentions: I.M. Crombie and Sir Michael Dummett. Philip Pullman lived in Jericho, which is just about North Oxford. But, if Eagleton thinks that Dawkins' atheism has this as its cultural context, then so too does the theism of C.S. Lewis, Alister McGrath and Antony Flew. Their conversions from atheism may have had some personal religious element, but their move was within a narrow cultural circle. They did not, once disenchanted with atheism, research diligently like Augustine, consider the Neoplatonists, or in today's full-access world, Buddhism, the Advaita or Taoism; they simply relaxed comfortably into the theism of their cultural context. It is not that different from moving house from the Woodstock to the Banbury road. With this metaphor in mind we can perhaps agree when Beattie says 'we need to find a different form of engagement between custodians of knowledge in the world's religious traditions, and the more recent claims to intellectual authority by advocates of various forms of scientific materialism and atheist rationalism'.[149]

Beattie's view of religion is postmodern, defining them as 'enacted stories . . . informed by a sense of transcendence'[150] – which is consistent with the importance she places on literature and the arts in the new debate. Her views on mysticism are somewhat similar to the postmodern views of Don Cupitt (in drawing on the linguistic turn). She says of the three Abrahamic religions: 'However close the relationship between God and the soul might be, it does not dissolve into undifferentiated oneness.'[151] This is to simply ignore the profoundly influential testimony of the (Christian) mystics, but she goes further: 'If one asks what transforms a political tyranny into a religion, then perhaps one has to look for signs of a transcendent vision, a mystical or utopian dimension, which breaks free of the restraints of a strictly materialist rationality and of the restraining influences of any historical religious tradition.'[152] Hence she finds Harris a heretic amongst atheists for believing in mystical experience. She also introduces the 'Radical Orthodoxy' – Christian postmodernist theology which we will discuss later on.

There is much in Beattie's book that is a good argument against Dawkins *et al.*, but NOMA is not the basis of it. Instead she focuses on creativity and culture:

> Theology may well be dead in the water for everyone but theologians, but God's story is alive and well. In cinema, popular culture, art, music and literature – even in the popularity of the new atheism – the story of God is an implicit theme running through the imaginative life of Western culture as pervasively as it ever has.[153]

As a case study she looks at Ian McEwan's *Saturday* (we will return to this and the issue of the religious and spiritual presence in culture later on). But another topic most valuably raised by Beattie is the position taken by the new atheists on violence. Given that religious violence was the catalyst for the entire debate, this is an important issue. She surveys their views, and concludes: 'So far then, the new atheists represent a spectrum of attitudes towards war and violence which is similar to the kind of spectrum one might find among religious believers.'[154] She found Hitchens, Harris and Hari to support the Iraq war, while Dawkins was against. We could also note that Amis is against the war. Amis contemplates what he considers to be the ridiculous claims of conspiracy theorists that 9/11 was orchestrated by the US Government, and adds quietly: 'The fact is that America didn't wound itself in September 2001, as the fabulists claim. It did that in March 2003, and thereafter.'[155]

Charles Taylor

We have already introduced Charles Taylor and his work *A Secular Age*, and have suggested that there is something postsecular in his thought. How then can one locate him amongst the new defenders of faith? He is neither a Christian apologist in the Lewis-Swinburne mould, nor does he target his work at the new atheists; indeed, he only recognises them obliquely. Yet he is an apologist for faith in general throughout *A Secular Age*, and in a later section in his book he puts forward an apologetics for Christianity in particular.[156] What marks his thought is a subtlety and generosity of position, making it perhaps the most hidden, yet profound, challenge to the extremism either of old religion or the new atheists.

John Humphrys

We now return to John Humphrys, perhaps an unlikely new defender of faith if we go by the title of his book, *In God We Doubt*. Its subtitle, 'Confessions of a Failed Atheist' may be compared with that of Flew: 'How the World's Most Notorious Atheist Changed His Mind', but Humphrys has not made Flew's 'North Oxford' journey from atheism to belief. Instead, we find an intellectual acuity that puts the professors to shame; at the same time he is warm, thoughtful, well-read, and with an eagle eye for dogmatism on both sides of the debate. He finds, as we did earlier, that Alister McGrath can be as intemperate in his language as Dawkins. Humphrys says of McGrath's polemic at one point: 'The truth is, there's a lot of dogmatism on both sides of the divide, but to call Dawkins non-thinking is a bit below the belt.'[157]

Humphrys may be not be a believer, but he is highly critical of Dawkins and Harris where he thinks they are wrong. Like C.S. Lewis and his follower Francis Collins his objection to atheism starts with the fact of altruism, though Humphrys frames his discussion in terms of *conscience*. Yet, unlike Lewis and Collins, his conviction that the 'Moral Law' of which they speak is real does not imply for him that he needs to suddenly sign up *in toto* to Christian belief. He doesn't, like Flew, move from the Banbury to the Woodstock Road, by which metaphor is meant moving from a culturally received middle-class atheism to a culturally received middle-class theism. He simply says of conscience, 'I have argued . . . that its existence is proof of something transcendent, beyond the material.' In this he defies Dawkins *et al.*, but doesn't have to join McGrath, Ward and Flew. He maintains his independence of thought. His isn't a middle ground of bland compromise; instead he is in favour of the debate itself: 'For all their differences there are a couple of propositions on which atheist and believer can agree. One is that their dispute goes to the core of what it is to be human.'[158]

Humphrys is also pretty sure of what is at the 'core of what it is to be human': love. And he finds no better expression of it than in St. Paul. Humphrys isn't interested in an evolutionary explanation of love which the new atheists offer, if they speak of it at all: 'We are more than the sum of our genes – selfish or otherwise – but you might not think so if you read only the works and listened only to the words of the atheist evolutionists. . . . Nor do they have much to say about love.'[159] He then goes on to cite the passage in 1 Corinthians 13 which concludes 'And now these three remain: faith, hope and love. But the greatest of these is love.'[160] Humphrys comments: 'That's it, isn't it? Has there ever been a greater description of love?' But Humphrys isn't now, like Francis Collins, in hock to an evangelical community that demands the Bible be inerrant. We saw that Keith Ward looked seriously compromised when he attempted to defend the 'Ban' in Deuteronomy. Perhaps the cultural capital locked up in the Bible for Ward, and for so many Christians, is too great to permit real critical distance. Humphrys in contrast can apply critical reasoning to any and all of it, saying 'the Bible, read by an agnostic, is as likely to fuel scepticism as it is to engender belief.'[161]

Humphrys is intrigued by a passage from Proverbs 16:31:

Grey hair is a crown of splendour; it is attained by a righteous life.

Jokingly, he tells us that his own grey hair is just such a sign of righteousness, only to puncture this claim by finding another translation of the same passage:

The hoary head is a crown of glory, if it be found in the way of righteousness.

How did the 'if' creep in, he asks? It now makes sense of the passage – that the visible signs of old age are a crowning glory, *if* attained by a righteous life. His answer is that the passage with the 'if' in it is the King James version, while the one without is from the New International Version, based on the work of hundreds of scholars, whose apparently more advanced linguistic skills suggested they drop the 'if'. He comments: 'the modern version is barking mad. . . . the seventeenth-century translators produced a version that made at least a degree of sense. They supplied a meaning they suspected the original authors had probably intended but expressed badly.'[162] What Humphrys is doing is what any person of independent mind should do when encountering the scriptures: check them against reason and proportion. By doing so in a sympathetic way he neither becomes an indentured apologist to Christianity, nor, like Harris, one who dismisses the scriptures as gibberish.

Issues in the New Defence of Faith

The new defenders of faith are clearly united in their belief that religion itself is of value, and that to attack it *in its entirety* is wrong. But their defence seems a little hampered by its parochialism, in that they seem to want to defend *the* faith (i.e. Christianity) instead of faith itself as the Prince of Wales puts it. The Prince also gets to the heart of the issue when he says:

> My belief is that in each one of us there is a distant echo of the sense of the sacred, but that the majority of us are terrified to admit its existence for fear of ridicule and abuse. This fear of ridicule, even to the extent of mentioning the name of God, is a classic indication of the loss of meaning in so-called Western civilization.[163]

What is interesting about this is the Prince's appeal to a general sense of the sacred, without tying it to any one tradition. Most of the new defenders of faith rather manage to miss this key defence of religion – that it is the expression of a sense of the sacred. This is partly because they seem to be defending the outer structures of their particular faith, perhaps for example the resurrection, rather than this more simple issue of the sacred which goes beyond such specifics. Also, we see some residue of the strategy adopted by Malcolm Muggeridge and the then-Bishop of Southwark when pouring scorn on the Monty Python team: the defence from authority. This is related to what Beattie points out and which is called here the 'North Oxford' factor – the rather cocooned world of middle-class Christian tradition, best represented perhaps by C.S. Lewis. What can be drawn from his now very dated *Mere Christianity* is the enormous attraction for the new adherent of accepting the authority of Christian tradition (though of course this applies to all dogmatic religion). This move – however genuinely religious its motivation – requires the end of critical thought in respect to the tenets of the religion, but yields an immediate payload of *reflected* authority. The hectoring and parental tone of Lewis may not be noticeable to those already swimming in the Christian middle-class stream, but it rings massive alarm bells to those outside of it. Hence, to the extent that the new defenders of faith pursue Christian apologetics as 'indentured intellectuals of faith' their counterblasts to the new atheists will not speak far beyond the already converted: these would include McGrath, Ward, Swinburne and Flew.

Lennox, Collins, Smith and Beattie, on the other hand, mostly avoid arguments from authority, while beyond doubt it is Charles Taylor and John Humphrys, vastly different thinkers that they are, whose open-mindedness is the best defence of faith that we have so far encountered.

Chapter 5:

Postsecularism and the New Debate

We can now summarise the new debate and at the same time return to the central theme of this book: postsecularism. We are asking: to what extent does the debate represent a renewed openness to questions of the spirit, while retaining the secular habits of critical thought? What the new debate has, which had been lacking for some time, is a real *energy* of engagement, in which old assumptions might break down and genuinely new insights arise. There is now certainly a renewed energy, but the question remains, is the new debate merely a recapitulation of arguments between atheists and religionists from the dawn of the secular age, or is there something new in it? The issues at stake can be grouped under three broad headings: firstly science and NOMA, secondly 'God' and mysticism, and thirdly moderate religion, apocalypticism and the 'Black Mass Fallacy'.

The Question of NOMA

The energy of the new attack on religion is undoubtedly based in the attack from science, meaning the superordinate question of the relationship between science and religion becomes crucial. What remit, if any, does science have to speak on religion? Or rather, as 'science' as an entity does not speak, how legitimate are the arguments raised by the new atheists against religion when drawing on science? The answer to this question has deep postsecular implications. If science, broadly defined, is a mode of enquiry which has in the past or is now developing to the point where it can *take the place of religion*, then we must seek any renewal of the spiritual impulse within science. If, on the other hand, we adopt the position of non-overlapping magisteria, then we must conclude that much of the new debate is talking at cross-purposes, and that the renewal of the spiritual impulse lies outside of science. But adjudicating on

NOMA is no easy task, because the issue lies at the heart of scientific, religious and philosophical controversies since Descartes. What we *can* observe is that the new atheists are resolutely opposed to NOMA. Hitchens, it is true, does believe that religion and science are non-overlapping, but considers them antagonistic, rather than complementary as Gould proposed. The new defenders of faith, as we saw, seem rather confused over the issue. There are many statements to be found that 'God' is not something open to scientific experiment, mostly based on the conviction that 'God' is not material, but these are then rather contradicted by a reluctance to explicitly adopt the NOMA position. Alister McGrath, as we saw, rejected NOMA but was in favour of 'POMA' – *partially* overlapping magisteria.

Perhaps the reason why the new defenders of faith do not adopt NOMA, even if they have a training in science and hence a clearer picture of science than the lay person may possess, is because, as mentioned above, the issue has such vast implications for contemporary thought. Hence it is worth briefly considering the climate of intellectual opinion that makes NOMA unappealing to most. Dualism since Descartes has had a bad name, though most recognise that Descartes at least usefully framed the debate with his division. The question he posed was inevitable with the emergence of Newtonian mechanics and optics, even though Descartes' version of these sciences was in error. Even more so was his idea that 'mind stuff' was in a two-way interaction with the 'extended stuff' of the body, the so-called upwards and downwards causations. The locus of his solution, the pineal gland, was not the major problem, but rather it was the failure to understand in terms of modern physics that *energetic* exchanges were required. For mind to influence body it would have to affect matter by pushing it or pulling it in some way. But if mind is defined as non-material then it cannot, nor can the pushing and pulling of sense organs affect the mind. The same argument, of course, applies to the posited Western 'God' – how could a non-material entity either know the world or act in it, if it was not also material? This, in essence, is the mind-body problem, which applies as much to human minds as it does to 'God'.

The solution to this for hard science is to deny mind. We saw in *Secularism* that Antonio Damasio sums up this denial when he says that the goal of scientific understanding is 'to move the spirit from its nowhere pedestal to a somewhere place',[164] that 'somewhere place' being the brain. This conviction amongst the scientists within the atheism debate, that a discourse of brain states is a sufficient discourse, is what allows many of them to reject NOMA. Sam

Harris seems to go further than most when he proposes that even mystical experience and ethics will in time yield their mysteries to neuroscience. Dawkins and Dennett focus more on genes and memes, but the message is the same: there is only extended stuff. Mind *is* brain. (In *Secularism* this was called 'Damasio's Error' as a riposte to his coining of 'Descartes' Error'.)

For other contemporary thinkers this is not good enough: it is palpably obvious that our subjective experience cannot be adequately approached by such a circumscribed narrative. But they largely balk at NOMA because of its Cartesian character, and their chief objection is perhaps philosophical: that there ought to be a unified system of human knowledge about the world and our experience of it. This desire to unify human knowledge seems to be a largely unacknowledged thread running through diverse fields of thought. Here are some examples from widely different backgrounds: Erwin Schrödinger writing on physics and biology in 1944; Paul Ricoeur writing on Marx and Freud in 1970; Robert Pirsig's philosophical novel *Lila* in 1991; and Ken Wilber in *A Theory of Everything* in 2003.

Schrödinger says 'We have inherited from our forefathers the keen longing for unified, all-embracing knowledge.'[165] He adds: 'We feel clearly that we are only now beginning to acquire reliable material for welding together the sum total of all that is known into a whole. . . .' Ricoeur says 'We have at our disposal a symbolic logic, an exegetical science, an anthropology, and a psychoanalysis and, perhaps for the first time, we are able to encompass in a single question the problem of the unification of human discourse.'[166] A large part of the efforts of the Frankfurt school can also be understood as the attempt to unify Marxist and Freudian thought.

Schrödinger and Ricoeur are poles apart in their worldviews, while Pirsig and Wilber live in yet another intellectual universe, bordering on the New Age. Pirsig says: 'Historically every effort to unite science and ethics has been a disaster.'[167] His division of thought is between science and the humanities as ethics, and he proposes a 'Metaphysics of Quality' in *Lila* to unite them. For Pirsig, when a scientist says that ethics is not part of his domain, he is committing schizophrenia. Pirsig's *Lila* is an extraordinary philosophical journey in the setting of a novel, pursuing issues dealt with at length by Carlos Castaneda and Ken Wilber, yet making no reference to them.

Wilber's entire oeuvre can be understood as the search to integrate all of human thought, specifically the arts, humanities and spirituality. Yet another example can be found in the attempt within physics to unify relativity and quantum mechanics, a venture that has become something like a grail quest for physicists. Everyone is in haste to 'unify' human knowledge, but few stop to ask whether this is achievable, desirable, or even exactly what it would mean. We saw that Francis Collins says that NOMA 'inspires internal conflict, and deprives people of the chance to embrace either science or spirit in a fully realized way.' Perhaps it is the anxiety about conflict that is the key here. We saw that Sam Harris is scathing of those who adhere to NOMA, those who suggest that there is 'no need to have all of our beliefs about the universe cohere.' One might be 'a God-fearing Christian on Sunday and a working scientist come Monday morning, without ever having to account for the partition that seems to have erected itself in his head while he slept.'[168] Harris finds this reprehensible, but on the same page states: 'There is clearly a sacred dimension to our existence, and coming to terms with it could well be the highest purpose of human life.'

Given this extensive philosophical quagmire, is not surprising that the new defenders of faith have not rushed to adopt NOMA as the mainstay of their strategy. But can we say that NOMA or something like it is essential to a postsecular worldview? Perhaps yes, because otherwise Damasio and all of neuroscience will circumscribe not only our discourse about the mind of humans but also the 'mind of God', to use a metaphor. Putting it another way, it seems essential to retain some kind of NOMA-like approach if the sacred is not to be reduced to the neuron (or the meme, which must be explicable in terms of the neuron). Harris clearly relishes this reduction, without seeing that it removes the sacred at a stroke.

The Defence from Hierarchy

The apparently overwhelming urge to 'unify' all of human knowledge requires some investigation, as it seems to be a major stumbling block in the rehabilitation of spirituality/religion as magisterium in its own right. Yet even a short consideration of the question of knowledge shows that knowledge grows within specific fields of enquiry: only by asking a specific question – that is, by skilfully narrowing the parameters of it – does knowledge arise. Clearly, humans are good at this. The result is a proliferation of knowledge in different fields, on a scale now so vast as to defeat any attempt by a single person to master it all. Naturally, what is then attempted is a kind of meta-question, seeking a meta-knowledge that will order or marshal the knowledge explosion into a manageable system. In a sense a library or a university does this by its divisions of subjects, the first and most obvious divide being between the sciences and the humanities. But, as we have seen, even this first step creates an intellectual anguish.

Why? Why should the division of human knowledge be a bad thing, and the putative unification of knowledge be a desirable goal? What could it mean, to walk into a university library and unify its contents?

Obviously, it would mean nothing. This yearning can only be understood as the seeking of the right thing, 'union', in the wrong place, 'knowledge'. This is the perspective, at least, of the mystics. The life of a mystic has three stages: the awakening of the yearning for union, the seeking of it – often a journey of great personal drama – and the final attainment of it. But it is not a journey through universities or libraries, or the domains of knowledge to be found there. Even the writings of other mystics, which can be found on a shelf in a corner of 'religious studies' in a corner of the 'humanities', are unlikely to help in the journey. And 'unifying' the knowledge on the rest of the shelves, whatever that might mean, wouldn't help either.

But the mystically inclined do venture schemes for unifying knowledge, based on *hierarchies* of various kinds. Such schemes have existed since before Plato, emerging in their Western form as 'the great chain of being' in Renaissance thought. Elements of this continue in Leibniz's *Monadology*, and are taken up by Arthur Koestler, E.F. Schumacher,[169] and then notably in the work of Ken Wilber. Other mystically-inclined thinkers who put forward quite independent versions of it include Robert Pirsig and the British architect-mystic Douglas Harding.[170] These hierarchies have no place, however, in mainstream thought. Reductionists like Dawkins and Dennett believe in only one kind of knowledge – that which is found in the so-called hard sciences, and which they conceive of as structurally flat. All scientific knowledge is tested by experiment, so all of it has the same character, according to this philosophy. Let us see how just one variant of the hierarchy approach challenges this.

Robert Pirsig's *Lila: An Enquiry into Morals* was funded by the Guggenheim Memorial Foundation as a follow up to his *Zen and the Art of Motorcycle Maintenance*. Both books pursue philosophy in the setting of a travel novel. In *Lila*, Pirsig contemplates various structural levels including the cellular, the personal and the societal, demonstrating that the 'morals' or goals of each are very different. What is good for a person may not be good for the cells that make up that person's body, or may not be good for society. What is good for society may not be good for the individual or their cells, and so on. What is crucial is that the kind of 'good' at each level is as different as the kind of 'knowledge' which pertains to it: anthropology is a form of knowledge that cannot be deduced from biology, for example. But when Pirsig homes in on a more precise location for this exploration he is at his most convincing. He addresses the relationship of hardware to software on a computer, and the novel that he might be typing into its word-processor. He starts by pointing out that the circuit designer needs to know almost nothing about software design and vice versa: their two worlds only intersect in the machine-code of the processor, a set of codes that can be printed out on a single page. But, he says: 'Even in this narrow isthmus between these two sets of static patterns called "hardware" and "software" there was still no direct interchange of meaning. The same machine language instruction was a completely different entity within the two different sets of patterns.'[171]

In fact, the stratification is more ramified than this: the printed circuit board is designed with only a very limited understanding of the processor, and the bistable transistors within the processor designed with limited understanding of the processor philosophy as a whole (is it a complex- or reduced-instruction chip). Software in turn is built out of a hierarchy that includes the BIOS, the operating system, and finally the application programme – the word-processor – in which Pirsig's novel is taking shape. Each level involves different software skills and knowledge domains. Such a division of labour was already lamented by Marx, and he naively thought that communist modes of production would 'unify' this fragmented labour – yet another example of a misplaced human yearning for unity. What Pirsig ends his account of the computer with is the observation that 'one could spend all of eternity probing the electrical patterns of that computer with an oscilloscope and never find that novel.' Likewise, Harris could spend eternity probing the neuron and never find his mystical experiences there, any more than Dawkins could find the works of William Blake – whose poetry he admires – in Blake's genes.

Pirsig's argument was cited earlier to show that the effort of Dawkins and Dennett amongst others to reproduce, anticipate, or replace the knowledge of domains at a higher level within the hierarchy – the human world of experience, for example – with knowledge of a domain at a lower level – the gene – is a futile one. To 'explain' either religion or poetry in terms of the gene is to attempt to explain software in terms of hardware, or a novel in terms of a hardware-software conglomerate (a computer).

All the hierarchical systems introduced above are potential defences for faith, because they help to rein in scientific accounts of human experience by showing that such accounts are at the wrong level in a hierarchy. Koestler, Schumacher, Pirsig, Wilber and Harding provide resources for the defence of faith which have not yet entered the new atheism debate to any degree. The analysis of the *Monadology* in *Secularism* does similar work; Leibniz stands as a great precursor to the others just mentioned. But the relevance of these systems to the new debate lies in their relationship to the concept of NOMA. They offer an important middle ground because, on the one hand, they refuse the complete separation of knowledge entailed in NOMA, and on the other, they refuse the complete elision of boundaries.

Intelligent Design and Fine Tuning

We have seen that some of the new defenders of faith, rather than drawing on either NOMA or hierarchical theories, are relying instead on the 'science' of Intelligent Design and fine-tuning, by which strategy they are drawn into the territory of reductionist science. Now it is true that some claims by scientists that such-and-such a problem will be solved 'real soon now' turn out well, and some don't. Maybe biogenesis and speciation will never have a convincing scientific explanation, particularly bearing in mind that 'narrative' forms of science such as Darwinism are always less convincing than the 'exceptionless natural laws' of physics. But neither side of the debate can predict the future development of human knowledge, and these gaps in evolutionary theory may well be filled one day. It is risky to hang questions of the spirit on these gaps.

The issue of fine-tuning is rather different however. Even though Stenger disputes some of the fine-tuning claims, it seems likely that at least some are supportable. What really divides a secular sensibility from a postsecular one is the response to the fine-tuning data. The secular mind can simply say: 'so what?' Coincidences are coincidences, and secularists aware of the New Age can add that reading anything into coincidences or 'synchronicity' is just more *Celestine Prophecy*-style psychobabble (more on the New Age later). The presecular mind insists that fine-tuning is an argument for 'God' whereas a postsecular mind – exposed to wider-ranging religious ideas, including that of Buddhism – might see something more broadly sacred or significant, not relying on the 'God' metaphor.

Cosmo-theophany and Cultural Autism

When contemplating fine-tuning there might well be a sense of awe at the fragility of our existence – that is, that it might so easily not be. For the would-be suicide or those convinced intellectually that life is not worth living – such as Schopenhauer, or South African philosopher David Benatar who attacks Dawkins for his optimism[172] – the fine-tuning argument would elicit no positive response. But for those open to questions of the spirit in a *via positiva* vein it speaks again of what is here called 'cosmo-theophany' – an awe or perhaps even an ecstatic mood of intellectual elevation on encountering such exquisite detail, structure, and balance.

Several key distinctions in spiritual life were pursued in *Secularism*, including *bhakti* vs. *jnani*, *via positiva* vs. *via negativa* and esoteric vs. transcendent. If there is to be a response to scientific discoveries that involves awe, wonder and even ecstasy (of a rather inner and non-demonstrative type), then this properly belongs to the clustering of spiritual impulses identified as *jnani via positiva*. We saw that the Enlightenment could be understood as the culmination of a move in Western religious thought from *bhakti via negativa* to *jnani via positiva*, in which religious 'love' is replaced by religious 'knowledge' and an inwardness replaced by an outwardness. The secular mind is then understood as a contracted and rather barren form of the *jnani via positiva* outlook, in which the search for spiritual wisdom is reduced to the search for mechanism, and the world-curious or embracive spirituality of the *via positiva* is reduced to the harnessing of the machine-of-the-world to purely material ends. Another way to describe this contraction is through the idea of 'cultural autism' – a societal move to posit life and self as mechanism.

While an empathy for science can be found in both the esoteric and transcendent traditions, and for example in Neoplatonism which is a mixture of these, any 'esoteric science' of the kind found in Rudolf Steiner's work is anathema to the reductionist scientist. Instead Dawkins writes often and movingly of his awe and wonder in confronting Nature in general, but specifically as revealed to him through Darwinism. Whatever his hatred of religion, we can still describe his response here as a form of cosmo-theophany, being aware of course that the 'theo' in 'theophany' has to be understood not as 'God' but as some broader elevating principle or sacredness. What Dawkins's metaphor of 'Mount Improbable' demands is an effort of scientific imagination; by the same token the metaphor of 'God' demands an effort of religious imagination. But it is clear that presecular religionists, in their often literalist conception of 'God', create a climate where such a religious imagination is discouraged. Likewise they find it hard to participate in the kind of scientific imagination found in 'Mount Improbable'.

Where the new atheists express something of a cosmo-theophany in their science, we can say that they are participating in something spiritual, having defined spiritual as a profound connectedness. When the mind encounters science this way, it resonates with this feeling of awe, eloquently and movingly described by Einstein, Schrödinger, Dawkins and many other scientists. In some way the human mind appears built to resonate with these insights; the Renaissance captured this idea in its concept of 'man as microcosm'. But a reductionist viewpoint denies the possibility that the human mind could encompass the universe, as the Neoplatonists would say, because reductionists are forced to believe that the human mind is the human *brain*. How could a lump of grey jelly the size of a grapefruit contain within it the universe? Ridiculous. But theophany of a cosmic kind, i.e. one arising in the context of Nature or its scientific exploration, shows that the *reductionism* is ridiculous. Where this reductionism is clung to, not just as an intellectual exercise, but as an emotional stance towards the world, one can characterise it as cultural autism.

To the extent that this kind of stance is cultural, it is universal, and no-one escapes it completely, beyond, that is, the possibility of any person standing outside the culture of their time. The point here is that if one finds that the work of a particular individual clearly demonstrates cultural autism, it is not to suggest that they can be clinically located on the autism spectrum. Hence, for example, the characterisation of the work of Daniel Dennett on memes as demonstrating cultural autism is not intended *ad hominem*. Instead, 'cultural autism' as a term is an attempt to capture the mood of a science-enthralled world.

Memes

The goal of reductionist reasoning is to explain everything, including human experience, in terms of mechanism. The first such attempts were found in La Mettrie's 1748 *Man a Machine*. There is a macho sanguinity about such works, suggesting a robust personality not inclined to introspection, ecstasy, or melancholy; the converse of the Romantic. This personality, represented in recent fiction by McEwan's Henry Perowne, is emotionally balanced and quite capable of enjoying the classical arts. But the search to describe everything in terms of mechanism has become so pervasive as to require a reductionist account not just of the arts, but of all interiority – an account now provided by meme theory. While Dawkins originated it, it is Dennett who pursues it to extremes in his work and in doing so reveals its poverty.

The poverty of meme theory, or a similar type of account, is in the idea that human culture, whether art or religion, can be understood in terms of evolutionary advantage. Somehow memes such as religious belief, a symphony, a cathedral, or democracy, can all be understood in terms of giving their carrier organism – human minds – competitive survival advantage. If one examines the competitive world of contemporary fine arts funding, one might suggest that it looks rather Darwinian. But what purchase does meme theory give us on a funding system that in Britain gives rise to such high-profile events such as the Turner Prize as well as the art that wins it each year? What does it mean to be inspired by this art, to stand in front of it, and to be transported in some way or another in the aesthetic equivalent to a cosmo-theophany? Where is the what-is-it-like-to-be in meme theory, compared to what a good art critic can convey in their writing? Nowhere. It is a biological metaphor operating at the wrong level in the hierarchy of our experience.

But meme theory is in its infancy, standing perhaps as Ptolemaic (proto-) science stood in relation to Newtonian science. We can see this in *Darwin's Dangerous Idea* when we compare part Three of Dennett's book, which deals with memes, to parts One and Two, which deal with genes. His useful and illuminating presentation of Darwinian theory for the lay person is rigorous and well-supported in the literature, whereas the speculative chapters on memes are meandering and far-fetched, much as when he applies memes to religion in *Breaking the Spell*. But we cannot tell whether a speculative proto-science will enter science proper, or take its place in the scientific dustbin along with vitalism, phrenology, and Einstein's cosmological constant (his admitted 'biggest blunder'). We know what it would take for meme theory to enter science: a neurological basis, in which case meme theory would look a bit like the language of 'neural correlates' discussed in *Secularism*. The argument is not against the possibility of such correlates in the brain, but that we have no 'experiential correlates' of brain, neuron, peptide and so on. We experience the redness of red, the painfulness of pain – the so-called qualia – but there is nothing in our experience that corresponds to brain, neuron, peptide – or meme. I experience my body, my feelings, and my sensations, but I don't experience my brain, my neurons or my peptides: they are concepts, not percepts. We need a jolt by which we could collectively recoil from the direction this neurological obsession is taking us in: perhaps the term 'cultural autism' creates an image sufficient for that.

Irrelevance of the 'God' Question

We have approached the issue of postsecularism and the new atheism debate by first considering the over-arching issue of NOMA and related ideas such as knowledge hierarchies. But for the general public the debate starts – and perhaps ends – with the existence of 'God'. Does he, or doesn't he, exist? We mentioned earlier the popular singer Gary Numan and will look later at his 'atheism' albums of recent years. We can examine here, however, a couple of non-contiguous lines from his song 'A Prayer for the Unborn' from his album *Pure*:

> If you are my father
> Then love lies abandoned and bleeding.
> If you are my answer
> Then I must have asked the wrong question.

Numan makes clear that his 'father' here is 'God' and that in this song he is expressing his rage against the universe in letting his first infant die. 'You were glorious,' he sings of 'God', 'but you were somewhere else.' This is the problem of theodicy that crops up so often in the new atheism debate, but the point we want to make here is that to ask whether 'God' exists or not is the *wrong question*. The answer 'yes' or 'no' is useless because the 'God' that Dawkins and other atheists construct is a straw man, and is easily brought down. The anthropomorphism of 'God' has dogged Western religion, and has been opposed by powerful elements within all three monotheisms. To the extent that religionists today cling to an anthropomorphic 'God' they will excite people such as Dawkins to attack it, which in fact *serves* religion. Beyond saying this, there is little in the argument over 'God' that is interesting in a postsecular sense. What is interesting in this aspect of the new debate lies in the non-anthropomorphic conceptions of 'God' amongst the new atheists. Although the term 'Einstein's God' is introduced by Dawkins to remove from his argument the parts of religion he might approve of, the term in itself is a useful contribution.

Negative Theology and 'Intellectual High Treason'

Dawkins says that to confuse the Abrahamic vengeful 'God' with 'Einstein's God' is 'an act of intellectual high treason'. Great weight should be placed on just this idea, that the various 'Gods' constructed out of differing spiritual impulses need to be carefully distinguished, but that no one of them is more correct than another. It was also shown that Flew made clear that his 'God' is 'Aristotle's God', but rather avoided the issue of whether this was the same 'God' that Bishop Wright was so pleased to discuss with him. Some atheists come close to spitting in indignation at the negative theology, insisting that it is either nothing to do with the 'God' that they are sure doesn't exist, or that theists are deliberately using obfuscating language – 'inspissated gloaming' – as a smokescreen to avoid criticism.

All this has postsecular implications because the genuine interest that Dawkins *et al.* may have in 'Einstein's God' represents a renewed interest in questions of the spirit in keeping with the scientific tenor of our age. Putting it another way, the new atheists seem receptive to a *jnani* concept of spirituality, especially when it rides on a sense of cosmo-theophany. As a 'divine disclosure', epiphanies in science reveal something of the deep structure of the universe, and, to the extent that we are a microcosm of the universe in the Renaissance sense of the word, it also reveals the deep structure of what it is to be human. This has a sacred feel to it, simply because it moves us along the vector of profound connectedness. What Dawkins *et al.* fail to understand is that worship of the Christian 'God' does the same thing, but using a different energetic source: devotion. It isn't intellectual high treason to conflate different paths to the divine, just clumsy. The same clumsiness led the Jews to anathematise the worship of idols: who can judge the interior movement of the worshipper towards profound connectedness when in front of a golden calf?

There is *nothing* in science that should stand against the religious impulse when more broadly conceived, and, if postsecularism is to mean anything, it must contain such a pluralism. This is the lesson – at one level at least – from secularism and postmodernism: pluralism is both possible and desirable. The secular era makes it possible to recover repressed religious streams of thought, and one such stream, generally termed Neoplatonism, or even more broadly 'Greek' or 'Hellenic', has never been inimical to science. Where science would be hostile to Neoplatonism is where this ancient confluence of spiritual traditions becomes an esotericism. All the more reason then, for NOMA: we simply say that science cannot adjudicate on the question of disembodied beings and subtle energies, because it only deals with the energetic exchanges between matter. It's *good* at that.

The Status of Scripture

For completeness a related issue in the new debate must be mentioned: the status of scripture. As a result of secular scholarship, we have access to all the world's great religious scriptures, and through the discipline called 'Religious Studies', as opposed to 'Theology', we can triangulate across these scriptures to find what is common and what is local colouring. Beyond this, there are modern rigorous disciplines such as history, archaeology, and ethnology which allow much light to be shed upon the origins of scripture and the events they purport to describe. If the mutual ignorance pact between secular scholarship and faith tradition is really breaking down, then the attack on scripture by atheists will not only increase in volume but accuracy.

The movement known as 'Higher Criticism', active about a hundred years ago, was applied to the Bible, and hinted at rather alarming results for Christians. The biblical sources, when subjected to modern methods of scrutiny, looked less and less reliable. But both the secular and the religious impetus for such enquiry faded over the twentieth century as secular scholarship turned to more interesting projects and faith tradition retreated to its intellectual ghetto. A postsecular era, on the other hand, will have no choice but to press such enquiries again, driven in the first instance by the atheists. Christopher Hitchens has usefully included extracts in his *Portable Atheist Reader* from the work of Ibn Warraq, who challenges biblical accounts as part of his attack on the Koran. The bland assurances of Bishop Wright regarding biblical accuracy and the historical nature of Jesus simply cannot stand alongside the work of scholars like Warraq, or even against more popular works by authors such as Freke and Gandy.[173] This is not to assume that either side has a monopoly on truth here, but rather that the suspended attempts to clarify the nature of scripture as man-made texts are resuming. No possible harm can come from this.

At the same time, the issue raised by Keith Ward's defence of scripture becomes crucial. If the utterly unacceptable passages in scripture are, according to his idea, updated and corrected by later scripture and by the 'general sense' of scripture, then how will this revision reach the general public? After all, Bibles still contain the 'Ban'. Warraq points out that Islamic scholars follow a doctrine of 'abrogation' by which 'certain passages of the Koran are abrogated by verses with a different or contrary meaning revealed afterwards.'[174] He then adds that this poses a problem because recent scholarship on the chronology of Koranic verses show that later verses are more intolerant than earlier verses. For example 'Slay the idolators wherever you find them' of sura 9.5 would overwrite many other suras that dictate toleration based on the new chronology. Ward's chronological scheme, which may work on a New Testament vs. Old

Testament basis, and even within the Old Testament to some degree, may not work within the Koran. What is left then is the 'general sense' of scripture as a tool for its correction and revision, but this has also has its drawbacks. What if a fundamentalist draws a different 'general sense' from scripture than the liberal and uses it to discard the tolerant passages?

Moderate Religion and the Religious Left

This brings us to the subject of the religious moderates, a group persistently opposed by the new atheists. While some, in more realistic moments, do accept that the only pressure that the religious extremists might respond to is from the moderates in their own religion, most of the new atheists give them short shrift. The motives seem to vary, however. The oddest is that of nostalgia, it seems: the desire for 'good old-fashioned religion' as somehow more *authentic* than the various modernisations the new atheists detect in moderate religion. More commonly the line of attack is expressed in Harris's dictum, that moderates only exist because of secular knowledge and scriptural ignorance. If they really knew the scriptures of their religion, the argument goes, they would be defenceless against the attacks from secularism. And in holding out against such exposure, they provide the extremists with the broad base from which to claim justification. Harris says: 'Religious moderates are, in large part, responsible for the religious conflict in our world, because their beliefs provide the context in which scriptural literalism and religious violence can never be adequately opposed.'[175] For scientists like Dawkins, the moderates also hold back the proper teaching of science in schools.

What the new atheists are doing is not just to associate religion with extremism, but also to associate it with right-wing conservatism. There are exceptions, such as those who characterise Islamism as a corruption of Islam through Marxism, in which case they are associating religious violence with extreme left-wing politics. But if we can say that in America at least, religious fundamentalism is a broadly right-wing phenomenon, then what about the religious left? Who are they and where are they?

For many people even the term 'the religious left' will have an unfamiliar ring to it. Historically this has two reasons: firstly, that left-leaning thinking has been broadly atheist since Marx, and secondly, that believers who are on the political left are a fragmented constituency compared to the political right. In Michael Lerner's *The Left Hand of God* he explains why many 'decent Americans' are attracted to the religious right: 'because it is the only voice that they encounter that is willing to challenge the despiritualisation of daily life. . . .'[176] Lerner's analysis of the American scene is most useful, showing that there is a much larger religious left than one might have anticipated. But his solution to the basic issue, the fragmentation and resulting political disempowerment of the religious left, is politically naïve. Despite this, the very interesting question remains: could postsecularism provide something of a coherent and unifying framework of thought for the religious left? If postsecularism implies a spiritual pluralism, would this not align itself to certain liberal principles of diversity and toleration?

The New Atheists and War

As we saw however, the new atheists are not necessarily old Marxists. Neither does either side of the new atheism debate align itself politically with the issue of war in general, nor more specifically with that of the war in Iraq, as Tina Beattie points out. But she is alarmed to find Sam Harris so bellicose: 'Harris stands out as someone who makes no attempt at all to mask his contempt, not only for radical Islamism but for Muslims in general, and who is willing to justify any violence, however extreme, to fight the threat which he thinks they represent.' Harris, as an American, is probably more extreme in his attitude than any European atheist might be, and one might account for this partly by his youth. But it is alarming indeed to find him write: 'Some propositions are so dangerous that it may even be ethical to kill people for believing them.'[177] These 'propositions' are just those contained in the Bible and Koran which are roundly condemned by all the atheists, such as the 'Ban' in Deuteronomy, hence Ward's half-hearted attempt to distance contemporary Christians from it is most unconvincing in this intellectual climate. Yet the views of Harris also represent a regression in our conception of moral law: the issue of what people *believe* as opposed to what they *do* has long been argued over, and a modern consensus reached that force can only be used against a person in respect of harmful acts, or when such acts include incitement to violence. To hold a *belief*, however, has long been regarded in Western law as no case for force.

Ideologies and Apocalypticism

The three monotheisms of the West are apocalyptic religions in their origins, though the adherence to this amongst contemporary believers varies widely. As a general rule, the more fundamentalist the believer, the more likely they are to hold end-time, millennial or apocalyptic views, in which ordinary human history ends in Judgement. More than any other religious belief, 9/11 brought to secular attention this aspect of monotheism, partly because the television footage of the attack showed destruction on a near-apocalyptic scale. More significantly, the religious ideology apparently behind the attack was apocalyptic, and the new atheists are uniform in their condemnation of this, often believing, falsely, that all religions are apocalyptic. Hence it is important to reiterate that Buddhism, Hindusm, Taoism, Confucianism, Shinto, Zen and the Bon Po, for example, are not.

Fuel to the atheists' outrage at apocalypticism is the idea that other millennial ideologies such as Nazism and Communism are somehow also 'religions'. This thesis finds most vivid expression in John Gray's *Black Mass*, which opens by saying that 'the new millennium is littered with the debris of utopian projects, which though they were framed in secular terms that denied the truth of religion were in fact vehicles for religious myths.'[178] He follows this up by stating: 'Modern revolutionary movements are a continuation of religion by other means.' This is a common move amongst some modern theorists, to conflate 'ideology' with 'religion', but as A.C. Grayling points out in his review of *Black Mass*: 'This empties the word "religion" of any meaning, making it a neutral portmanteau expression like "view" or "outlook".'[179] Gray's analysis is not to be completely dismissed however because there is no doubt that Marxist teleology is, to some degree, in its outward form at least, inherited from Christian millenarianism. But Gray wants to make apocalypticism both the heart of Christianity and its departure from Judaism, neither of which is supported by a more careful reading of scripture (particularly if we include the Gospel of Thomas). To the extent that Gray does conflate religion with secular teleologies, however, it is fair to call this move the 'Black Mass Fallacy'. The first element of this fallacy is to believe that religion *equals* apocalypticism, and the second element is to conflate religious and secular apocalypticisms. While McEwan and others rightly point out that Revelation is at the core of Christian apocalyptical belief,[180] this is mostly true of extreme Protestants: Catholics are largely embarrassed by Revelation. Nor do religions with their origins east of Iran have anything resembling apocalypticism in their creeds: they are more likely to hold to a cyclical view of time, in which all things renew themselves (rather as in Heraclitus). When we look at millennial assumptions in Marxism we see the basis for an extreme ideology that has absolutely no common ground with religion. What we should learn from extreme secular ideologies is not that they are religions in disguise, but that there is a universal human tendency to go to extremes. It is not that religion is the common factor in secular and religious extremism, but that extremism is the common factor in the corruption of widely differing human endeavours, including religion.

Amongst the new atheists we find that both Ian McEwan and Philip Pullman stumble into something like the Black Mass Fallacy as key to their rejection of religion, though Pullman more closely follows (or perhaps anticipates) Gray when he says 'You don't need a belief in God to have a theocracy.'[181] Marx will do, though this muddies the waters, as Grayling is quick to spot. Yet the new atheists, if they keep out of the Black Mass Fallacy, are possibly doing a great service to monotheist religion by exposing what is undoubtedly a canker in it. Although the discipline of religious studies was founded with the principle that it could not adjudicate between the competing truth-claims of different religions, by the mere act of placing them on an equal footing – which theology by its very nature cannot do – one is led to the act of *triangulation*. If apocalypticism were equally prominent within Buddhism as it is in Christianity, one would be forced to conclude that it was an essential of religion. Instead, a wider acquaintance with far-Eastern religion suggests the opposite conclusion, that apocalypticism is an historical accident of the West. It could be removed from Western religion with no detriment to its core values at all.

Postsecularism and the New Debate: Summary

Having summarised the thinking of a range of both new atheists and new defenders of faith, we are now in a position to estimate how 'new' the current atheism debate actually is. It was suggested in *Secularism* that the Enlightenment brought about a divorce of intelligence from religion; the former pursuing the arts, science and politics, while the latter sank into a kind of cocooned slumber. Charles Taylor puts it slightly differently; he says of the collapse of religion, which had previously been the principal force that ordered society: 'A great energy is released to re-order affairs in secular time.'[182] That great energy has shaped the modern world, while religion appeared to mark time in its cultural ghetto. But did it? Of course not; that would be an enormous over-simplification. Christianity has modernised to the extent that theologians can venture ideas never possible in the presecular era, including – infuriatingly for the new atheists – such concepts as the 'death of God' theology. An existential theologian like Paul Tillich can venture radical ideas that are widely acclaimed. But the overall cultural pressure on mainstream religion was so muted, due to the mutual ignorance pact, that Sam Harris can *almost* legitimately describe Tillich as a 'blameless parish of one'.[183]

Tillich can be understood as a mixture of presecular and postsecular thinking, and Harris's acknowledgement of such innovation in religion can be understood as a kind of pressure for mainstream religion to follow suit. To this extent the new debate is postsecular and not a recapitulation of late Enlightenment arguments. As pointed out earlier, the atheists are reading religion and the theists are reading science in a way unparalleled throughout the secular era. The secular energy brought to the debate, partly fuelled by the moral outrage against religious violence, gives the debate a cultural importance that was largely unknown through the secular age. The scholarship on world religions carried on steadily through the twentieth century also provides the new debate with far greater opportunity for triangulation on key religious concepts. Harris, for example, draws on the Jain religion to provide a non-violent contrast to monotheism (an irony considering his bellicose stance).[184]

We leave the new atheism debate with one last question: how will it develop? It could just degenerate into a dialogue of the deaf, and a retrenchment on both sides to the secular détente of the last century: a return to mutual ignorance. Or is Humphrys right in suggesting that the West is losing its *reticence* about religion? Will this guarantee that a constructive dialogue has to take place, that there is no hiding place for the excesses of religious belief, or for that matter the excesses of atheist dogmatism?

We turn now, away from the new atheism debate, towards a series of other cultural contexts in which a postsecular sensibility can be sought as an answer to some of these questions. These contexts are a little similar to what Charles Taylor calls the 'nova' – the proliferation of means by which the religious impulse found new expression after the collapse of old religion as the central structuring principle for society.

Part Three:
Some Postsecular Contexts

Chapter 6:
Postsecularism and Physics

Even though Enlightenment philosophers rarely understood either the emerging science of that period or its real implications, the cultural impact of science was to be enormous. We can now consider the irony: science seemed to underpin the secular revolution (despite all the caveats that this was no simple process) – and now appears to underpin the *postsecular* revolution. But we need to be more precise: it was *physics* that started the revolution leading to secular atheism, and it appears to be physics that has started a renewed argument for mysticism, and from thence to a softening of the secular stance. We have found that the biological sciences are hotly contested in the new atheism debate, with secular Darwinism on the one side and theistic Intelligent Design on the other. Physics has a different role in this debate, playing out in the area of the anthropic principle or fine tuning, where the arguments for and against are more balanced. But beyond fine tuning, the physics of quantum theory has inspired new thinking about consciousness and spirituality.

Biologists today largely pursue a reductionist materialism untouched by revolutions in scientific discovery at atomic or cosmic scales. The scientist Paul Davies (whose work we examine shortly) quotes psychologist Harold Morowitz:

> What has happened is that biologists, who once postulated a privileged role for the human mind in nature's hierarchy, have been moving relentlessly toward the hard-core materialism that characterised nineteenth-century physics. At the same time, physicists, faced with compelling experimental evidence, have been moving away from strictly mechanical models of the universe to a view that sees the mind as playing an integral role in all physical events. It is as if the two disciplines were on fast-moving trains, going in opposite directions and not noticing what is happening across the tracks.[1]

This explains why it is hard to find vituperative atheists amongst physicists, while one veritably falls over them in biology. But what is it in modern physics that has caused such a revolution in thought? We can look to three new branches of physics that emerged in the twentieth century: quantum theory, relativity, and chaos theory. All of these *appear* to counter the notion of the universe as a machine, separate from the human mind, and with a linear chain of cause and effect. It took perhaps seventy years from the foundations of these new disciplines for the implications to permeate popular culture, but there is no doubt as to who started the wider perception that physics has spiritual or religious implications: Fritjof Capra, and his seminal text of 1975: *The Tao of Physics*. This can be called the first postsecular text of 'New Age science' with a basis in physics; it has sold over a million copies in many languages. A flood of such writings followed, some examples of which are listed here:

- Gary Zukav, *Dancing Wu Li Masters*, 1978
- David Bohm, *Wholeness and the Implicate Order*, 1980
- Paul Davies, *God and the New Physics*, 1983
- John Barrow and Frank Tipler, *The Anthropic Cosmological Principle*, 1986
- Danah Zohar, *The Quantum Self*, 1991
- Frank Tipler, *The Physics of Immortality: Modern Cosmology, God and the Resurrection of the Dead*, 1994
- John Gribbin, *Schrodinger's Kittens and the Search for Reality*, 1996

More recent volumes include:

- Lynne McTaggart, *The Field*, 2003
- Ervin Laszlo, *Science and the Akashic Field: An Integral Theory of Everything*, 2004
- Chris Clarke, *Ways of Knowing: Science and Mysticism Today*, 2005
- Hollick, Malcolm, *The Science of Oneness: A Worldview for the Twenty-First Century*, 2006

These books and their authors are typical of a revolution in popular science writing. These can be best sellers and find their way onto outlets like airport bookstalls, but they can be strictly divided between books by scientists writing on their own field, and books by outsiders to science.

Nobel Prize physicist Niels Bohr famously said: 'Anyone who is not shocked by quantum theory has not understood it',[2] while Richard

Feynman, one of the greatest physicists of recent times, used to say that *no one* understands quantum theory. Be that as it may, the shock has reverberated in contemporary culture through the writings of pioneers like Capra. We can list the three well-known issues that are raised by these discoveries of the sub-atomic world: quantum indeterminacy, quantum holism, and quantum non-locality.

The first of these, quantum indeterminacy, simply says that in the case of a sub-atomic particle like the electron we cannot know both its position and momentum. This sounds very technical and uninteresting, but boils down to the fact that we cannot take measurements on such tiny objects in the way that we can, for example, with planets. The shattering (to a physicist, at any rate) real-isation was that this was nothing to do with poor instruments, but that this was a structural issue: you cannot know things about a very small object with any precision because you have to chuck another small object at it to investigate it. The very act of observation changes the object being studied. You can shine a torch into a dark room to observe things in it, and they aren't changed by the act, because the light beam is made of very tiny things, and the objects in the room are enormous in comparison. The vase is not knocked off the mantelpiece by the light beam. But shining the equivalent of a torch into the darkness of an atom disturbs the parts of the atom because the objects making up the light (known as photons) are the same size or bigger than the sub-atomic objects. Annoyingly, although there are smaller objects (particles) to be had, they are so energetic that they behave with even more intrusive results. Impasse.

The Enlightenment rationalist project breaks down here because the confident prediction that human intelligence and endeavour would progressively reveal the workings of the physical universe is undermined. Einstein himself could not accept quantum indeter-minacy – stated more formally as Heisenberg's uncertainty principle in 1927 – even though he was one of the principle founders of the new science. To this day there are those scientists, following Einstein and others like David Bohm, that don't accept the uncertainty principle, but they have not succeeded in disproving it. Physics has had to live with the fact that we *cannot* know some things, a state of ignorance not just the result of inconclusive laboratory experimentation, but actually part of the fabric of scientific theory. We remember that the attack on religion from science was largely based on the idea that science held *explanatory* powers simply unattainable by religion. The *uncertainty* principle suddenly challenged that notion, as did a host of other discoveries such as wave-particle duality. This is a limit to scientific knowledge built into the very structure of that knowledge, a little like Gödel's incompleteness theorems in mathematics.

Quantum holism – or 'entanglement', as it is known – means that it is possible for a particle separated from its pair, and at the other end of the universe, to somehow 'know' what happens to its partner. This is again the subject of great debate, but challenges another important scientific principle: that one can isolate one part of the universe from another in order to study it. This postulate of the interconnectedness of all things is fundamental to New Age thinking, and was anticipated by Leibniz in his *Monadology*, though not on scientific grounds at all.

For many contemporary thinkers, the overall implication of quantum theory is that the human experimenter is intimately bound up with the experiment, and that human consciousness is intimately bound up with matter. This contradicts the Cartesian notion of matter and mind as separate substances, and, for many, requires the reintroduction of the language of spirit, or at the very least a close examination of consciousness. The idea that physics has such implications is called the anthropic principle, as we saw earlier. Scientists John Barrow and Frank Tipler have explored the anthropic implications of a wide range of findings in modern physics in *The Anthropic Cosmological Principle*, listed above as amongst the key writings in this field. (Interestingly they did not highlight the anthropic implications of Einstein's relativity theory, possibly because even fewer people understand that than do quantum theory.) Whether the more recent challenge from Stenger and others to the anthropic or fine tuning argument will prevail is hard to say. In any event, the relationship between the actual science of, for example, physical constants, and the meta-science of what meaning we give to them, is itself crucial to the debate.

Chaos theory, the study of complex systems, is often thought of as the third 'new' science of the twentieth century, and also offers a challenge to the reductionist worldview. Chaos theory challenges cause-and-effect in a different way to quantum theory, which says that there is an indeterminism at the heart of matter, but it rarely impinges on the macro-world in which human experience takes place (though it might just do in the *brain*, as we shall see in the next section). Chaos theory says that while in principle the behaviour of atoms and molecules in complex systems operate by strict laws of causality, in practice it is impossible to predict the outcome *even with the most powerful computers imaginable*. Furthermore, complex systems seem to generate higher-order patternings focussed around 'strange attractors' which can be thought of as analogous to

Plato's 'forms' or Jungian archetypes. All these ideas suggest a very different cosmos to the image that science had earlier created of a clockwork mechanism with regular, precise, and predictable motions.

Both relativity and quantum theory may engender a solipsistic interpretation. From these starting points it is easy to see a range of parallels with the teachings of the mystics, and even to see theological implications. One well-known series of texts that deals with 'God' and the new physics is by the British astronomer Paul Davies; indeed one is even entitled *God and the New Physics*. Davies was awarded the Templeton prize for the advancement of religion for his efforts (then worth a million dollars). Sir John Templeton is a philanthropic billionaire who approached the Nobel committee with a proposal for a category for progress in religion, but was turned down and so created his own annual award. Given the generally Christian context of Sir Templeton's work it is intriguing that the award should go to Davies, whose book starts and ends with the assertion that 'science offers a surer path to God than religion.'[3] As of the year 2008, the Templeton prize has been awarded thirty-eight times, thirteen of those to scientists. Of these, ten broadly speaking work in the field of physics, and only three in biology. Again, this suggests that of the two, physics is more congenial to religion.

The sense of shock that the Western mind has experienced with quantum theory may be a result of this realisation that there are possible limits to what we can know. But we have collectively never asked the simple question of what would we do with 'complete', 'absolute', and 'unlimited' knowledge of the physical world? Physicists themselves, committed to the search for 'a theory of everything' (which at this point in history takes the form of the search for what is known as the unified field theory), find it hard to explain what success would mean. The most famous attempt is perhaps contained within the last lines of Stephen Hawking's well-known popular science book, *A Brief History of Time*:

> However, if we do discover a complete theory, it should in time be understandable in broad principle by everyone, not just a few scientists. Then we shall all, philosophers, scientists, and just ordinary people, be able to take part in the discussion of the question of why it is that we and the universe exist. If we find the answer to that, it would be the ultimate triumph of human reason – for then we would know the mind of God.[4]

What can this mean? The 'triumph of human reason' here would merely restore the conception of the Universe as a machine, a concept at present in some doubt.

To 'know the mind of God' is, for the *jnani*-type mystics, an experience whose theoretical underpinning comes from traditions of thought like Neoplatonism in the West, or Buddhism and Advaita in the East. Their methodologies rely on the interiority of introspection, not the exteriority of the cyclotron. But in his introduction to *God and the New Physics* Davies says:

> For the first time, a unified description of all creation could be within our grasp. . . .
>
> It may seem bizarre, but in my opinion science offers a surer path to God than religion. Right or wrong, the fact that science has actually advanced to the point where what were formerly religious questions can be seriously tackled, itself indicates the far-reaching consequences of the new physics.[5]

The idea that Davies has put forward, that science can tackle formerly religious questions, is not, it is true, held by many scientists, or if they do, they may be convinced like Dawkins and Stenger that it *disproves* 'God'. However, it is a false assumption that explanations of natural phenomenon have anything to do with the core of religion. For the *bhakti* no such explanations are needed for the religious life, and for the *jnani* on the *via negativa* the same holds. It is only *jnani* on the *via positiva* who may find their energies engaged with scientific explanation, but they will read 'God' *into* the science, not deduce 'God' *from* it, because their spirituality has a pre-existing source which has nothing to do with science. Ken Wilber, in his book *Quantum Questions*, set out to show this from the writings of the pioneers of quantum science, including Erwin Schrödinger. In the introduction Wilber says: 'The theme of this book, if I may briefly summarize the argument of the physicists presented herein, is that modern physics offers no positive support (let alone proof) for a mystical worldview.'[6] At the same time he acknowledges that the idea of physics-supports-mysticism is so entrenched in the New Age that no one book could possibly reverse the tide.

But let us look a little harder at what 'explanation' means in the first place to a scientist like Davies. Quantum indeterminacy puts a great 'I don't know' at the heart of science, and prompts a possible rethink of our assumptions about its entire project. Gary Zukav includes the following thoughts on Newton and gravity in his *Dancing Wu Li Masters*:

Newton clearly felt that a true understanding of the nature of gravity was beyond comprehension. In a letter to Richard Bentley, the classical scholar, he wrote:

> that one body may act upon another at a distance through a vacuum without the mediation of anything else, by and through which the action and force may be conveyed from one to another, is to me so great an absurdity that, I believe, no man who has in philosophic matters a competent faculty of thinking could ever fall into it.

In short, action-at-a-distance could be described, but it could not be explained.[7]

Zukav stresses in his book the absurdity or counter-intuitive nature of many scientific theories, an absurdity already commented upon by Newton in the above passage, and central also to the paradox born along with Newton's optics: the wave-particle duality. Newton put forward a particle theory of light, while his contemporary Huygens put forward a wave theory, and although fashion tended to favour either one or the other at different times, in the end science came down firmly in favour of . . . *both*. Such paradoxical and uncomfortable views about science had never been put into the popular domain prior to Capra. Zukav points out that 'Newton was the first person to discover principles in nature which unify large tracts of experience', which may be a better way to understand science than in terms of pure explanation. Given the existing mysteries and indeterminacies posed by science it looks increasingly impossible that a 'theory of everything' would one day *explain* everything – more likely it will unify a certain limited tract of experience. Whether that particular domain or magisteria of experience has any overlap with the magisterium of spiritual, mystical or religious experience is open to debate.

What is even more intriguing about Hawking's closing remarks in a *Brief History of Time* is his suggestion that a complete theory will illuminate the question of 'why we and the universe exist.' This flies in the face of all experience of the development of fundamental science in the twentieth century, which shows that attempts to find meaning in the equations become progressively more frustrated, as perhaps Wolpert was driving at in his remarks about science and meaning. (In the daily application of quantum science in consumer electronics engineers cheerfully admit that they don't know what the equations mean, but that they *work*.) Why should an equation of 'everything' deliver the results that Hawking suggests? And, against all the evidence that shows how few people, either at the time of

Newton or now, understand physics, why should he imagine that this theory would now become understandable by not just scientists, but everyone,? Again, what is notable in all this is the deep desire to unify human knowledge, an impulse we earlier suggested is valid but misplaced.

Leibniz was adamant in the *Monadology* that the scientific method of posing and answering questions would merely create an infinite regress. We have seen this in the idea of the 'atom', originally conceived of as the end of such a chain of enquiry, an indivisible particle. Modern science showed that it *was* divisible into proton, neutron and electron, which in turn are made up of more fundamental particles, leading to what is known fondly as the 'particle zoo'. Murray Gell-Mann tells us that the number of fundamental particles may be infinite, but only several hundred have 'sufficiently low masses to be discoverable in the laboratory'.[8] The implication, when thought through, is that humanity will discover precisely as many of those particles as it has collectively the wealth and will to *afford* – it is a matter of ever larger particle accelerators, soaking up billions of dollars. So is it likely that this process could possibly bottom out in a theory of everything, and if so what would it mean? Leibniz says: 'And as all this detail involves other prior or more detailed contingent things, each of which still needs a similar analysis to yield its reasons, we are no further forward. . . .' How prescient he was! Leibniz, perhaps the only man in Europe to have the mathematical skills to understand the *Principia*, and possessed of a deeply *jnani* religious impulse, was well placed to pass a balanced judgement on science as a project. 'God' is not an explanation of the universe in the way that science is: there is a category mistake here. 'God' is immediate, direct and intuited – there is no chain of reasoning, no potentially unterminated regress of cause and effect.

The Cultural Reception of Science

We saw in *Secularism* that the Enlightenment philosophers, largely ignorant or disdainful of the empirical science of Newton, were, on the other hand, mesmerised by its success. Hume wanted to be a 'Newton of the mind' and Leibniz believed that something *akin to* the scientific method could be used to resolve political issues, and in particular the political problem of religious difference. Locke, having read his friend's *Principia*, was unable to follow it.[9] Hence we can say that science became the domain of a few trained specialists who could properly understand and pursue its development, but at the same time science became public property in the form of nothing more than a grand (and confused) metaphor. The cultural reception of science in the Enlightenment created one image in particular: the image of the clockwork universe, and of 'man a machine'. This became central to the secular mind.

Science in the late-twentieth century, mainly due to the new physics, created the possibility of a radically different cultural reception, one which apparently *promotes* religion (even if only to a relatively small cultural grouping). If we contrast the cultural reception of 'man a machine' to the cultural reception of the anthropic principle, then we are looking at the difference between the human reduced to insignificance, and the human raised to centre stage again. In the former vision, the human being is an alienated, microbe-like biological replicant on a vanishingly tiny corner in the cold space of cosmos; in the latter the human being is joyously co-extensive with and co-creator of that cosmos. But does the science itself bear either of these extremes of interpretation? Where in the equations of the inverse-square law of gravitation and the equations of quantum mechanics are such meanings apparent? Put this way we are forced to the conclusion that meaning is *read into* the science, and that we should focus, not on the science, but on the cultural movements that force such readings.

There are broadly three cultural movements today that press science hard for meaning: one was identified earlier as 'scientism', the next as the New Age, and the third as the new defenders of faith. Scientism is mainstream and secular, includes writers like Stephen Jay Gould, Richard Dawkins and Daniel Dennett, and extracts mostly bleak and reductionist meanings largely from biology. The New Age is countercultural and spiritual, includes Ken Wilber, Fritjof Capra and Gary Zukav, and turns largely to the new physics. The new defenders of faith, as we saw, draw on Intelligent Design and fine tuning arguments.

Writers well beyond the New Age, including many postmodernist thinkers, are persuaded that science no longer requires an abandonment of spirituality or religion. Australian academic David Tacey is outspoken against the New Age, yet says this of the 'spirituality revolution':

> Significantly, the new revolution is found at the heart of the new sciences, where recent discoveries in physics, biology, psychology, and ecology have begun to restore dignity to previously discredited spiritual vision of reality. Science itself has experienced its own revolution of the spirit, and is no longer arraigned against spirituality in the old way.[10]

Scientists like Richard Dawkins and Victor Stenger vehemently disagrees with this point of view, but what counts is not whether science supports Tacey's position. What counts is that there is clearly a cultural movement amongst significant shapers of opinion that science supports religion, regardless of the fact that science was incomprehensible to the generalist in Newton's time, and is infinitely more so today. Culturally speaking, secularism cannot rest on science as it used to, so, whatever the final verdict on the new science itself, it has clearly contributed to a shift in opinion.

That modern science should have created the cultural context for *both* the supposed birth and supposed death of atheism provides ammunition for the NOMA position – the separation of science and religion as non-overlapping magisteria. John Polkinghorne, quantum scientist, ordained minister in the Church of England, and Templeton prize-winner, supports a separation of science and the spiritual life as parallel and complementary *enquiries into what is*.[11] One of his suggestions is to put the achievements of science into perspective, or in other words to refuse to allow its brilliance to dazzle us. He writes on science:

> Success has partly been purchased by the modesty of its ambitions. Only a limited range of questions are addressed, relying on a correspondingly limited technique of inquiry, dependent upon the possibility of the manipulation of impersonal reality and reliant on the marvellously powerful but specialised language of mathematics.[12]

While Newton would surely have agreed with this, the New Age, due to its Neoplatonist heritage, opposes such a separation. John Polkinghorne's writings on physics and religion are that rarity: they derive from a single person equally qualified in both, and are far from New Age in their tenor. Despite this distance, however, both his work and the more serious of New Age writings on physics and religion raise three important issues: firstly the renewed engagement with questions of the spirit, secondly the stimulus to contemporary intelligence that this meeting of disciplines can engender, and thirdly the need for this encounter to be understood in terms of the *jnani via positiva* impulse.

The cultural reception of science plays out quite differently in various communities of thought. For example, another interesting juxtaposition of science and religion lies in the literature on Buddhism and physics, introduced by Capra and Zukav, and expanded on by other authors. B. Alan Wallace is well known in this field.

His first book on Buddhism and physics is called *Choosing Reality* (1996), and his most recent is *Embracing Mind: The Common Ground of Science and Spirituality* (2008). He essentially seeks to find a middle ground between physics and spirituality, but, as Buddhism is the background to this, there is no need to run aground upon arguments about 'God'. Wallace is not trained in physics, but Jeremy Hayward, who also writes on Buddhism and physics, is. He asks: 'Is Buddhism a possible belief system that can provide a context for science as it recognizes the relativity of universes and for extending the range and depth of scientific understanding?'[13] Hayward is pursuing the demand, felt perhaps most keenly amongst New Age thinkers, for extending science into the realms of spirituality. We saw that Sam Harris, perhaps because of his interest in Eastern mysticism, also believes this to be possible. Clearly, however, such a move is in opposition to NOMA-style thinking which is content to let science remain within its materialist circle.

Chapter 7:
Postsecularism and Consciousness Studies

In April 1996 over one thousand delegates packed the convention hall in Tucson, Arizona for the 'Tucson II – Towards a Science of Consciousness' conference. Most of the world's leading thinkers on consciousness were speaking, including David Chalmers (philosopher), Sir Roger Penrose (mathematician), Stuart Hammerof (anaesthesiologist), Susan Greenfield (biochemist and director of the Royal Institution), Susan Blackmore (psi researcher) and many others including Daniel Dennett. There was a palpable air of excitement generated by the coming together of so many different disciplines (which included the visual arts and mysticism) and the possible birth of a new science. The University of Tucson, Arizona, has become a focus for this emerging discipline, and is home to the research team of Stuart Hammerof, and the *Journal of Consciousness Studies* (JCS). The breadth of discourse within the conference, its openness to spiritual traditions, and its willingness to somehow transcend reductionism meant that there was one notable absence in 1996: Francis Crick.

The Tucson conferences, the JCS, and the discipline as a whole can be seen as a remarkable battleground for the very meaning of the word 'science'. The battle is between concept pairs like: reductionist / holistic, materialist / anthropic, objective / subjective and so on, the first of each pair belonging to conventional science, and the second representing a new direction. To the reductionist materialists the words 'anthropic', 'holistic', 'subjective', and so on have no meaning, and have no place in science. To the other camp – those one might term postsecular – these words represent a new direction, not just for the emerging discipline of consciousness studies, but for science as a whole. They are seeking nothing less than a 'holistic' science, one which is broad enough to explore areas previously off-limits to science, such as consciousness, spiritual experience, the paranormal, and even 'God'. It was pointed out earlier that biologists tend to fall into the reductionist camp and physicists into the holistic camp. What is remarkable about the new discipline is that physics and biology meet here, with the potential for the reductionist biologist having to encounter the more mystically inclined physicist – all within the arena of quantum theory.

Quantum theory and Microtubules

It is not clear whether consciousness studies as a science would have emerged without quantum theory. As far back as 1970 the idea was being put forward that consciousness might emerge in the brain via quantum phenomena. Two objections to this have been raised: firstly that the relationship is based on nothing more than the assumption that 'quantum theory is mysterious and consciousness is mysterious, therefore they are related', while the second, more scientific objection has to do with the question of scale. The operation of the brain in terms of cells and neurons is, at a molecular level, vastly greater than the scale of operation at the subatomic level where quantum phenomena are observed. How, then, could these effects be 'amplified' up to the cellular and neuronal scales? (Schrödinger gives a good account for the layperson of this issue.)[14] It is true that the laser beam is an existing example of amplification of quantum effects to the macro level, but there is no reason why such technologies should have a counterpart in Nature. It was the discovery of microtubules in the brain – tiny structures which might demonstrate quantum effects – that suggests possibilities for consciousness. Stuart Hammeroff (at Arizona) and Sir Roger Penrose (at Oxford) have been working on the physiology and quantum theoretical aspects of these microtubules for some time, and, for them, therein lies the best hope yet for a scientific account of consciousness. However, Dr Susan Blackmore, a known sceptic, says:

> If quantum computing does occur in the brain this would be very important, but it only adds another layer of complexity to the way the brain works. So we must still ask 'How does subjective experience arise from objective reduction in the microtubules?' The strange effects entailed in quantum processes do not, of themselves, have anything to say about the experience of light or space or pain or colour or time.[15]

The 'Easy' and 'Hard' Problems

But what precisely *is* the scientific problem of consciousness? Consciousness is notoriously hard to define, and certainly cannot be delivered up for investigation in a test tube. In *The Essence of*

Christianity Feuerbach radically redefined religion as 'nothing else than the consciousness which man has of his own, not finite and limited, but infinite nature.'[16] He goes on: 'Consciousness, in the strict or proper sense, is identical with consciousness of the infinite; a limited consciousness is no consciousness; consciousness is essentially infinite in nature.' This 'infinity' is not that of the mathematicians or logicians, but of the *jnani*-oriented mystic. So how could consciousness become a scientific problem?

Early in the debates presented in the *Journal for Consciousness Studies*, philosopher David Chalmers helped to define the questions being investigated. He proposed a division in consciousness studies between the 'easy' problem and the 'hard' problem. The 'easy' problem was functional: how parts of the brain worked, and could be related to the contents of experience. He was not suggesting that such science was easy, far from it, but that steady progress would be made within existing scientific paradigms, and with increasingly powerful instruments for non-invasive scanning of the brain. The 'hard' problem was conscious *experience*:

> The really hard problem of consciousness is the problem of *experience*. . . . It is widely agreed that experience arises from a physical basis, but we have no good explanation of why and how it so arises. Why should physical processing give rise to a rich inner life at all? It seems objectively unreasonable that it should, and yet it does. . . . If any problem qualifies as *the* problem of consciousness, it is this one.[17]

Chalmers focuses on conscious experience, while acknowledging that for others the hard problem is represented by the idea of 'qualia', which means the redness of red, the painfulness of pain and so on. Qualia cannot be explained by brain activity according to those who recognise the 'hard' problem: there is an explanatory gulf, as Susan Blackmore points out. Chalmers' account of conscious experience is reminiscent of Descartes' definition of 'to think'.[18] Descartes makes it clear that while it is possible to doubt the veracity of the contents of consciousness, the one thing that he cannot doubt is that one 'thinks' – which he describes, a little like Chalmers, as the sum total of his experiencing. The *via negativa* traditions of India, including that of the Buddha, likewise doubt the validity of 'extended stuff', the material world which is termed *maya* or *samsara* – illusion. In Hinduism the process of doubting or stripping away the confusion of manifest sensation is termed 'neti, neti' – not this, not that – while the Buddha called it the 'end of I-making tendencies'. As in all traditions of antiquity, the Buddha was the subject of mythologizing, so the simplicity of his teachings and his own nature as a human person can be lost. Sutra 123, 'Wonderful and Marvellous', in the *Middle Length Verses of the Buddha* is a good example: it opens with Ananda (the Buddha's cousin and closest assistant) recounting the wonderful and marvellous qualities of the Tathagata to the other monks. ('Tathagata' is a term the Buddha uses to refer to himself.) The Buddha himself joins them and inquires as to the nature of their discussion. On hearing its topic he suggests that Ananda 'explain more fully the Tathagata's wonderful and marvelous qualities.' This might sound odd, even if we are to discount the Buddha's habit of referring to himself in the third person (a habit widespread amongst Eastern teachers). Jesus, however, does the same in the *Gospel of Thomas*,[19] asking his disciples what they believe him to be, presumably to see what, if anything, they have understood of him and his teachings.

Ananda recounts the supposed supernatural conditions surrounding the birth of the Buddha. This account is repeated elsewhere in the Pali Canon, and is part of the folklore of the Buddha's life. After a lengthy exposition from Ananda on these miraculous circumstances, including the heavenly conditions leading up to it, the Buddha responds as follows:

> That being so, Ananda, remember this too as a wonderful and marvellous quality of the Tathagata: Here, Ananda, for the Tathagata feelings are known as they arise, as they are present, as they disappear; perceptions are known as they arise, as they are present, as they disappear; thoughts are known as they arise, as they are present, as they disappear.[20]

The contrast between Ananda's emphasis on the supernatural, and the Buddha's emphasis on what is essentially the state of conscious awareness, is stark. The Buddha's statement here is the essence of both the goal and the method: by 'knowing' feelings, thoughts and perceptions as they arise, are present, and disappear, the identification with them is broken, and the self is liberated. The word 'know' in this context is not of course the normal meaning of the word, but a ferocious quality of attentiveness built up through the continual practice of meditation. The parallel between the Buddha's terse statement of awareness – the attention to the flow of perceptions – and Descartes' description of what it is to 'think' is striking. Descartes' account of how he rigorously prepared himself and pursued his 'meditation' is also remarkably close to Buddhist practices of meditation. That the Buddha fails to explicitly deny the supernatural qualities attributed to him has led of course to the accretions of mythology, and to interpretations of his system as occult or esoteric. But, when triangulated against modern *jnani* Masters of the *via negativa* in the Advaita tradition, we can only conclude that the Buddha's emphasis was firmly on the simple discipline of conscious awareness, in which 'feelings, perceptions, and thoughts' come and go.

The Buddha, Descartes and Chalmers agree that conscious perception, or simply 'experience' in Chalmers' account, is *important*, though for Chalmers as a philosopher it becomes the site of an important question, which may be engaged with only intellectually, while for the spiritual seeker of enlightenment it becomes the site of essential practice. In the context of Eastern *jnani* traditions – and in Descartes' personal account – the focus on conscious awareness is central to the enquiry, to the practice, and to the goal. Feuerbach likewise makes it central, and declares its intrinsic nature to be infinite. Chalmers' 'hard problem' thus attracts attention and critical engagement from Eastern traditions such as Buddhism present in the West. However, the reductionists, having no familiarity with the language and priorities of such systems, simply deny the 'hard problem' altogether.

Daniel Dennett is perhaps the most extreme, using the analogy of vitalism from biology to discredit non-materialist theories of mind. For him the reductionist answer to the 'hard' problem is simply to say: *the sum total of all the solutions to the easy problem will be the solution of the hard problem.*[21] But being alive *is* something over and above all the component workings of the organism. Consciousness *is* something over and above the component workings of the brain. Dennett's attack is based on the wrong defence of vitalism, that one could imagine something that exhibits all the behaviour of a living organism and yet was not alive (known as the 'zombie problem' in consciousness studies). The same defence of consciousness – that one could imagine something that exhibits all the behaviour of a conscious organism, and yet was not conscious – would likewise fail. For the reductionist the organism that is alive or conscious can be regarded as a machine, and all its workings discovered. Leibniz effectively countered this idea in his *Monadology* where he proposes an imaginary machine like a mill which was a scaled up organism. He pointed out that by entering the organism like a mill, one does not discover perception (or consciousness) in the workings of the parts: these exist at the level of the *monad*, i.e. at the level of the whole. This is the argument from hierarchical knowledge.

By making the analogy with vitalism, Dennett certainly appeals to reductionist biologists, for whom 'vitalism' was the greatest embarrassment of nineteenth-century biological theory. Francis Crick likewise believes that the solution to the hard problem will simply follow from his proposed line of attack: neural correlates. He points out that we have begun the process of mapping out which neuronal complexes are involved in which experiences, thus being able to correlate Chalmers's list of conscious experiences with different neuronal activities. By focussing on those neuronal activities involved with conscious experience, rather than those involved in maintaining bodily functions, like the heart rate, to which we have no conscious access, Crick assumes that we will eventually explain consciousness. This is more 'nothing buttery'. Hence one line of counter-attack is to point out the lack of 'experiential correlate' to neuron, peptide, brain, etc, thus turning the arguments of 'neural correlate' on their head. There is nothing in lived personal experience that corresponds to neuron, peptide, or even brain (the science actually confirms this: there are no nerve endings in the brain).

IONS and the SMN

Another leading organisation involved with consciousness research is the Institute of Noetic Sciences (IONS), set up in 1973 by Apollo astronaut Edgar Mitchell. While on his lunar mission he watched the Earth suspended, glowing in the darkness and experienced an epiphany, a sense of mystery and conviction that the universe itself is alive with consciousness. One might call this a postsecular experience: the moment when a trained scientist, propelled through the collective scientific project beyond the confines of our planet, turned to look at it, and saw it not as an object to be understood in terms of mechanistic reduction but through spiritual experience. Mitchell experienced in a very direct way the outcome of the scientific project initiated by Newton, just as those contemplating the mysteries of quantum theory do. Where these encounters lead to the sense of the numinous, spiritual or mystical, we can call them postsecular, because they required the secular materialist project in the first place. Earlier we coined the term 'cosmo-theophany' as somehow more profound than an epiphany, because a theophany has the quality of the sacred revealing itself, not through some anthropomorphic conception of 'God' or a god, but through the cosmos itself.

The mission of IONS is to explore the inner world of the mind as rigorously as the science leading to space travel had explored the outer world. The Institute has gathered leading thinkers from all over the world – thinkers that we can characterise as postsecular – including two that will be mentioned here: physicist Amit Goswami from India, and biologist Rupert Sheldrake from Britain. Goswami has pursued the idea of expanding the very nature of science: a most radical scheme, which he calls a 'Science within Consciousness'. Goswami tackles Chalmers's 'hard problem' head-on by positing an idealist science which takes consciousness as the ground or starting point, rather than matter.[22] One might say that Goswami, with his background in quantum science and cultural inclination towards Vedantist philosophy, represents a particularly Indian contribution to postsecular thinking.

Rupert Sheldrake is that great rarity in biology: a non-reductionist thinker. His seminal work *A New Science of Life* was greeted with hostility by *Nature*, the premier science journal and de facto arbiter of what is and what is not science. The editor wrote: 'This infuriating tract . . . is the best candidate for burning there has been for many years,' and Sheldrake himself was included in a national TV series on 'heretical' scientists. Predictably, when a physicist writes a popular science book explaining that quantum theory is mysterious and has analogies in the world's spiritual traditions, people sit up and take note. When a biologist attempts to point out that the vitalists have left biologists with unanswered questions even after a hundred years of collective and massive research, he is ostracised. Interestingly from our postsecular perspective we can observe that while a physicist like Schrödinger has a well developed instinct for the transcendent, Sheldrake's writings display an animist leaning that is more easily located within a shamanic tradition.

A close equivalent to IONS in the UK is the Scientific and Medical Network (SMN), with a number of shared high-profile members across the two organisations. The SMN explains its origins and history thus: 'The Network was founded in 1973 by George Blaker, Dr. Patrick Shackleton and Sir Kelvin Spencer, based on their collective desire to reconcile scientific investigation and scientific models of reality with the spiritual dimension of life, and so to open dialogue between scientists and spiritual luminaries of all backgrounds.' Amongst its early members were eminent figures such as Sir John Eccles, David Bohm, Ilya Prigogine, E.F. Schumacher, and Arthur Koestler; today its ranks include Sir John Polkinghorne, Sir John Houghton, Sir Crispin Tickell , Rupert Sheldrake, Edgar Mitchell, Lord Rees-Mogg, Karl Pribram, and Mary Midgley. The SMN has perhaps more of an interest in the field of medicine and the application of non-reductionist approaches to it, but, as with IONS, the issue of consciousness is central to its concerns.

IONS and the SMN represent practical embodiments of Taylor's 'nova', organisations which pursue the religious impulse in ways that are radically different from, and sometimes unrecognisable to, old religion, and with consciousness as a common goal of enquiry. As such they are quintessentially postsecular.

Introspectionism

When the Buddha urged his followers to pay attention to the arising, presence and disappearing of feelings, perceptions and thoughts, and when Descartes retired to his stove to investigate the same, we might characterise such investigation as 'introspection'. The German physiologist and psychologist Wilhelm Wundt, generally acknowledged as the founder of experimental psychology, set up the first laboratory in 1897 in Leipzig based on introspection as a method. The tide of scientific opinion was against him, however: Auguste Comte, founder of Positivism, held that a single mind cannot be both the agent and object of research, and this and other objections prevented Wundt's methods from prevailing. In psychology, first behaviourist, and then cognitive, research methods became the norm, and it is only now, in the emerging field of consciousness studies, that introspection is being taken seriously again.

From a postsecular point of view the revival of introspectionism is important: it gives a new cultural weight to an activity closely related to the *jnani* practice of meditation, and allows for a renewed interest in the reports of the mystics on their inner journeys, whether recorded in the East or West. Consciousness studies is having a broader cultural impact, however, as shown by the inclusion of artists at 'Tucson II'. An art exhibition on the theme of conscious-ness accompanied the conference, and there was a presentation by a group of artists involved in lucid dreaming. This is a form of dreaming where the practitioner trains to act in a volitional way, and the artists concerned had used their dreaming to explore the imagery then deployed in their painting. As a group they had been influenced by the surrealists Roberto Matta and Gordon Onslow Ford, and their methods also touch on American painting that draws on shamanic native practices, such as Rothko's work.[23] The 'existentialist' film *Waking Life* (Richard Linklater, 2001) also pursues this rather postsecular theme.

Literature has also been influenced by consciousness studies, as mentioned earlier in the work of novelist David Lodge, whose reputation earns him comparison with John Updike and Philip Roth. It was suggested in *Secularism* that *Thinks* . . . as a novel is virtually a primer in consciousness studies. Lodge is exploring consciousness, not only as central to the professional activities of one of the protagonists, but also in terms of the baffling inability to enter another's mind: Ralph and Helen each ultimately find they cannot know what the other thinks. Beyond this Lodge has written articles claiming that novelists have always placed consciousness at the centre of their enquiry,[24] and has published an essay-length treatment on this theme in *Consciousness and the Novel*. In *Thinks* . . . Lodge puts Messenger forward as a reductionist who, like Crick, dismisses the 'hard problem'. It is for Helen Reed to focus on it, drawing, as Chalmers does, on the famous essay by philosopher Thomas Nagel 'What is it Like to be a Bat?'[25] In the novel she sets the question as a creative writing exercise for her class to explore. Nagel has provided the West with a construction for identifying what consciousness is by suggesting that when we ask, is such-and-such an organism conscious, what we should really ask is: 'what is it like to *be* that organism?' Nagel admits that the resources of his own mind are inadequate to the task of imagining what it is like to be a bat, principally because he does not have sonar, and does not spend the day hanging upside down in a cave. Despite this, he is convinced that it is a valid question, and from the position of asking 'what is it like to be an organism' of almost any organism, one is entering into the question of consciousness. As a Western philosopher, Nagel has three handicaps in pursuing this line of enquiry: he is not familiar with the fundamental assumption of shamanism that it is not only possible to empathetically know what it is like to be a bat, but crucially important; he is not immersed in an introspectionist tradition like Buddhism; and he is not a creative writer like Helen Reed. Lodge is way ahead of philosophy here in pointing out that it is almost the core task of the novelist to pursue the what-is-it-like-to-be? question. Although the Buddha rejected any shamanic mode of consciousness, his system of practice and insight led him and his tradition to the conclusion that all 'beings' are sentient. This is not a tautology, but a direct contradiction of Descartes' conclusion that animals were not conscious. One only speculate that Descartes' meditation did not go deep enough, or that his personality somehow shut out bats and other animals from 'thought' as he defined it. Leibniz, by contrast, makes it explicit in his *Monadology* that monads at all levels are conscious because they have perception.

Some novelists in the West, and some spiritual traditions in the East, place the 'hard problem' at centre stage. Western science however denies it altogether, or, like Descartes, would deny consciousness to a bat. In chapter eight of *Thinks . . .* we are presented with Helen Reed's students' essays (which are partly a satire by Lodge on a range of other authors' styles). Messenger simply dismisses each student's attempt to enter the consciousness of a bat as 'hopelessly anthropomorphic'.[26] Yet Buddhist compassion for all sentient beings relies precisely on the human quality of empathy for living creatures, which may derive from the protean Mirandola-like ability to enter imaginatively into the world of other beings. Such a preoccupation with consciousness is part of spirituality, philosophy and the arts: Lodge is exposing the question of whether science has any remit to venture into this field. But the question hangs over the novel: will the subjective 'feminine' realm of the creative arts be overwhelmed by the objective 'masculine' certainties of science? Lodge certainly *believes* that it should not be the case, saying: 'The contest is unnecessary. Literature constitutes a kind of knowledge about consciousness which is complementary to scientific knowledge.'[27]

Beyond the surfacing of 'consciousness' as a topic finding its way into culture in these various ways, we can speculate that many who are becoming interested in it are using it as a way to explore the spiritual. The gap left in our languages of the interior, seemingly only filled with the language of the Freudian unconscious, has now an alternative grammar and mode of enquiry. Ironies abound of course, particularly that Crick's commitment to the science of consciousness was explicitly undertaken to undermine what he understood to be the domain of religion. It is not, of course, the reductionist approach of scientists like Crick that contribute to the postsecular, but we can see in the debate as a whole the emergence of many new ways of thinking about what used to be called 'spirit' – a re-engagement of the best of contemporary intelligence with such long-neglected questions. The preoccupations of consciousness studies are those of the *jnani*, and, to the extent that it focuses on pure ('infinite') consciousness, moves from a *via positiva* of the physical sciences to a *via negativa* of Eastern introspective traditions. There is also an element of the esoteric where research touches on altered states of consciousness and the paranormal.

Chapter 8:
Postsecularism and Transpersonal Psychology

Transpersonal psychology and its broader field of thought, transpersonal theory, represent one of the most hospitable postsecular fields for the spiritual, but at the same time its impact on culture has not been as visible as with the two previous examples: physics and consciousness studies. The fact remains that, when it comes to psychology, Freudian ideas reign in popular culture despite cycles of academic debunking. Transpersonal psychology as a tradition stems not from Freud but from Carl Gustav Jung (though earlier work by William James and others was also formative). The essence of transpersonal psychology is that it recognises the spiritual dimension of the human being, placing it centre stage in both its theorising and in its psychotherapeutic interventions. We can see it as an essentially postsecular context because it involves both a paradigmatic secular invention – psychology – *and* a broad engagement with the spiritual.

We saw in *Secularism* that Freud's momentous contribution to the secular atheistic worldview was a reductionist psychology, providing a mechanistic language of interiority that replaced the religious. From the perspective of the spiritual, Freudianism is harshly scientific in that it reduces all of the inner life to two 'drives' – eros and thanatos – while from the perspective of the hard sciences it is wildly unscientific, having no empirical basis. All systems of psychology suffer to some extent from both these objections. Transpersonal psychology thus becomes a typically postsecular site of debate, providing a new language of the spiritual, but at the same time having its roots in reductionist thought. Transpersonal psychology emerged as a discipline in the 1960s through the pioneering work of Stanislav Grof, Abraham Maslow and others. Another earlier pioneer was Roberto Assagioli, contemporary of Freud and Jung, but not as well known because he did not write as much or as vividly. Assagioli and Jung, both enthusiasts for the psychoanalytical techniques of Freud, differed in one major respect from their master: they were both committed to the spiritual life and its positive role in psychoanalysis. They regarded psychological crises as at least *potentially* spiritual crises, and therefore in need of a much greater vocabulary of the inner life. Although Taylor does not mention transpersonal psychology as part of the 'nova' he discusses, he does say: 'The struggle between a "spiritual" and therapeutic reading of our psychic suffering doesn't only oppose religion to unbelief.'[28] He sees within the 'nova' a battleground where even totally secularised higher aspirations for such things as 'fulfilment' might be treated by drugs. Transpersonal psychology might not oppose some chemical interventions, but it fully accepts the spiritual.

Jung could not dismiss the spiritual impulse as Freud had in terms of compensation and regression. Jung's spirituality followed a certain limited pattern, however, and it was later thinkers in the field who gave transpersonal psychology its broader spiritual underpinning. Jung had an essentially *atavistic* outlook, despite his great care to present his work as modern and scientific. He was an 'archaeologist' of the soul, looking, like Freud, into the dark and unconscious origins of human behaviour. However he found in the unconscious a much richer set of dynamics, one that he explained through the introduction of the 'archetypes', which are generally hospitable to religious thought and mythology. In terms of the Two-Fold Model of Spiritual Difference, Jung's instincts were shamanic and esoteric, and temperamentally more inclined to *jnani* than *bhakti*, as his scientific interests suggest. It is well known that Jung was nervous of the 'transcendent', effectively remarking once that he saw *nirvana* as an 'amputation'.[29] Beyond a certain point of intensity in the spiritual life he was inclined to treat the accounts of mystical experience as indicating an 'inflation', a term he used to express overextension of personality through identification with the archetypes.

It was much later developments that really created the basis for transpersonal psychology as a discipline. In the UK it is today recognised as a section of the British Psychological Society (BPS), and in the US it is the Association for Transpersonal Psychology (ATP) that leads the field. The ATP website sums up the discipline in this way: 'It combines insights from modern psychology with those drawn from traditional spiritual practices, both Eastern and Western.' Transpersonal psychology was formally founded by Abraham Maslow and Anthony Sutich in 1969 with the publication of the *Journal of Transpersonal Psychology*, followed by the founding of the Association for Transpersonal Psychology in 1972.

Abraham Maslow

Abraham Maslow (1908-1970) was an atheist who became interested in healthy psychology rather than psychopathology. He studied what he called 'self-actualisers', individuals whose lives suggested the pursuit of needs that lay beyond mere 'getting along'. He characterised ordinary psychological needs such as the desire for love and recognition as 'deficiency-needs' – one step up from the physical needs of the body – and the higher needs as 'being-needs', including: truth, rather than dishonesty; beauty, rather than ugliness or vulgarity; unity, wholeness, and transcendence of opposites, rather than arbitrariness or forced choices; simplicity, rather than unnecessary complexity; and meaningfulness, rather than senselessness.[30]

Maslow was led to explore what he termed 'peak experiences', previously the domain of religious studies. Peak experiences were moments that not only held in them an intensity of positive feeling or a 'high', but had a positive transformative impact on the individual. In the language of William James these were recorded as 'conversion' experiences, but Maslow effectively updated that concept for a modern secular world, effectively allowing the spiritual a new entry point into contemporary discourse.

Another way to look at where Maslow (and transpersonal psychology) was heading is in terms of reducing *alienation*, a suggestion from Amit Goswami. If the normal person is considered to be 'normally alienated' then that person lives a balance between the alienating sense of being a separate person and the opposite sense of community or communion, experienced through friendship, relationship, family and community. A normal rhythm is experienced, alternating between the loneliness of isolation and the loss of individuality in the warmth of community, and feelings remain within tolerable boundaries in either direction. Psychopathology can be understood as the investigation of increasingly alienated states, where, paradoxically, the sense of self is both fractured and increasingly rigid, with the ultimate extreme represented by the catatonic schizophrenic. In this condition no meaningful exchange with others or the universe is possible, a state of desolate, loveless isolation that is irrevocable and irredeemable. In contrast the transpersonal spectrum starts with the normally alienated person and moves through increasing levels of self-actualisation to the extreme of the enlightened mystic. This ultimate condition – the mirror-image of the catatonic schizophrenic – represents the opposite paradox to the pathological. There now arises the contradiction of a flowering of the personality and at the same time the complete transcendence of the separate sense of self in mystical union. The exact nature of 'transcendence' is of course a central debate within transpersonal psychology – the question of what precisely is the transpersonal self? For now the idea of transpersonal psychology can be represented as the right-hand half of the diagram in fig. 2.

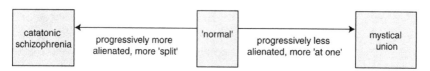

Fig.2 Transpersonal psychology in terms of decreasing alienation

Although it is not so common today to talk about psychological states in terms of alienation it was much more so in the nineteenth century (psychologists were then called alienists). It is useful in terms of the presecular / secular / postsecular periods we have been looking at, because we can talk about a presecular lack of alienation, a secular twentieth-century alienation (analysed in *Secularism*), and a postsecular healing of that alienation in the new millennium. Psychology can play a central role in this, through its journey from the alienating new reductionism in Freud to the transcendent in transpersonal psychology.

Stanislav Grof

While Maslow was essentially a theoretician, Stanislav Grof has pursued transpersonal psychology as a clinical practice in addition to his seminal writings on the subject. Born in Czechoslovakia in 1931, he came of age as an atheist in a Communist country, and was trained as a Freudian psychoanalyst. His journey from the nexus of atheism – scientism, Marxism and Freudianism – is an exemplary postsecular journey into spirituality. In this particular case the catalyst was LSD. In 1954, the Sandoz Pharmaceutical Laboratories in Basel, Switzerland sent a sample of a newly-developed substance called lysergic acid diethylamide to the lab where Grof worked. Because LSD seemed to trigger symptoms similar to schizophrenia the thinking was that researchers could take the drug to investigate the illness. Grof discovered instead that the drug initiated positive results rather than negative ones, results that could only be described in the previously rejected language of the spiritual. Grof's work on LSD was eventually terminated by new laws on the use of hard drugs, and he developed instead a method called 'holotropic breathwork' which can induce some of the same altered states of consciousness.

Grof's and Maslow's spiritual journeys from atheism have taken them, in our terminology, into two different areas: in Grof's case the shamanic (esoteric or occult), and in Maslow's case the transcendent. The whole field of the transpersonal demonstrates something of a division between these two spiritual impulses, and at the same time demonstrates that the boundary between them is often blurred. However, some simple pointers may confirm our characterisation of Grof and Maslow above, for example the advocacy of 'sacred medicines' in the Grof camp is typical of the shamanic (or, one might better say, neo-shamanic) rather than the transcendent or non-dual traditions.

Roberto Assagioli

Grof and Maslow are typical of the US scene in the 1960s, a time of flower power, drugs and hippy love. Jung and Assagioli operated in the much more constrained and sober continental European atmosphere between the wars. Jung's spiritual influences were hermetical, alchemical and Gnostic, i.e. Western esoteric, whereas Assagioli had inherited from his mother an association with Theosophy and more Eastern ideas. Both men are recognised to have their greatest strengths in their clinical application of psychotherapeutic ideas, which means that in a way their ideas live most strongly within clinical practice rather than in the broader cultural world of ideas. While Jung preferred to absorb his spiritual influences from the more ancient past – through reading – Assagioli was more inclined to explore the spiritual movements of his day, including Theosophy and Anthroposophy, in a direct encounter with their proponents. Assagioli met Alice Bailey, initially a Theosophist and later a founder of the Arcane School, and became her 'leading emissary' in Italy.[31] His principles of 'psychosynthesis' are partly based on the esoteric teachings of Bailey, and have in turn influenced Maslow's thinking. Assagioli was imprisoned for a while by Mussolini during WW2, and it was not until the 1960s that his work became better known. His system of psychosynthesis was unusual because it grew in an organic way over a period of time and through the influence from many workers in the field. His influence and imagination was an important part of the transpersonal scene right up to his death in 1974 and beyond.

The UK post-war scene also threw up its innovators, including John Heron and John Rowan. John Heron founded the Human Potential Research Group at the University of Surrey, while John Rowan, author of the well-known text *The Transpersonal*, is active in writing and clinical practice. Several British universities are involved in the transpersonal scene, including Liverpool John Moores, which offers an MSc in Transpersonal Psychology and Consciousness Studies. On the teaching team is Michael Daniels, who has offered a number of systematic overviews of the transpersonal field, and in one paper makes a useful summary of seven models of the transpersonal self:

1. The Metamotivational Theory of Abraham Maslow
2. The Analytical Psychology of C.G. Jung
3. Roberto Assagioli's Psychosynthesis
4. The Holotropic Model of Stan Grof
5. The Structural Model of Ken Wilber
6. The Analytic Model of Michael Washburn
7. The Feminist Theory of Peggy Wright[32]

Daniels' approach is interesting because he represents a trend in this field towards creating spiritual maps or taxonomies (similar to the Two-Fold Model of Spiritual Difference used here). There is possibly no other field of academic discourse that does this so thoroughly, or casts such a wide spiritual net. Daniels is not the first, of course, to attempt a massive integration or systematisation of the spiritual in transpersonal terms: that place goes to Ken Wilber.

Ken Wilber

Wilber has been mentioned before, and we can now take a look at his work in its rightful context. John Rowan considers Wilber to have transformed the field of transpersonal psychology, and there is no doubt of Wilber's far-reaching influence. His output is prodigious and his followers many, and his collaboration with Andrew Cohen has introduced him to a group with a neo-Advaitan origin. This suggests already that Wilber's instincts are closer to the transcendent than to the shamanic / esoteric, aligning him better with Maslow than Grof. Wilber's core preoccupations however are with *developmental* psychology, evolutionary theory, and integration. We will look here mostly at his early work, but have mentioned earlier how his ideas have developed into a hierarchical 'theory of everything' in what he terms the 'Four Quadrant' model.

Wilber's first book, *The Spectrum of Consciousness*, was written at the age of twenty-four, and was financed by working as a dishwasher in a restaurant. A request to fund his work had been regretfully turned down by the Institute of Noetic Sciences, just a year after it had been founded by astronaut Edgar Mitchell (IONS had its own funding problems). The book began an extraordinary series of writings, which, taken as a whole, could be called the 'Fourth Organum' – i.e. a work as far reaching in its synthesis as Aristotle's *Organum*, Bacon's *Novum Organum*, and Ouspensky's *Tertium Organum*. It may then come as no surprise to find that Wilber has considerable respect for Aristotle, or that one of Wilber's recent books is called *A Theory of Everything*.

The Spectrum of Consciousness outlines a developmental model for consciousness consisting of an 'outward arc' and an 'inward arc', or, in more psychological terms three phases: pre-egoic, egoic, and trans-egoic. Wilber was one of the first to identify the trans-egoic – a term constructed out of entirely Western notions – with the Eastern concepts of Enlightenment, liberation, *moksha*, or *nirvana*. His second book, the *Atman Project*, developed the two-arc model further, identifying a sequence of stages from the infantile, through normal adult development, and on through a further sequence of stages to the non-dual. Wilber's own continual development in his writings and his status amongst his readership has led him to identify three stages in his own thinking: Wilber-I, Wilber-II, and Wilber-III.[33] Wilber-I has its roots in a Romanticism that Wilber-II rejects, while Wilber-III refines the stages leading up to enlightenment or the non-dual stage.

John Rowan, in adapting the two-arc model in his book *The Transpersonal*, has suggested that the main concern of transpersonal psychology should be the middle band of progression, termed the 'centaur' by Wilber.[34] The centaur stage of development, preceded by the 'mature ego' and the 'biosocial bands', relates to Maslow's self-actualiser. The centaur is so-called because the image of half-man, half-horse suggests a mind and body in a profound harmony. Rowan suggests that psychotherapy of some kind is essential to reach this stage, and also that it is a preparation for the later, more spiritual stages. Wilber in his *Spectrum of Consciousness* devotes a chapter to the centaur, and details how work on the body at this stage can lead to psychological integration. It is these later stages which are both the most interesting from a postsecular perspective, and also the most difficult to categorise and describe. One such difficulty, introduced earlier, relates to our distinction between the occult and the transcendent.

In Wilber's first book there is a chapter called 'no-mans land', which gives an account of the post-centauric levels. At this stage in his thinking Wilber calls this stage as a whole, leading to the non-dual or transcendent, the 'Transpersonal Bands' (though this terminology is modified later on). He says this about them:

> These Bands historically have not been as widely studied as the others, for several reasons: (1) They scare the living daylights out of most people; (2) Orthodox psychiatry considers them as signs of a very disturbed psyche; and (3) Enlightened Masters consider them as makyo – illusions of the most deceptive nature.[35]

In the terminology adopted here, Wilber is assuming that the path to the transcendent (Enlightenment, *nirvana, moksha*, liberation, the non-dual) is *through* the occult or esoteric (which is also related to the shamanic). This is despite the cumulative evidence from many teachers of the non-dual that the esoteric played no role in their self-realisation. His second assumption is that the non-dual is the inevitable and only developmental goal of a human being, thus aligning himself to the transcendent more, say, than Jung or Grof. In the passage above we see that Wilber takes seriously the idea that Enlightened Masters dismiss the occult as a distraction, and one can certainly find examples of this, including the Buddha, Ramana Maharshi, Krishnamurti, and the entire neo-Advaita tradition. Rowan solves this problem in an interesting way: he suggests that what is here broadly called the occult could be seen as *extra-personal*, rather than transpersonal,[36] because it largely deals with spirit entities. This might suggest that the occult could lie outside a linear model of development, supported, for example, by the observation that occult experiences and abilities have been documented in children. Wilber, however, wedded as he is to a progressive model of human development, insists that the occult area of experience lies between the centauric and the non-dual stages. As his model developed it refined these stages into two main bands: the subtle and the causal. The subtle band itself is divided into low subtle and high subtle, as is the causal band. Within these four levels are potentially further levels, for example the low subtle contains an astral and a psychic level. Yet it is clear that Ramana Maharshi, for example, went through none of these stages in his own enlightenment.

The precise descriptions of these various levels is not as important here as the recognition that Wilber's 2-arc model has firstly been highly influential, and secondly is intended to give a complete map of the human psyche from birth to transcendence. Psychologists of a more reductionist outlook will reject these transpersonal models, as will religionists of transcendence for whom the psychological constructs are inappropriate. However Wilber must be credited with the extraordinary achievement of having brought the psychological and the spiritual together in an elegant conceptual framework, one that is at the core of much postsecular thinking. We will look at just one of many insights that the model yielded in Wilber's hands: his idea of the 'pre-trans fallacy'.

Pre-trans fallacy

Freud dismissed everything that Romain Rolland had suggested to him concerning the 'oceanic', the core of the spiritual life, as merely a pre-oedipal infantile state. Wilber's two-arc model helps explain both conceptually, and via the circular nature of the diagram he uses, that Freud has committed a fallacy, mistaking some similarities in the pre-egoic state with some in the trans-egoic state, principally the sense of oneness. Wilber has called this the 'pre-trans fallacy' and it is a valuable contribution to postsecular thinking. Wilber has also been able to show, via his developmental model, that Jung has made a related mistake, taking the collective unconscious to be the transcendent. Wilber calls Freud's error reductionist, while Jung's error is 'elevationist'.[37] To take the animistic, atavistic part of the unconscious, whether individual or collective, and elevate it to the level of the transcendent is to possibly confuse again the occult / shamanic with the transcendent / non-dual. Whether we agree with these analyses or not, Wilber has given us a language to debate these important issues. He returns to it in *The Eye of Spirit* where he reminds us of the Buddhist insight that enlightenment can only be attained from 'this precious body'.[38] This is central to the Buddha's thought: that spirits, fairies, demons, angels – no matter what kind of disembodied being we encounter or posit – are all at a disadvantage next to the ordinary human mortal. They have to become embodied to transcend.

Jorge Ferrer

Transpersonal psychology has developed throughout the twentieth century, though its proper beginnings may be found in the 1960s. It is still a rapidly evolving field however, and to demonstrate this we look briefly at a book by Jorge Ferrer, *Revisioning Transpersonal Theory*. By using the word 'revisioning' Ferrer is acknowledging the seminal *Re-Visioning Psychology* by James Hillman (first published in 1976). Hillman's well-known work extended Jungian ideas through a deliberate attempt to draw on *polytheism*, rather than monotheism, shamanism or the transcendent, making it unique in psychology, and also an interesting critique of monotheism. Ferrer's work turns out to be a critique of the *entire foundations* – as he sees them – of transpersonal theory, and shares with Hillman an emphasis on pluralism.

Ferrer believes that transpersonal theory is dominated by three elements: experientialism, inner empiricism, and Perennialism. For Ferrer, these exhibit the following faults: 'experientialism' involves a misplaced emphasis on personal spiritual experience; 'inner empiricism' involves an inappropriate borrowing of the scientific method; and Perennialism is too restricted a spiritual tradition to do justice to the full range of spiritual experience that transpersonal psychology encounters.

Dealing with the last point first, one can say that Perennialism, as defined by Aldous Huxley for example, may leave out the devotional (the *bhakti* element), and, even more likely, the shamanic. Ferrer's real objection is more to do with his postmodern emphasis, an unease with the universalist assumptions of Perennialism. But, beyond this assumption that spirituality is a universal experience and impulse of the mind, there is no real 'orthodoxy' in Perennialism. Transpersonal theory would mean little if it did not have some version of this spiritual universalism, and Perennialism in the hands of the transpersonal tradition appears elastic enough to encompass the variety of spiritual impulse argued for here.

But Ferrer, by applying ideas from postmodern thinking, wants to give transpersonal theory a more *participatory* framework. He believes that there is an over-emphasis on personal experience – epitomised in Maslow's peak experiences – at the expense of what is called here the *social* dimension of the spiritual life. Ferrer calls this social dimension the *interpersonal*, as opposed to the private *intrapersonal* emphasis on experience. He suggests that the emphasis on personal experience leads to increased egotism,[39] but this is to ignore a key element in the accounts of such experience: their humbling tenor. The hallmark of a genuinely spiritual experience – as opposed to any form of heightened ego-gratification – is that it cannot be manufactured. It often arises when the striving for such experience has been exhausted, when it is least expected, and it is clearly beyond personal will. In other words, to use a language older than psychology, it is a matter of grace. Maslow's key insight is that such experiences are transformative of the individual in a spiritually positive manner, and that can only mean: a greater connectedness, a lessened imperative to oneself, and a deeper love for others. A genuine spiritual experience leads to what Ferrer is looking for – the interpersonal – but may well arise in a solitary moment. The Two-

Fold Model suggests that this is a matter of spiritual temperament.

Ferrer's further objection to 'inner empiricism' is a natural outcome if one objects to the emphasis on inner experience in the first place. However, it flies in the face of developments in consciousness studies, where introspectionism is beginning to gain credibility as an empirical method, and it ignores the exhortations from many great Masters, Socrates and the Buddha included, to 'know oneself'. It is possible however that Ferrer is simply concerned that the spiritual will be 'colonised' by the scientific, a genuine danger of inappropriate methods. The resolution of this issue lies in the recognition that the 'empirical' already diverges widely between the hard and social sciences, and that the transpersonal and spiritual fields can deploy an empiricism entirely appropriate to themselves. After all, if the initiate in any of the traditions does not *test* their experience in some way, then, as Ferrer fears, they are vulnerable to all kinds of fantasy and delusion.

Debates within transpersonal psychology are relevant to the emergence of postsecular discourse in general, and transpersonal ideas are increasingly entering mainstream psychotherapy. Although referrals from family doctors may still be small in proportion to conventional CBT (cognitive-behavioural therapy), it has wider acceptance in the private sector – that is, in the case of self-referral. More than this, the transpersonal provides an extensive secular language for the spiritual, and in doing so is quintessentially *postsecular*.

Chapter 9:
Postsecularism and the New Age

The New Age represents perhaps the largest cluster of contemporary re-engagement with the spiritual; in Taylor's terms it is an important social imaginary. It is characterised by an openness and enthusiasm for the spiritual life that separates it from the secular mainstream. To the extent that this is made possible by secular freedoms, while rejecting key secular shibboleths, it is *postsecular*. To the extent that it avoids critical self-awareness, it is merely a mixture of presecular millenarianism and secular therapies, and may fall into the trap of the narcissism of difference denied. It is by nature very diverse in its spirituality, partly as a reaction against the narrowness of the traditional monotheism which it rejects. However we can characterise its spirituality as broadly *jnani, via positiva* and with a strong leaning to the esoteric, thus making it a mirror-image to the core Catholic tradition of *bhakti via negativa* and anti-esoteric. The New Age is therefore also similar in many of its impulses to Neoplatonism, though it differs in one marked respect: its teleology, i.e. its particular vision of spiritual purpose, goal and vision of the near future for mankind. One can trace New Age ideas back through Swedenborg to Ficino, but its full emergence in the twentieth century ensured that it roams free of the pervading Christian contexts of those earlier times. It is, however, free to re-absorb Christian ideas on its own terms; one example would be Neale Donald Walsch's *Conversations with God* book series and film.[40]

The New Age differs markedly from the three postsecular contexts just discussed in that it is a popular movement, often led by practitioners, teachers and thinkers demonstrating in a marked degree a postsecular intelligence, but also populated by the markedly gullible. This gullibility may hold within it a certain emotional or spiritual intelligence, but it lacks the typically secular grounding in critical enquiry. In particular it is missing a critical distance from the founding principle of the New Age, a specific form of *millenarian- ism*. This has an astrological basis in the epochal transition to the 'Age of Aquarius' (from the 'Age of Pisces', the Christian era) in which it is believed there will be a collective global transformation of human consciousness. The astrological belief is based on the location of the pole star in different constellations in a 2,000 year cycle. Millenarianism as the belief in a coming age of peace and human advancement is in its most benign form simply hope, optimism, and a willingness to work towards such goals. At its worst it involves the justification of apocalyptic behaviour – isolated communities, stockpiling of weapons and food, authoritarian cults – and adherence to fantastical beliefs and conspiracy theories. At some levels New Age millenarianism is not so different from Christian apocalypticism.

Because of this general tenor of New Age beliefs it is largely ignored by secularization theorists. Steve Bruce calls its spirituality 'diffuse religion', while Paul Heelas calls it 'self-spirituality' and considers it to be the '*lingua franca*' of the New Age.[41] Bruce believes that 'diffuse religion has little social impact'[42] and states that he cannot believe that 'a shared faith can be created by a low-salience world of pick-and-mix religion.'[43] He adds that he also believes that the children of New Age parents will not inherit the 'faith' in the way that happens in older faith traditions. We saw, however, that Bruce is determined to prove that religion will disappear; interestingly he seems to share the prejudice against the New Age held by con- servative religion. Charles Taylor, working in a less sociological vein and a more sympathetic mode, considers such hostility to the New Age as 'myopia'.[44] In a balanced small-scale study of a single British town, Kendal, Paul Heelas and Linda Woodhead label faith tradition and the New Age respectively as 'congregational' and 'holistic' milieus, finding that five times as many people were involved in the former as the latter.[45] Whether this ratio is true across the Western world, and how it is changing over time, is unclear, but Charles Taylor gives us a useful concept by which to consider New Age ideas; that of the 'social imaginary'. There can be no doubt that the New Age has an impact on the collective social imaginary – even if only, for example, as a way to label the preoccupations of Cherie Blair, wife of the former British Prime Minister. But on a larger scale, the New Age as a social imaginary is bound up with the three postsecular contexts so far discussed: physics, consciousness studies and transpersonal psychology. The common factor is the 'self'.

Origins of New Age Thought

It is of interest to explore the origins of New Age beliefs in the confluence of ideas that include Neoplatonism, Romanticism, German
Idealism, Theosophy, Anthroposophy, and Eastern traditions. In toto
they represent everything that the Christian tradition rejected, all
the modalities of the spirit that were either persecuted as different or
elided as the same. The millenarianism of the New Age cannot come
from the East, as such teleologies are foreign to Hinduism, Buddhism
and Taoism, so it must have its roots in the Christian apocalypse, the
German Idealism of thinkers like Fichte and Hegel, and evolutionary
theory. It is not clear that the astrological origins alone would suggest
the dawn of a new era so dramatically an advance on previous astrological ages without such powerfully teleological influences.

Paul Heelas in his 1996 study *The New Age Movement* traces some
of its historical influences, and its emergence in the 1960s as part of
the flower power scene. He says 'If New Agers themselves have got
it right, we are in the realm of the koan, not the Ten Commandments.
That is to say, religion, as normally understood in the west, has
been replaced by teachers whose primary job is to set up "contexts"
to enable participants to experience their spirituality and [own]
authority.'[46] As the East is more a tradition of teachers than texts,
Heelas has put his finger on it with the koan: this is quintessentially
part of the teacher-pupil relationship, and is not handed down
through a canonical text like the Bible. In Transcendental Meditation
(TM), for example, each student is given a mantra (a phrase to chant
internally) in secret by their teacher, chosen specifically to assist
that student. Hence, while the teleology of the New Age is Western,
much of its spirituality is drawn from the East. Again, it is noticeable
that Steve Bruce, whose thesis predicts that religion will end in
about twenty years, can't hide a presecular prejudice against Eastern religion that can only have its origins in the Christian tradition
he anticipates the end of with so much relish. He says, for example:
'The preference for the East over the West stems from a desire to
compensate.'[47]

Heelas also makes an interesting point about New Age scholarship
in general – that it is based in the wider academic tradition of religious
studies. He says:

> Following the principles emphasized by Ninian Smart – who
> has done more than anyone else to develop the discipline in this
> country [Britain] – the academic study of religion *must* remain
> *neutral* with regard to matters of ultimate truth. I am often

criticised, by New Age friends and critics, for not attempting to distinguish between the genuine and the false. My reply is that if people say that they are Enlightened, for example, the academic simply does not have the tools to assess the claim. The spiritual realm – as adherents like to attest – lies beyond the compass of intellectual enquiry.[48]

The development of religious studies as an outcrop of theology in Western universities has only been possible because of the neutrality of this very cautious approach, initiated by Smart, and summed up here by Heelas. But, as stated, it is tantamount to an abdication of intelligence, a reduction of critical enquiry to the mere recording of phenomena. In fact, in the work of Maria Caplan in *Half Way up the Mountain*, for example, a serious attempt is made to distinguish between true and false claims of enlightenment.[49] Such claims are probably the most difficult in the spiritual life to approach critically, but the fact that it has been attempted at all suggests that Heelas and Smart are much too cautious. So what happens if we tackle a less problematic question than enlightenment, for example the millenarianism at the core of the New Age? It is perfectly legitimate to record that such beliefs exist, and to explore their variation and nuance in different groups, but to leave it at that is surely unsatisfying. Why not seriously consider its truth claims? The New Age is dismissed by secularists as deluded Romanticism, but both its best and worst aspects raise questions that need to be *engaged* with, to the benefit of the spiritual life.

Heelas makes a useful distinction between the 'prosperity wing' and the 'counter-culture wing' of the New Age, and believes that it is largely middle-class people who are drawn to it.[50] If this is the case then it is a largely educated group, though pulled in two different directions. The prosperity wing sees their spirituality as part of, and a contribution to, being successful – this is perhaps more common in the US than Europe (and the fact that it fails to critique capitalism is perhaps why Bruce is so hostile to it). The counter-culture wing sees their spirituality as part of a larger rejection of modernist capitalist values, and turn to alternative life-styles drawn to Nature and self-sufficiency. The Roman Catholic Church places Jesus and 'Aquarius' as an either-or choice, while Wilber agrees with those who reject the New Age as shallow and narcissistic. Given that the New Age is dominated by teachers rather than the Bible, it is of interest to ask where the corrective to spirituality-as-narcissism may be found within the New Age?

This counterbalance was termed the 'Kierkegaard Corrective' in *Secularism*, based on his essay, 'Works of Love'.

Heelas's distinction between the counter-culture and prosperity wings is useful here. The counter-culture wing, as in Eastern traditions of teachers, has a natural corrective: simplicity and poverty. In India, renunciation was the simplest, though not the sole, guarantor of ethical behaviour in the spiritual life, best understood as part of the entire world-view of the *via negativa*. In pre-modern *jnani* spiritual traditions the *via negativa*, as defined here, means the placing of emphasis on the unmanifest, the infinite and eternal, the imperishable, the 'still centre of the turning world', as expressed in these and countless other metaphors. But the New Age, as part of the historical shift since the Enlightenment – in particular the evolutionary, teleological Idealism of Hegel *et al.* – is intensely *via positiva*. This is also true of the counter-culture wing: it is not usually renunciative of life itself, merely holding a different prescription of the good life, or 'flourishing' – one that is bound to Nature. If we look in the counter-culture New Age lifestyle for a corrective to spiritual narcissism, then it is not just the negative quality of simplicity, but rather the positive affirmation of Nature and ecology that stand out. When New Age spirituality seeks wisdom in ancient nature religions, then the Kierkegaard Corrective becomes translated from 'love thy neighbour as thyself' to 'love Nature as thyself', and its articulation comes not from Christianity and Kierkegaard, but from what is known as 'deep ecology' or 'ecosophy' (to be discussed in chapter ten).

But what of the 'prosperity wing' of the New Age? Its natural corrective cannot lie in renunciation, obviously, nor is it necessarily committed to the environment or to Nature. We can better understand the dynamics within it by looking at a key early text of the New Age: *The Aquarian Conspiracy* by Marilyn Ferguson.

The Aquarian Conspiracy
First published in 1980, *The Aquarian Conspiracy* opens with these lines:

> A leaderless but powerful network is working to bring about radical change in the United States. Its members have broken with certain key elements of Western thought, and they may even have broken continuity with history. This network is the Aquarian Conspiracy. It is a conspiracy without political doctrine. It is a manifesto. With conspirators who seek power

only to disperse it, and whose strategies are pragmatic, even scientific, but whose perspective sounds so mystical that they hesitate to discuss it.[51]

Ferguson then presents an optimistic summary of the radical changes she sees taking place in science, politics, religion, education and human relationships which are in the process of transforming America. She includes as precursors to this revolution some of the thinkers discussed in *Secularism*, including Pico della Mirandola, Swedenborg, Teilhard de Chardin and Aldous Huxley; in fact a wide-ranging survey of historical sources. Reading from this perceived historical trajectory, Ferguson tells us: 'The proven plasticity of the human brain and human awareness offers the possibility that *individual evolution* may lead to *collective evolution*.'[52] The book presents a vision of unbounded optimism, introducing the last chapter with stirring words from the past: 'Victor Hugo prophesied that in the twentieth century war would die, frontier boundaries would die, dogma would die – and man would live.'[53]

Hugo died in 1885, roughly a century before *The Aquarian Conspiracy* was published. Yet such is the optimism – infectious, charming and sorely needed – of the New Age, that it fails to be tempered by the sobering fact that in the hundred years after Hugo's death two world wars engulfed the planet, and national boundaries have proliferated in the wake of the collapse of Communism rather than disappeared. The approach of Ferguson to history is typical of the New Age: it is a selective reading on the one hand – supporting the idea of an imminent global transformation – and an unconscious historicism on the other. That the New Age may have 'broken continuity with history' as she claims is true to the extent that it shakes off many assumptions of an absolutist past. However the old structures of thought and power have already been challenged by the Enlightenment, modernism, and postmodernism, and there is a strong case that most New Age ideas are better understood as a re-emergence of the suppressed Neoplatonist tradition (using the term in an umbrella sense). When Ferguson claims 'that *individual evolution* may lead to *collective evolution*' she does, however, dramatically update the language of Neoplatonism, propelled by the cultural reception of Darwinism and the train of thought that works through Hegel, Sri Aurobindo and Teilhard de Chardin. The image of evolution has a mesmerising impact on the New Age, suggesting progress towards a better future (an assumption entirely unwarranted by the *science* of Darwinism), an inevitability of that beautiful future, and the impossibility of regression. But how can one cite Victor Hugo's optimism without noticing that events showed it to be completely groundless?

Reading Susan Jacoby's *Freethinkers* alongside *The Aquarian Conspiracy* makes an interesting contrast. Jacoby's thesis, that free thought in America is less politically discernable after 9/11 than during the eighteenth-century writing of its Constitution, would suggest that 'collective evolution' is a much slower process than Ferguson imagines. It even suggests the possibility that the periods of genuine advance in values that the New Age represents, visible perhaps in the 1970s, are small, and susceptible to reversal, just as the Reformation, with its promise of radical religious freedoms, led to the burning of Servitus, judicial torture and murder of Roman Catholics, witch-hunts by Protestants, and the destruction of priceless church art. John Gray's thesis running through many of his books (including his *Black Mass* mentioned earlier), despite the obviously exaggerated pessimism of it, is nonetheless a useful statement of the fact that advances can be reversed.

Yet the New Age remains a significant cultural and political presence in America, having had an impact through its prosperity wing on business management and ethos, resonating with the 'can-do' instincts of a country founded on the entrepreneur. It also represents the opposite spiritual extreme to the renunciative *via negativa* instincts of many key religious movements that emerged in the period 500 BCE to 1500 CE, including Buddhism and Christianity. Neoplatonism, if we understand it as a broad confluence of non-Christian ideas, also included strongly *via negativa* elements, made visible in such thinkers as Dionysius and Eckhart. However, Aquinas, as we saw, was part of the early shift to *via positiva*, flowering in the Italian Renaissance, and finding later expression in the Enlightenment. Hence we can see the New Age as part of that growing momentum towards the *via positiva*, one that exerts a strong pull on contemporary Christian thinkers like the Catholic theologian Matthew Fox. But is this an *evolution* or merely the swing of a pendulum? Any examination of the earlier modalities of the spirit, including shamanism, Goddess polytheism and warrior polytheism, must conclude that these were also intensely *via positiva* traditions. This much larger and less selective historical sweep than Ferguson is prepared to undertake might well suggest that the 'New' Age be better understood as a revisiting of much older principles, submerged by a vast collective experiment in the *via negativa* lasting nearly two thousand years.

The Celestine Prophecy and *The Field*

It is worth looking at two more recent books that purvey core New Age beliefs: *The Celestine Prophecy* (1994) by James Redfield and *The Field* (2001) by Lynne McTaggart. *The Celestine Prophecy* is a novel barely constructed as such to convey a set of spiritual teachings in the form of 'Nine Insights'. The novel conveys the worst of the New Age in its uniquely American manifestation, through its naivety and pandering to the shallowest of 'spiritual' impulses. It is useful however in its presentation of what amounts to three key beliefs of the New Age. The first of these is the unfounded millenarianism already discussed, the second being the 'physics-supports-mysticism' thesis, and the third a naïve synchronicity. 'Synchronicity' was a term devised by Jung to describe the operation of the archetypes, and has a spiritual dimension to it because it suggests that we as individuals are connected to the whole, and that the whole engenders meaningful situations for us according to our needs. As a spiritual construct it is a two-edged sword, however, because it can either diminish our self-absorption through a vision of the whole as organic and connected, or it can radically boost the narcissistic ego by making the self the prime subject of all events. In the latter case it can easily fall into paranoia, where every event in the immediate surroundings, or even in the entire world, is read as negatively targeted at the self. Redfield, in presenting an entirely optimistic vision, makes synchronicity achingly self-absorbed, though he avoid falling into the trap of paranoia. The protagonist of the novel undergoes a series of adventures in Peru in which the requirement to be exposed in succession to each of the 'Nine Insights' necessitates a synchronicity on such a ludicrously linear and massive scale as to be absurd. It merely conveys that the whole world appears to revolve around the protagonist, perhaps a tellingly accurate portrait of American self-absorption. It is also uncannily, though probably unwittingly, Hegelian.

Lynne McTaggart's *The Field*,[54] on the other hand, is not fiction, and serves a more serious purpose: the deeper elucidation of the 'physics-supports-mysticism' thesis. In the *Celestine Prophecy* Redfield has one of his characters say:

> In other words, the basic stuff of the universe, at its core, is looking like a kind of pure energy that is malleable to human intention and expectation in a way that defies our old mechanistic model of the universe – as though our expectation itself causes our energy to flow out into the world and affect other energy

systems. . . . Unfortunately, most scientists don't take this idea seriously. They would rather remain sceptical, and wait to see if we can prove it.[55]

Redfield is merely mouthing a widespread misconception about quantum theory, alongside the quintessentially New Age and unscientific use of the term 'energy'. Amusingly – perhaps touchingly – his character regrets that scientists would rather remain sceptical until the hypothesis is proved. That scepticism is of course the basis of all scientific method and of the very success of science. Lynne McTaggart, a British journalist, has a better grasp of the scientific process, and hence her book *The Field* represents a more serious essay on the relationship between the new physics and mysticism. On the front cover science fiction writer Arthur C. Clarke endorses the book, adding 'We are on the verge of another revolution in our understanding of the universe.' Dr Wayne Dyer, a New Age psycho-therapist and self-help author proclaims: 'McTaggart presents the hard evidence for what spiritual masters have been telling us for centuries.' The evidence that McTaggart marshals is extensive, up-to-date, and as well-informed as a journalist with no science training can hope to provide, but by no stretch of the imagination is it 'hard evidence'. What the book should do is provoke all those who are interested in the separate worlds of physics and mysticism to rigorously pursue the difference between scientific speculation and scientific fact. Newton was clear on the difference; it should be a core part of a general education (and Richard Dawkins is well-placed to promote such understanding of science). McTaggart has selected a number of controversial scientific papers from the vast emerging literature. Are these scientific *speculation*, chosen to persuade us that an unlimited free energy source waits to be tapped, and that the physics of it supports mysticism? Or are these scientific *facts*, that suggest an imminent breakthrough in cheap non-polluting energy and the incontrovertible proof of mysticism? The sobering question really posed by *The Field* is: who is competent to decide between these two interpretations? At worst the New Age will buy the entire thesis without any attempt to distinguish between speculation and proven science, but at best it will persuade a reader to seriously study the physics involved.

On one of McTaggart's conference flyers she claims that her work, i.e. the new physics, 'has given thousands of people "permission" to hold spiritual beliefs.' The text that started this movement, *The Tao of Physics*, has sold over a million copies, and has entered the social imaginary by also spawning a series of 'Tao of' books. Capra makes clear to us in the afterword to the third edition that his book evoked a similar response of a sense of 'permission' to pursue spiritual beliefs in his audience. He records: 'Again and again men and women would write to me or would tell me after a lecture: "You have expressed something I have felt for a long time without being able to put it into words." '[56]

Alpha Males of New Age Enlightenment

The work of Ferguson and McTaggart, and similar writings, even if they are overly-optimistic, represent the engagement of a significant postsecular intelligence with spiritual issues (Ferguson is editor of the *Brain / Mind Bulletin*, a report on brain research and consciousness). Another example of a well-researched and thoughtful presentation of New Age ideas is found in the magazine *What is Enlightenment?* (*WIE*) edited by spiritual teacher Andrew Cohen, and often featuring the thought of Ken Wilber. Articles in WIE range from the naive style of prediction of Ferguson, to balanced and factually accurate accounts of key spiritual and political thinkers pertinent to its mission: 'redefining spirituality for an evolving world'. Its quarterly publications are often themed on a single issue, with interviews and articles representing a wide range of views on it. Rather than the incautious assumption that society is on the threshold of immediate global change, WIE engages in critical debate around its central preoccupation: evolutionary spirituality and evolutionary consciousness. Andrew Cohen's teachings have changed since his emergence from under the wings of his Advaita teacher Punjaji, the emphasis shifting progressively from a teaching of enlightenment, to impersonal enlightenment, to evolutionary enlightenment. The Advaita is intensely *via negativa*. Cohen, in the direct lineage of its greatest modern teacher, Ramana Maharshi, has effectively made a journey from a vision of enlightenment that is Eastern and *via negativa*, to a vision of enlightenment that is Western and couched in the *via positiva* terms of Hegelian historicism and Darwinian evolution.

Issue 26 of *WIE*, August-October 2004, was devoted to the issue of peace and war 'in a post 9/11 world'. It included a regular feature called 'The Guru and the Pandit', a discussion between Cohen and Wilber, and interviews and articles on war and peace. The general standard of editorial research, imagination and openness rank *WIE* with other prestigious mainstream world affairs magazines, and it also adheres to high production values in its design, all of this in the context of its New Age leanings (as its advertising copy alone indicates). Issue 26 included a page on 'The Lessons of India' with quotes on the subject of peace from Ramana Maharshi, Mahatma Ghandi and Sri Aurobindo, arguing that India was particularly blessed to produce this trio at the same time in history (approximately 1870 to 1950). Maharshi's statement is quintessentially Advaitan: 'To bring about peace means to be free from thoughts and to abide as Pure Consciousness. If one remains at peace with oneself, there is peace everywhere.'[57] This conception of the non-dual is at the core of Cohen's *jnani via negativa* spiritual heritage, and the articles in WIE since its inception often articulate the struggle that the modern Western mind has with this passive or quietist *via negativa* stance. By adopting the core New Age belief in the evolution of consciousness, and the articulation of it by Ken Wilber, Cohen has effectively cut his Advaitan roots. Yet the continual *via negativa* impulse shows in Cohen, particularly in the discussion feature with Wilber on the issue of war. Cohen says:

> Now our notion of what God or the Absolute is depends very much on whether our view of reality is biased toward the unmanifest domain or the manifest domain, or whether it transcends and includes both.[58]

In this single sentence Cohen has got to the heart of his dilemma, of the creative tension between the *via negativa* (as a bias to the unmanifest) and the *via positiva* (as a bias to the manifest). In his dialogues with Wilber he often pulls the discussion back to the unmanifest, perhaps motivated by the experiential origins of his personal spiritual journey in the Advaita of his teacher. Yet his commitment to *evolutionary* spirituality, *evolutionary* consciousness and *evolutionary* enlightenment is complete. To accept the idea of the evolution of enlightenment is to suggest that the enlightenment of the Buddha (for example) was primitive or incomplete or undeveloped. The portrait of the Buddha as a man that emerges from the Pali Canon is neither bland nor lacking in detail, and the articulation of his enlightenment is not at all vague. So how is it possible for Cohen, in the lineage of a modern enlightened master like Maharshi, and Wilber, adherent to the Buddhist tradition, to assert that enlightenment has evolved either since the Buddha or since Maharshi? Laying side by side, on the one hand, the relevant passages in the Pali canon and the recorded sayings of Maharshi, and on the other, the writings and recorded dialogues of Cohen and Wilber, what case can be made for an evolution of enlightenment? Only one answer can be given: the New Age imaginary.

Wilber says: 'But sometime in the modern era – it is impossible to pinpoint exactly – the idea of history as devolution (or a fall from God) was slowly replaced by the idea of history as evolution (or growth toward God).'[59] The exact date is not possible to identify, but it was certainly in the eighteenth century that the idea of progress gripped the Western mind and was applied to the spiritual life. But this arose from the confluence of quite arbitrary factors: the industrial revolution, German Idealism, Darwinism, and the re-awakening of Abrahamic teleology. It is only because Cohen, Wilber and the New Age are in thrall to the deceptive glare of *historicism* that they fail to apply any critical distance between evolution and spirituality. The great beauty of evolutionary theories is that proponents can be legitimately vague as to the time-scales for change, so it is impossible to prove the theory wrong. However, the alternative analysis is much simpler and open to critical debate. Instead of suggesting that enlightenment has evolved from the Buddha to Andrew Cohen, we can see that there is a simple shift in bias: from the *via negativa* to the *via positiva*; from a spirituality of the unmanifest to a spirituality of the manifest. Neither can this be interpreted as any kind of historical development: the *via negativa* of the Buddha, the Advaita, and of early Christianity was not a primitive state of spirituality, but a revolution against a previously *via positiva* context. The *via negativa* of these traditions may be represented as either a massive mistake, or a genuinely rich period of experimentation, according to inclination, but it cannot be represented as less developed than preceding or subsequent spiritualities. Nor, of course, can the exploration of *via positiva* spiritualities in the New Age take the identical course that it did in shamanism, Goddess polytheism, and warrior polytheism, despite the neo-shamanic and neo-pagan revivals that are part of the New Age. Hence Wilber and Cohen do represent the genuinely new, because their experimentation is not a revival but an intense polymath engagement with the spiritual life in a period of accelerated change. Its insistence on evolution is open to critical challenge, however. As a metaphor it appeals very widely to the imagination of the time, but it has a negative effect in marginalising ancient spiritualities, and even recent Masters like Maharshi.

But the Buddha, Cohen and Wilber have something in common: their masculine dominant personalities. To call Cohen and Wilber the 'alpha males of New Age enlightenment' is to draw attention to this feature of their work, their insistence on their supreme position. Cohen throughout his talks and writings gives no credibility to any other contemporary spiritual teacher, and shares in the popular habit of emphasising the alleged abuses of discredited gurus like Osho. Yet storm-clouds are gathering over Cohen's own reputation. Wilber is remarkable for a modern thinker in the lengths he goes to counter criticism of his work, devoting large sections of his web site and current writings to detailed refutations of those who disagree with him.

Amusingly, considering that allegations of sexual abuse are the most common form of criticism of fallen gurus, the same issue of WIE that was devoted to the question of peace and war also carried an article entitled 'Women Who Sleep with Their Gurus'. It was a long-overdue presentation of the woman's side of the story, researched by Jessica Roemischer after having an affair with her own Korean guru.[60] It is frank and in many ways typically American: an admission that the guru has power, that women are attracted to power – as much in the spiritual life as in any other – and that adult women can positively own and initiate these relationships. Whatever one's opinions on this, or on Cohen and Wilber in general, one has to conclude that WIE represents some of the most intelligent, well-informed, challenging and creative writing in the New Age domain; a considerably *postsecular* writing.

The Mantra of Integration
The comparison between Andrew Cohen and the Buddha (as re-vealed in the Pali Canon) is a good one: both have devoted followers, create rules for the *sangha*, dismiss other spiritual teachers, and are somewhat authoritarian. Hence if the Buddha is called a 'lion roaring in the forest' one can call Cohen a 'lion roaring in the urban jungle', each an image that epitomises the masculine. Ken Wilber however should be understood as a philosopher rather than as a teacher, hence he is the 'pandit' to Cohen's 'guru'. They share a commitment to evolutionary consciousness, while Wilber adheres also to another New Age construct: the mantra of 'all is one'. This is not the same as the 'not two' principle of the Advaita, but rather a yearning to bring together all that was sundered in the modern mind, a yearning for *integration*. As we saw earlier, this is often a desire, possibly futile, for integration of *knowledge*. Integration is the key word and concept for Wilber, manifesting itself for example in the establishment of his ambitious Integral Institute. Wilber is unique as a late-twentieth-century philosopher for his radical engagement with questions of the spirit, making him closer to the Rationalists, in particular Leibniz, whose *Monadology* enters Wilber's thought via Koestler's ideas of 'holons', and Hegel, whose historicism is central to

Wilber's evolutionary principles. Wilber's work represents a massive attempt to intellectually integrate what he calls the 'big three': the arts, science, and the spiritual (let us call them *magisteria* after Gould). It is instinctive to a philosopher to believe that they officiate at the court to which all other disciplines must submit their truth-claims, and to attempt grand theories of everything. It is therefore instinctive for a philosopher to reject a theory like Gould's of non-overlapping magisteria. Wilber even suggests a similar approach that he calls 'epistemological pluralism' but backs off from the idea very quickly, claiming that modernity wouldn't hold with it.[61] Gould as a scientist certainly did hold with it, but Wilber is right that most do not – Richard Dawkins, for example.

But the issue here is what does it mean to *integrate* the arts, science and religion? Certainly by constructively engaging with all three an individual overcomes the notion that one of them should dominate or subsume the other two. (On this basis we will see that the attempt by Dawkins to subsume the poetic into science as far from a *constructive* engagement.) But Wilber's problem is that any theory that brings together such vastly disparate domains of human experience is inevitably going to result in a trivialisation of all of them. This is the key feature of the New Age, that it avoids *difference*. This may be a natural historical reaction to the Inquisition, where the identification of difference so often led to ecclesiastical imprisonment, torture and murder. But the bland integration of difference has its natural counterpart in the reluctance to engage in critical enquiry, and in the apparent intellectual paralysis that Heelas insists on in the academic study of the New Age. As humans we must take New Age ideas and subject them to critical examination, as we do all other domains, and neither should we adopt the methods of science, the arts . . . or philosophy. Integration of opposites has always been a central part of the discourse of mystics from Heraclitus to Maharshi, but that integration is not presented at an intellectual level as in Wilber's philosophy. Rather, the mystics assert that it is at the level of consciousness itself that integration takes place. As T. S. Eliot says, there is a still point at the centre of the turning world, but seen from that still point the vista shows a turning world of *difference*, not identity. Wilber is seeking a profound integration in the manifest domain, where difference reigns, instead of resting in the profound integration of the unmanifest domain, where unity reigns. He seeks the healing of the sundered spirit in an intellectual integration of vastly different and extensive domains of human knowledge, instead of an experiential integration in the immediate and simple locus of the non-dual. Knowledge cannot be other than fragmentary, atomising.

Without a critical approach to the New Age, and even its foundational millenarianism, we are left with an anxiety regarding its natural spiritual correctives. Where does the prosperity wing of the New Age end and selfish consumerism begin? Where does the counter-culture wing of the New Age end and passive quietism begin? In giving up the central pathology of monotheism – control – the New Age is susceptible to the pathology of self-absorbed narcissism. Yet spiritual pluralism does not inevitably lead to narcissism: India has shown this down the millennia. The hard part, in considering the lessons of India for the spiritual life, is that the *via negativa* came to dominate its thought since the time of the Buddha, and provides a natural corrective in its adherence to simplicity and poverty. How do we find parallel correctives in the spiritual pluralism of the New Age when the focus is so intensely on the *via positiva*, even on material prosperity? This is a question for our age perhaps, not just for the New Age.

The 'Shallow' and the 'Deep' New Age

British University libraries rarely stock the works of Ken Wilber because he appears too New Age. With rare exceptions the academic world dismisses the New Age as a whole, reacting to the extreme and uncritical naivety of works like *The Celestine Prophecy*. Instead it should distinguish between the shallow and deep ends of the New Age, and critically engage with authors like Wilber, Ferguson and McTaggart. Andrew Rawlinson's work on contemporary spiritual teachers also covers the deep end of the New Age, and represents a critical engagement with the difficult issue of Eastern religious ideas in the West.[62]

But the real significance of the New Age lies with the vast majority of its adherents who are sincere in their searching, and have the courage to step outside of the smug secular mainstream. David Tacey criticises the New Age, saying: 'not "follow your bliss," but "thy will be done." '[63] 'Follow your bliss' is a New Age exhortation voiced by author Joseph Campbell, but it helped the Buddha, no less, to attain enlightenment. But 'thy will be done' stands for what the Buddha found: the transcendence of ego, the extinguishing of the separate volitional self, the ending of I-making tendencies, the beginning of compassion. If the New Age represents the nursery slopes of the spiritual life, then it is the task for a movement or sensibility such as postsecularism to encourage the more arduous journey up the mountain. The metaphors are mixed here: 'higher' in one image is 'deeper' in another. Either way, the challenge posed by the New Age for postsecularism is to provide a natural pathway from the shallow to the deep, from self-absorbed spiritual questing to a sensibility marked by 'thy will be done' or, as in the Kierkegaard Corrective, 'love thy neighbour as thyself'.

Chapter 10:
Postsecularism and Nature

The twentieth century can be thought of as the century of alienation. A whole new language had emerged to describe this condition, and depression can be seen as a symptom of this alienation, along with its method of treatment by Prozac. Spirituality as the experience of a profound connectedness can be understood as both the diametrically opposed condition to alienation, and a more secure alleviation of it than Prozac or other chemical interventions. Hegel had introduced the word at the beginning of the nineteenth century in the sense of 'alienation from Spirit' or 'alienation of Spirit from itself'. But modern Western alienation can also be examined from the perspective of alienation from *Nature*, and a re-engagement with Nature considered as a reclaimation of the spiritual. This re-engagement with Nature needs to take specific forms for it to be understood as having a spiritual basis, but more as a matter of degree than of category shift. The secular argument against the notion of spirituality as connectedness places a range of secular activities of expansion, including sexual love, identification with community, art, football, science, and so on, as forms of connectedness of varying depth. If they become sites for a repressed spirituality then they become part of Taylor's 'nova', but more generally they are the sites for what he calls a purely secular human flourishing.

Nature too, as representing places and activities that are expansive of self, can be theorised in an entirely secular way. But Nature pushed a little harder than a weekend, artistic, sporting, or leisure activity quickly provides a connectedness so profound as to be irrevocably spiritual. To the degree that contemporary intelligence has re-engaged with Nature at this deeper level, we can discover within it possibilities for a postsecular spirituality. Charles Taylor considers Nature to be an important locus for a reframed religious or even moral impulse: 'the moral significance of nature that I have been describing is clearly also widely felt: the awe at wilderness; the sense of kinship and ecological concern with nature; the desire to renew oneself by leaving the city and visiting wilderness, or living in the country; all these are features of our world.'[64]

But historically Nature has been actively denied as a site of spirituality in the *via negativa* traditions of both East and West. In terms of the five historical modalities of the spirit it is clear that shamanism and Goddess polytheism were deeply bound to Nature; that warrior polytheism began the process of prioritising human-human relationships over human-Nature relationships, and that monotheism and transcendent modalities of the spirit completed that denial of Nature, at least in their *via negativa* manifestations. In the West, at the time of the Industrial Revolution, there was already in train a profound shift back from *via negativa* to *via positiva*, but that re-engagement in the physical world was not necessarily a return to Nature. Political power became deeply wedded to a material wealth that necessarily required the subjugation of Nature, so while the Romantics voiced the aching sense of loss of wilderness, mountain and forest, they, like everyone else, used steam trains to get there and the telegraph to signal their intentions. Descartes is credited with providing the intellectual underpinning for the view of Nature as mechanical; the first atheist texts by La Mettrie and Holbach took Descartes' ideas further in proposing 'man a machine' and 'Nature a machine'. Yet the early twenty-first century provides new possibilities for viewing Nature in a holistic, rhapsodical and spiritual light. Nature is also now the site of an ethical imperative, perhaps *the* ethical imperative for humanity, as ecologists are insisting.

Brody and Abram

Two interesting contemporary writers on Nature, Hugh Brody and David Abram, both of Jewish parentage, have contemplated the role of Abrahamic religion in the subjugation of Nature. Brody is an anthropologist and documentary filmmaker whose book *The Other Side of Eden* recounts his work with the hunter-gatherers of the Arctic. Abram is an ecologist and philosopher whose influential *The Spell of the Sensuous* is a polemic for a return to the senses. The professor of Jewish mysticism Gershom Scholem says: 'Religion's supreme function is to destroy the dream-harmony of Man, Universe and God, to isolate man from the other elements of the dream stage of his mythical and primitive consciousness.' This is because Scholem sees certain stages in the development of mysticism: 'In this first stage, Nature is the scene of man's relation to God.'[65] The second stage for Scholem is the classical period of monotheism, one in which the abyss between 'God' and man

> can never be bridged. To them the scene of religion is no longer Nature, but the moral and religious action of man and the community of men, whose interplay brings about history as, in a sense, the stage on which the drama of man's relation to God unfolds.

In the third stage, which he calls the romantic period, mysticism arises which 'strives to piece together the fragments broken by religious cataclysm, to bring back the old unity which religion has destroyed, but on a new plane, where the world of mythology and that of revelation meet in the soul of man.' Scholem's account is a little like Hegel's, though making it clear that religion (monotheism) represents a cataclysm for the older nature religions. Neither is the old unity to be restored in its original locus – Nature – but on a new plane. It is true of all three monotheisms that Nature figures only as that which is overcome, and this is one of the greatest differences between monotheism and religions of the Far East.

However, Brody and Abram are part of a widespread Western re-evaluation of Nature which places it and embodied consciousness centre-stage again, and hence they are interested in its historical marginalisation at the hands of the Judeo-Christian tradition. Brody asks of the book of Genesis: 'Whose way of life does it reflect and endorse?'[66] Later on: 'Genesis is the creation story in which aggressive, restless agriculture is explained, is rendered an inevitability. Its first eleven chapters are the poem of the colonizers and the farmers. They are not the story of Anaviapik and his people.'[67] Simon Anaviapik was an Inuit who had helped Brody in his research and filmmaking, and who had confirmed for Brody what was emerging as a revolution in white man's thought within the anthropological studies of hunter-gatherers. This revolution suggested that hunter-gatherers represented the 'original affluent society',[68] having ample resources for survival, and leisure time for cultural activities, particularly story-telling. This completely over-turned Western notions of the lives of so-called primitive peoples, summed up by Hobbes as 'nasty, brutish and short'. Brody is not in the first instance interested in the spiritual life of the Inuit, but he quickly understands that not only is theirs a shamanic culture, but that the very openness of shamanism allowed it to readily accept Christian ideas. The white coloniser did not of course reciprocate, but proceeded instead to insist that the Inuit religion was idolatry, to forcibly educate (indoctrinate) children away from their families, and to ridicule their close relationship with Nature.

David Abram, sensitive to the accusation from ecologists that the Judeo-Christian tradition is responsible for the ravaging of the ecosystem, makes a forcible case that Judaism is much closer to Nature than usually assumed. It is the Greeks, he suggests, that created the rift between the world of the senses and the world of the written word, when they adapted the Semitic alphabet and introduced vowels. Hebrew is written using only consonants, with the reader participating in constructing the meaning of a sentence by aspirating the vowels according to context: according to Abram it is the specific use of the breath that gives reading a Hebrew text its sacred character. Furthermore each consonant in Hebrew stood for a concrete object in the natural world, a correspondence that was entirely lost when the Greeks adopted the alphabet. The Greek alpha, beta and gamma were originally *aleph*, 'ox', *beth*, 'house' and *gimel*, 'camel'.[69] Abram claims that the transition to an abstract thinking that denied the senses and Nature was completed by the Greeks, quoting Socrates in the *Phaedrus*: '...I'm a lover of learning, and trees and open country won't teach me anything, whereas men in towns do.' But somehow, Scholem is more persuasive on this issue.

Brody's encounter with the shamanic culture of the Inuit was full of surprises. Pien Penashue, a hunter in his sixties, practiced scapulamancy, the use of a burnt animal shoulder blade to predict the future. He also told Brody about 'the shaking tent, the most powerful of all Innu shamanic techniques.'[70] The missionaries had attempted to eradicate these practices which they saw as devil worship, and the Inuit were only slowly recovering their old traditions. It fell to Penashue to explain to Brody why the older Inuit were also Christians and sang hymns some evenings: 'The Innu religion is the religion of life. Christianity is the religion of death. We have to follow Innu ways in order to get our food here on our land, to live. But we have to follow the Christians in order to get into heaven. When we die. So we need them both.'[71] The Inuit were able to recover much of their way of life once the zeal of the Christian missionaries had been dissipated by modern secularism and the (limited) recognition of human rights. However Brody makes it clear that this recognition is only to the extent that the Inuit range over land unfit for farming or generally useless to the white man. He regards the destruction of the hunter-gatherer way of life by agriculture a 'holocaust'.[72] Yet it is clear that Christianity was not the only culture to have marginalised (literally pushed to the margins) the shamanic way of life. Abram defends Judaism when he says 'Such pantheistic notions equating God with nature – common to many practitioners of Kabbalah – would startle the various environmentalists today who charge that Hebraic religion expelled all divinity from the natural world.'[73] But the natural world was already diminished as the locus for the sacred by the emergence of large-scale agriculture along with a warrior-polytheism that abstracted the specific spirits of place into anthropomorphic deities, whose antics mirrored the increasing focus on human-human relationships. In the later monotheisms, and in the religions of transcendence in Greece and India, it was the emergence of the *via negativa* transcendent spiritual impulse that established the core spiritual relationship to be between the human and a non-localised abstract absolute. Nature became the site of the *fall* in the West, and *samsara* – illusion – in India.

Shamanic and Transcendent Nature Spiritualities

The re-awakening of Nature spiritualities in the contemporary West is not simply a recognition of how precious the shamanic modality of the spirit is, but an attempt to rekindle its traditions through study of shamanic cultures surviving at the margins. There appear to be two quite different Nature spiritualities: an ancient shamanism and a more recent nature mysticism. The latter appears in the West in the nineteenth century in the work of writers like Ralph Waldo Emerson (1803-1882), Henry Thoreau (1817-1862), Walt Whitman (1819-1892), John Burroughs (1837-1921), John Muir (1838-1914) and Richard Jefferies (1848-1887), while some equivalent is discernable in Japanese nature writing in the work of the seventeenth-century poet Matsuo Basho, for example. In the twentieth century the natural heirs in the Western tradition are Aldo Leopold and Annie Dillard. This form of nature mysticism is quite unlike the shamanic, because it is not predicated on contact with the spirit world, is not animal-focused, and not intercessionary. Instead its impulse appears as initially aesthetic, but pushed far beyond an appreciation of the beauty of Nature. Nature mysticism has been studied by scholars of mysticism for over a century, though many of those scholars, such as Evelyn Underhill and R.C. Zaehner have been Christians unable to shake off their instinctive horror of 'pantheism'. Yet it is clear that the nature writers we have listed have been able to pursue the unitive goal of the mystic through a direct engagement with Nature (rather than withdrawal from it). They pursued neither the *jnani via negativa* of the anonymous 'Cloud of Unknowing' and the 'Divine

Darkness' of Dionysius, nor the *bhakti via negativa* of focus on 'God' or other devotional objects. Neither was theirs a *bhakti via positiva* as expressed in the cataphatic tradition by celebration of the world in praise of the Christian 'God'. The nineteenth-century nature writers had mostly set their face against the Christian tradition, for example John Muir thought the great canyons of the High Sierra quite the best 'cathedral' for him. Their writings are mystical, but they are not mystics in the traditional sense of someone devoting their entire life and energies to the mystical path of union. Yet the distinction cannot be so clear-cut, between say Meister Eckhart and Teresa of Avila on the one hand, and Richard Jefferies and Henry Thoreau on the other. The writings of Jefferies and Thoreau show that their spirituality was no passive appreciation of an aesthetic natural realm, but an active form of spiritual *practice*. Both men would walk in forests and fields, or by lake or sea, in order to capture a certain 'something' in those moments, with no certainty in advance of success or failure. They did this in the same way that a Zen or Christian monk or nun enters a period of meditation or prayer, hoping for *satori*, or a moment of grace. Spiritual autobiographies are full of detailed and richly specific accounts of such unexpected twists and turns of the spiritual life.

Henry Thoreau would stride for hours through the woods and fields of Concord, Massachusetts, owned by his friend Ralph Waldo Emerson. Reginald Lansing Cook, in his interesting analysis of Thoreau as nature mystic, says this of him:

> He realised that it was wise to be outdoors early and late, travelling far and earnestly in order to recreate the whole body and to perceive the phenomena of the day. There was no way of knowing when something might turn up. He had noticed that when he thought his walk was profitless or a failure, it was then usually on the point of success, 'for then', he surmised, 'you are in that subdued and knocking mood to which Nature never fails to open.' One late August day, in 1851, when it appeared to him that he had walked all day in vain and the world, including field and wood as highway, had seemed trivial, then, with the dropping of sun and wind, he caught the reflex of the day, the dews purifying the day and making it transparent, the lakes and rivers acquiring 'a glassy stillness, reflecting the skies.' His attitude changed, and he took what Keats called 'the journey homeward to habitual self.' He exulted in the fact that he was at the top of his condition for perceiving beauty.[74]

In the following passage from Richard Jefferies' *The Story of My Heart* he is lying on the grass by a tumulus, the burial-place of a warrior of some two thousand years previous:

> I dip my hand in the brook and feel the stream; in an instant the particles of water which first touched me have floated yards down the current, my hand remains there. I take my hand away, and the flow – the time – of the brook does not exist for me. The great clock of the firmament, the sun and the stars, the crescent moon, the earth circling two thousand times, is no more to me than the flow of the brook when my hand is withdrawn; my soul has never been, and never can be, dipped in time.[75]

How does Descartes arrive so confidently at the conclusion that his soul is immortal? How does Jefferies know that his soul can never be 'dipped in time'? One rejects Nature as a machine, the other is transported by it. Yet one of the marks of mystical writings from all the traditions, East and West, is a sense of timelessness as described by Jefferies in this passage. For the nature mystics the trigger for this mystical condition is Nature, but for the *via negativa* mystics it arises from a withdrawal from the senses, rather than a heightened receptivity to them: the spiritual life is rich in its variety. It can be objected that the nature mystics of the nineteenth century were merely pursuing a heightened Romantic sensibility, and there is of course some common ground. There is also a great difference, however, and one could go so far as to say that Thoreau, Burroughs, Muir, Jefferies and Whitman are anti-Romantic to a considerable degree. Burroughs and Muir were naturalists, Jefferies and Whitman were journalists, and Thoreau and Jefferies were decidedly political in their thinking. None displayed the self-absorbed and self-pitying Romanticism epitomised in Goethe's Werther, for example, and keenly saw in Nature its unforgiving cycles of death and predation, as well as its lyrical and transcendent heart.

If the term 'Arcadia' sums up the Romantic vision of Nature, a place that the aristocracy, after Rousseau, visited with their servants and picnic-hampers; if it sums up the vision which underpinned the Highland clearances, allowing for ordinary families on the land to be replaced by the ultimate Enlightenment profit-making machine, sheep, then the term 'anti-Arcadian' represents its opposite. 'Arcadia' drove Capability Brown to demolish unsightly villages at the far end of the view from the aristocratic drawing room, and to dig out the ha-ha at the near end to prevent those very sheep spoiling the lawn. Nicholas Poussin's mid-seventeenth-century painting 'The Arcadian Shepherds' pursues the classical theme of *et in Arcadia ego*, which means that 'even in Arcadia I am' where 'I' is death. To the Romantic the existence of death in Arcadia is a betrayal, nowhere more harrowingly described than in Tennyson's *In Memoriam A.H.H.*, which introduced the phrase 'nature red in tooth and claw' into the English language. Tennyson was writing in 1849, contemporaneous with the nature writers we are discussing. Yet the nature writers are anti-Arcadian because their view of Nature is not of a place for weekend picnics and painting, for profit from shooting and sheep-farming (even if Muir works as a shepherd), or to be viewed from the drawing room. As Whitman says of most people: 'Very few care for natural objects themselves, rocks, rain, hail, wild animals, tangled forests, weeds, mud, common Nature. They want her in a shape fit for reading about in a rocking-chair, or as ornaments in china, marble or bronze.'[76] But the Nature mystics were sanguine about death and predation, paradoxically finding eternity in the very cycles of Nature that whisper chill mortality and cold betrayal to the self-absorbed, effete Romantic.

Ecology and Ecosophy

John Muir was not only a naturalist, writer and nature mystic, but also the founding father of ecology as a discipline and political force, instigating the American National Parks system. Ecology is a branch of the biological sciences, but has within its vision that which the mystic sees in Nature: a holistic understanding of Nature as both competition and *cooperation*. The reductionist biologist finds in the term 'cooperation' an unsupportable anthropomorphism, as though the term was suggesting that organisms somehow *agree* to support each others existence, much as we agree in human cooperative ventures. Leaving aside the findings of science for the moment, we can turn to one of the key ecological thinkers of the late-twentieth century, the Norwegian Arne Naess, born in 1912. Naess was appointed to the chair of philosophy at Oslo University at the age of 27 and was a keen mountain climber, having enjoyed the solitude of the Norwegian fjords and forests in working out his key theory of Ecosophy-T. This is a philosophy of ecology based on a meaning of the word 'philosophy' that is not the formal one taught in the university, but 'one's own personal code of values and a view of the world which guides one's own decisions (insofar as one does fullheartedly feel and think they are the right decision).'[77] An ecosophy therefore is a personal theory of living grounded in the perception of the full interdependency of all living things, which deeply guides personal conduct. Naess called his own version of this 'Ecosophy-T' (where the 'T' is said to stand for the name of his mountain hut Tvergastein) in the hope that a multiplicity of such ecosophies would emerge from others in the ecology movement. Naess studied the thinking of Spinoza and Ghandi, and after his resignation from Oslo University developed his ecosophy out of a wider range of sources including Gestalt theory. He was keenly aware of the nature of scientific thinking – having been an honoured guest amongst the Vienna Circle – but was drawn to Gestalt ideas because of its emphasis on the whole picture. Naess says:

> Gestalts bind the I and the not-I together in a whole. Joy becomes, not my joy, but something joyful of which the I and something else are interdependent, non-isolatable fragments. 'The birch laughed / with the light easy laughter of all birches. . . .' This gestalt is a creation which may only incompletely be divided to give an I which projects laughter into a non-laughing birch tree.[78]

Naess, as a philosopher deeply bound up with the Kantian tradition of scepticism toward the 'thing-in-itself', has exquisitely teased out in the above passage the problems of the scientific-philosophic difficulty with Nature. If we believe that we merely project our human emotions, in this case laughter, into Nature, then we can retain our separation between the human and the non-human, and Nature remains to be exploited according to our need or whim rather than encountered in the humility of a holistic recognition of interdependence. To the Western scientific-philosophic tradition the idea that the birch laughs is absurd. Even the idea that the robin or blackbird sings joyfully is an anthropomorphism, while the perception of beauty in Nature is relegated to the domain of the artist, and only the Romantic artist at that. Yet the shamanic traditions and later developments in the East like Shinto, Taoism, Tibetan Buddhism, and Zen never made this break with Nature.

Ecology then is a science which looks in one direction at co-operation, holism, Gestalt, and Eastern and ancient traditions of Nature-awareness, but also looks in the other at the biological sciences, predicated as they are on the view of organism-as-machine, digitally encoded with DNA. An ecosystem, viewed from the hard science perspective, becomes no more than a second-order machine in which the fundamental resource, energy, is exchanged through predation amongst the first-order machines, themselves built out of other machines at the level of the eukaryotic cell. Here lies the dilemma of all attempts at 'holistic' science. As a science it must start with the laborious analysis down to the fundamentals – as Dawkins would have it to the 'selfish' gene – and then slowly build up levels of complexity to arrive at the forest sloping down to the Norwegian fjord. But the holistic view of that forest, the gestalt view, is immediate, sensed at the deepest level of being. Naess in his mountain hut perceives the gestalt as beyond the ratiocinative labouring of analysis and synthesis – he perceives it in the immediacy of the moment. If he perceives it as the nature mystics do, then there is nothing prior to that moment, no history to that holistic sensibility – otherwise it would fall into fragmentation again. Jefferies perfectly describes such timeless states of consciousness. Yet, like John Muir a hundred years previous, Naess is also a scientist, able to draw on the cumulative history of scientific endeavour of many centuries and countless intellects. To the extent that Muir and Naess are mystics, they draw on the universal human capacity to merge at a profound level with existence, and to find in that moment that the birch is laughing with them, to experience a joy that is not their selfish joy but 'something joyful of which the I and something else are interdependent, non-isolatable fragments.' To the extent that Muir and Naess are also scientifically-minded, *they can read into* the forest, mountain and river the accumulated rational knowledge of the human analytical endeavour, and are richer and wiser for it.

Dawkins and the Argument from Design

To approach Nature with only the weapons of analytical science is to 'unweave the rainbow' as Keats puts it:

> Do not all charms fly
> At the mere touch of cold philosophy?
> There was an awful rainbow once in heaven:
> We know her woof, her texture; she is given
> In the dull catalogue of common things.
> Philosophy will clip an angel's wings,
> Conquer all mysteries by rule and line,
> Empty the haunted air, and gnomed mine . . .
> Unweave a rainbow. (*Lamia*, 1820)

Although we ought to sharply distinguish philosophy and science in the modern era, for Keats they were the same thing, Newton being the 'natural philosopher' whose work on the visible spectrum had robbed the rainbow of its mystery. Richard Dawkins is much exercised by this accusation, and devotes an entire book, *Unweaving the Rainbow*, to the defence of science as a poetics. Ian McEwan has the protagonist of *Enduring Love* tell us that Keats was 'A genius no doubt, but an obscurantist too who had thought science was robbing the world of wonder, when the opposite was the case.'[79] This is Dawkins' argument. It was earlier suggested that Dawkins is a nascent *jnani* of the *via positiva* orientation, and there is no doubt that in his writings his awe and wonder at the natural world (as framed by the sciences) are expressed with a literary, poetic and even numinous quality. Dawkins is moved by the beauty and complexity of the natural world in a way that the Buddha for example is patently not, but which the nineteenth-century mystical nature writers are.

John Muir's description of trees as he ascends the Sierra is moving for his capacity to wonder at each new species of oak that he encounters.[80] He is both a mystic and a scientist as these extracts show:

> These earthquakes have made me immensely rich. I had long been aware of the life and gentle tenderness of the rocks, and, instead of walking upon them as unfeeling surfaces, began to regard them as a transparent sky. . . .

> We had several shocks last night. I would like to go somewhere on the west South American coast to study earthquakes. I think I could invent some experimental apparatus whereby their complicated phenomena could be separated and read, but I have some years of ice on hand. 'Tis most ennobling to find and feel that we are constructed with reference to these noble storms, so as to draw unspeakable enjoyment from them. Are we not rich when our six-foot column of substance sponges up heaven above and earth beneath into its pores? Aye, we have chambers in us the right shape for earthquakes.[81]

When Muir says that he has 'some years of ice on hand', he was referring to his scientific study of glaciers. Yet his response to the earthquake is astonishing: he shows no fear, but marvels instead that the human frame, the human soul, 'is constructed with reference to these noble storms.' The Romantics of course always praised wilderness and storm, though preferably from a safe distance as Kant says: 'But the sight of them is the more attractive, the more fearful it is, provided only that we are in security; and we willingly call these objects sublime, because they raise the energies of the soul above their accustomed height. . . .'[82] Muir spent years in the wilderness alone, or just with his dog, and documents his travels with the enthusiasm of a scientist and the expansivity of soul of a mystic. Muir in his cabin and Naess in his mountain hut share with Dawkins a lyrical, rhapsodic appreciation of Nature. But Naess uses both the language of science and the holistic language of Gestalt to convey his sense of 'deep' ecology. This sensibility recognises that ecology faces in the Dawkins direction, towards the analytical-synthetic understanding that builds the higher machinery of ecosystem from the lower machinery of gene, but also in the Gestalt direction of the whole. This Gestalt perception makes possible Muir's sense of pure *capacity*, the capacity to be the earthquake, to contain the mountain. Without this sense of identification with Nature, it remains a machine. Further: it is not a question of 'mountains' plural for Muir and Naess, but of 'mountain' singular as a specific mountain, a specificity of place. Naess says: 'In non-nomadic culture, especially agrarian ones, a geographic sense of belonging is crucial. More specifically: rooms, interiors, stairs, farmyards, gardens, nearby trees, bushes – all these things become, on the whole unconsciously, a part of that which is ours, a powerful kind of gestalt.'[83]

While Dawkins responds to the rainbow as the nature writers and the Romantic poets also do to the wonders of the natural world, he is disturbed that Keats believes that the rainbow's 'charms fly / At the mere touch of cold philosophy.' Dawkins says: 'Could anyone seriously suggest that it *spoils* it to be told what is going on inside all those thousands of falling, sparkling, reflecting and refracting populations of raindrops?'[84] Clearly for Muir and for Naess such scientific explanations of natural phenomena do *not* spoil them; on the contrary we find in Muir every bit the enthusiasm of Dawkins for *explanations* and he actively seeks them for glaciers and earthquakes. But Naess's point about a sense of geographical belonging is true also for the rainbow. When Newton abstracts the rainbow into the repeatable scientific experiment – the *experimentum crucis* that changed the world for ever – it loses its sense of place, and enters the 'dull catalogue of common things'. For the poet this is the start of the *reduction* that science performs on Nature, the extraction of the principle from the place. Our experience of rainbows is always situated: whether in the mountains of the Lake District or driving through a city street, the rainbow is precisely so audaciously moving because it is contrasted against a lowering sky or located as a fraction of coloured arc between grey office blocks. It is always unexpected, vivid, and set, like music, against the counterpoint of landscape, whether natural or man-made in its specificity. Once it is repeatable, divorced from Nature, found shimmering in the glancing light on the recording surface of a CDROM, it is no longer a rainbow. When a child *first* sees a CD he or she may turn it over and over to see the colours, but the next day the magic is gone. Once it is a repeatable matter of spectrum, wavelength, reflection and refraction, a matter of mechanism, it is no longer a rainbow, no longer *the* rainbow. The mystical and poetic sensibility gives way to the scientific sensibility. The rainbow *is* unwoven.

Yet we see that a Muir or a Naess go beyond Keats: they can move between these sensibilities without claiming for either one a supremacy; the science does not spoil the rainbow for them. This means that they go beyond Dawkins too. He says uncompromisingly, with La Mettrie, that 'we, and all other animals, are machines created by our genes.'[85] His science is classical, pure, mechanistic, and is derisory towards holism or Gestalt concepts, yet, as his writings demonstrate, his soul is filled with poetry. He reads the Romantic poets, eager to find a place where the awe and wonder that he feels towards science has a counterpart; is delighted where the poets appear to praise science and is despondent when they dismiss it, as Yeats does as the 'opium of the suburbs'.[86] When Blake rails against Newton – Dawkins' greatest hero after Darwin – Dawkins says: 'what a waste of poetic talent.'[87] He is supremely confident of the utility of science, but desperately anxious that we see more, much more in it – that we see its poetry.

Dawkins shares the rhapsodical *via positiva* instinct of poets like Thomas Traherne, William Blake and Walt Whitman that existence is good, that it is a blessing to be born. (We saw that this very optimism of Dawkins has made him subject to the attack from Benatar.) But Dawkins' thesis is that it is the science itself that generates this felicity, that science has inherent within it awe, wonder, beauty and poetry. But examination of any university science curriculum or text-book quickly dispels that notion. To find writings like Dawkins' we have to look at the *private* lives of the scientists, not their peer-reviewed scientific findings; in other words we have to find awe, wonder, beauty and poetry in the hearts of men and women, not in their published science.

In addition to the elements he dislikes within it, Albert Einstein finds within Judaism:

> A sort of intoxicated joy and amazement at the beauty and grandeur of this world, of which man can just form a faint notion. It is the feeling from which true scientific research draws its spiritual sustenance, but which also seems to find expression in the song of birds.[88]

This is not the science of Einstein but the private thoughts of a man made known through autobiography. Dawkins says: 'And the heart of any poet worthy of the title Romantic could not fail to leap up if he beheld the universe of Einstein, Hubble and Hawking.'[89] But which universe? The college physics text-book doesn't quote the poetic, rhapsodical thoughts of Einstein, but places instead the equations of the Lorenz transformation on the page. Algebra is a dead thing. The Copenhagen interpretation of quantum theory states that the mathematics alone is valid, while any attempt to read into it an anthropic principle, or hidden variables, or multiple universe theories is unscientific – it is meta-science. It is invalid *science* to read a human meaning into the equations. Dawkins is quick to debunk those who see holistic and mystical implications in Schroedinger's equations. He says they are pursuing bad scientific poetics, and insists that there is such a thing as good scientific poetics.[90] But the poetry cannot come from the science, it must have its source elsewhere. The poetic, aesthetic and mystical sensibilities arise from a direct cognition of the *whole*, or wholes, also termed monads or holons by Leibniz and Koestler respectively. The poetry comes from the specificity of a given whole, not the generalisability of the machine-like workings of the parts. Science does the latter – and its very success relies on it – while poetry begins and ends in a radically different sensibility. Muir and Naess can move easily between the two magisteria, giving proper voice and weight to each, while Dawkins, ideologically driven to deny religion and mysticism their voice and weight, attempts to conflate them. His attempt to arrogate to science what is the proper domain of a quite different human impulse – the poetic and mystical – represents the ultimate march of scientism.

Postsecular Nature

If we follow Gould's idea of non-overlapping magisteria (NOMA), then science, religion and the arts are the expression of three very different impulses, all equally valid (Wilber calls them the 'big three'). When Dawkins rejects religion and attempts to arrogate poetry to the domain of science he distorts the multiple nature of human consciousness, effectively applying an absolutist monotheism of science. If we reject this monoculture of the mind and allow the three domains under discussion their equal gravitas, then there still remains the question: what happens along the boundaries? If each domain is confident and secure in its own legitimacy, and does not seek to conquer the territory of the other, then what happens to the ambassadors of any one region when posted to one of the others? They create, not the false synthesis of New Age mysticism-and-physics, nor the false victory of science over all other domains, but a movement of ideas and metaphors. It is this very human capacity to take the image or idea of one domain and use it to illuminate another – the gift of the poet – that has bewitched Dawkins, at the same time that he rejects its use in what he derides as primitive superstition. His rejection of the wisdom of shamanic cultures is only made possible by a selective accumulation of their worst practices. It is as if one were to judge science on thalidomide, Chernobyl, Bhopal, Hiroshima, Nagasaki, and the unregulated availability of antidepressants on the Internet.

But the shamanic view of Nature, which shares nothing with that of the modern biologist, provides precisely that Gestalt sense of the whole, permeated by living spirit. Is it a metaphor that a mountain has a spirit? That metaphor is very alive in the Scandinavian languages, where 'giants' are always on the fjord just the other side of the ridge. Or is the spirit of a mountain to a shaman a genuine 'other', to be engaged in a discourse of mutuality? What is clear, as scholar of shamanism Michael Harner says, is that modern peoples in cities across the West are engaging in a shamanic revival, not concerned with philosophical niceties, but convinced through ritual that there is a spiritual practice of nature-engagement. We can see this as a postsecular openness to spiritual practices of the *via positiva* engaged specifically with Nature. At the same time the nature mysticism of Muir, Whitman and Jefferies represents a vision of Nature that is not shamanic but living alongside the scientific world view, as we have seen, though not deriving from it.

Robert McFarlane, writing in *The Guardian*, says of nature writing today:

> In or around November 1932, nature writing in Britain was dealt a death-blow by Stella Gibbons. *Cold Comfort Farm*, one of the finest parodies written in English, took as its target the rural novels of Thomas Hardy, Mary Webb, the Brontë sisters and DH Lawrence. Mercilessly Gibbons sought out and sent up the hallmarks of the rural genre: all those characters called Amos or Jeb, all those idiots savants, all that loam, and especially all those gushingly naïve descriptions of 'nature' and 'landscape'. Gibbons's book was such a brilliant skit it became that rare literary object; a parody that remained standing once the genre it mocked had collapsed.[91]

But McFarlane sees a recovery of the genre, a new English nature writing, and concedes that in America the tradition of Thoreau was maintained through writers such as Aldo Leopold and Annie Dillard.

Perhaps the huge physical presence of the American wilderness, the legacy of Muir, kept alive an instinctive feeling for the gestalt of the open spaces. It was also in America that the shamanic achieved academic status through the discipline of transpersonal anthropology. Founded in the 1970s, partly due to the work of anthropologist Carlos Castaneda and his popular novels, its scientific wing became the Society for the Anthropology of Consciousness (SAC) when it became a unit of the American Anthropological Association in 1990.

Taken collectively, such a range of Nature-oriented sensibilities can be described as postsecular, even if some of them derive from the most ancient of cultures and others from nineteenth-century thought. Without the humbling of Christianity as an exclusive cultural force none of this would have been possible. At the same time, Nature spiritualities, whether neo-shamanic or Nature-mystical, are an easy entry into the spiritual life for the secular mind with its growing preoccupation with the environment. As suggested, when considering the counter-culture New Age, Nature is increasingly the site of a new ethical imperative, while also remaining that of the profoundest of spiritualities.

Chapter 11:
Postsecularism and the Arts

It is the creative outpourings of twentieth-century Western culture that create the impression of an intensely secular worldview. If the United States as a society is more religious, say, than Britain or France, then its cultural production does not betray that: the vast bulk of contemporary mainstream literature and visual arts from the US is clearly secular, often aggressively so. One can explain this as the historical outcome of the divorce of creative intelligence from religion that began in the Enlightenment, resulting in Martin's 'centre-periphery' division between cultural producers and society in general. In the visual arts the legacy of extreme Protestant iconoclasm also reinforced the rupture between the flow of religious ideas and the flow of aesthetic inquiry.

A work of art is judged in terms of the particular art: great novels, great poems, great paintings, great films, all acquire the reputation for being 'great' within the canon of that art on the specific grounds of its tradition. The judgement is ultimately *aesthetic*, with the proviso that the work must also be *original*. From the perspective of the spiritual, a work of art may be aesthetically beautiful and daringly original, but at the same time morally ugly and spiritually bereft. Goethe's *Faust* is a cultural landmark for the German-speaking people, because of its daring originality and vigorous aesthetic expression. Yet the self-absorbedness of the protagonist denies the larger ethical view that places the concern for the happiness and suffering of others as paramount; by our definition of spirituality as a profound connectedness it is spiritually arid.

To the conventionally religious, even disregarding any directly offensive anti-religious themes, the extreme secularism of Western cultural production lies in its almost total disengagement with the spiritual. There are exceptions, of course, but they are rarely sympathetically engaged, or if they are, such as in film versions of

Christian themes, they are often merely anodyne costume dramas, along the lines of Franco Zeffirelli's *Jesus of Nazareth* (1977). A challenging interpretation of Christ's life, like Martin Scorsese's *The Last Temptation of Christ* (1988), is both rare and condemned by the religious right (and ultimately only reinforces secular values). Alternatively, as we find in Goethe's *Faust*, there may be a strand of titillatory occultism, one that works through to New Age cultural productions, TV science fiction like the *X-Files*, and novels like Dan Brown's *The Da Vinci Code*. The novels of Philip Pullman, Tolkien and the entire Harry Potter phenomenon tap into this sub-culture, as do films like *Raiders of the Lost Ark* (1981) and countless derivatives. Artistically such productions might be ranked from masterpieces to New Age pap, but occult powers and secret fraternities are the common theme, culturally unbelievable, but providing a frisson of anti-secular pseudo-spiritual excitement. Once the novel is finished or the spooky music of the *X-Files* ends, disbelief returns from its enjoyable suspension, or if belief is retained, it is expressed in a culturally accepted secular form like Star Trek conventions or *Da Vinci Code* tours of cathedrals and chapels.

To a Muslim, for example, attempting to understand Western society from its creative cultural outpourings, the overwhelming impression must be of a world largely indifferent to religion, occasionally hostile to it . . . and superstitious at the margins. Yet Western culture is so vast that we *can* find creative works that meet the definition of the postsecular: a critical re-engagement of creative intelligence with questions of the spirit, a re-engagement that is neither the costume-drama re-enactment of religion's mythologized foundational events, nor pseudo-occultist fantasy.

Examples of postsecular cultural production are so dispersed within the mainstream that their existence does not easily become visible as a significant movement. Yet by collecting them together a picture emerges of how a critical creative intelligence, forged in the secular revolution of the last three hundred years, can express its engagement with the life of the spirit. This picture is of no comfort to the religious conservative, but refutes the assumption that secular culture must always dismiss, disparage and set its face against the spiritual.

The bulk of twentieth-century Western cultural production became the locus of the subjective, of the crying out of the self that refused to become the machine that science, since La Mettrie, insisted was the complete image of the human. From *Man a Machine* to the genetic neurologised self of Dawkins and Crick, reductionist science has denied the subjective interiority of the human being, so it became the role of the arts in general, and the novel in particular, to explore and defend the inner world. That world was, of course, increasingly alienated, hence the acceptance of Sartre's *Nausea* as a literary masterpiece: it was an honest representation of the bewildered position of self in the twentieth century. We saw in *Secularism* that David Lodge's *Thinks* . . . brings up to date for the twenty-first century the entire 'two cultures' debate. His protagonist Ralph Messenger effectively stands for Richard Dawkins in the attempt by science to arrogate to itself the last bastion of the humanities: the inner world of self, potentially available in such delicate intimacy in the novel and the poetic. Novels answer the question 'what is it like to be . . . ?' a bat, or more likely a person, possibly even a terrorist, by asking a question about *being* that science can neither ask nor answer. The novel asks that question, and the answer is *never*: 'like a machine'. Even if the novel is about a robot it asks the question 'what is it like to be a robot?' as a *being* and, as with Leibniz's mill, the answers are not to be found in its cogs, but in the preoccupations and drama of what-it-is-like-to-be a robot. Yet in the twentieth century the portrait of the Western soul in literature is a composite of alienation, of a struggle, heroic but usually failed, to find the roots in being that were severed by the destruction of religion. Literature largely adopted the language of psychology, a discipline abounding in mechanistic metaphors; or it acquired the socialist politics of Marx; or it retained its roots in the past via Romantic notions of the sublime and sexual love.

But it is the written Word that was at the heart of the rejection of monotheism; it was the absolutist clinging by the religions of the Book to its canon that made that canon both the only source of religion and the locus of disgust for it. The character Helen Reed in *Thinks. . .*, defending the domain of the novel as the proper exploration of the subjective, of consciousness itself, is wrong-footed because she has only a tenuous Roman Catholicism to draw on. David Lodge's analysis is very telling of the secular mind: how can it resist the encroachment by Messenger/Dawkins on that intimate sensibility of the poetic when the only religious text that it can draw on, the Bible, is culturally discounted? When Sartre 'read the mystics', as de Beauvoir tells us, he was forced to locate Teresa of Avila within the approval of the Roman Catholic Church, and thus he is forced to disapprove of her. He has no way to engage critically with her spirituality, because the Roman Church requires uncritical acceptance; he has no way critically to engage with the text of the Roman Church because it is fixed and cannot speak to the modern world. Perhaps David Abram is right: as the West adopted the Greek alphabet rather than that of the Hebrews, it lost contact with the sacred as it lost contact with the breath.

The arts are a vast 'third magisteria', and only a rather haphazard survey can be given here of how the spiritual emerges in the different areas of fine art, cinema, the novel and music, but the survey, such as it is, has a strict criterion: the spiritual must go beyond the secular narcissism of self-sufficiency. We will see that Hitchens uses the term 'numinous' and 'mystical' in respect of McEwan's novels, but that McEwan is in fact intensely secular. Taylor uses the term 'anthropological' to mean such a secular framework of thought that has no transcendent dimension: 'The idea is: the mystery, the depth, the profoundly moving, can be, for all we know, entirely anthropological. Atheists, humanists cling on to this, as they go to concerts, operas, read great literature.'[92] Later, he adds: 'People begin to listen to concerts with an almost religious intensity.' We shall be looking for something more explicitly spiritual – an explicit exploration of questions of the spirit.

Fine Art

Fine art in the twentieth century presents us with a history of revolt, with artists leading on many fronts the struggle to shake off the shackles of the past, including religion, or at least organised religion, and later, capitalism. But artists, in continual revolt against the art of the previous generation, or even season, came to take on the role of providing a continual challenge to *all* the assumptions of the modern world, including those of secularism. In art colleges at the turn of the twenty-first century, it is implicit that the role of the artwork is foremost to challenge, to subvert and to be socially engaged, and only secondarily to provide the more traditional functions of art, such as an aesthetic enquiry, narrative, ornament or celebration. Yet this is a matter of emphasis: artists, like musicians, have as their first allegiance their art. Romanian sculptor Constantin Brancusi (1876-1957) well represents the antinomian position of twentieth-century artists: he wanted 'an art of our own', meaning an art that belonged to the artist, and was not in the service of religion or state.[93] He made the journey on foot from the Romanian Orthodox country of his origin to Paris, where he studied with Rodin. He rejected both the classical art style of his mentor and numerous aspects of the religion of his youth (though retaining a deep respect for both), while, typically for many artists of the twentieth century, being drawn to the mystical, his favourite bedtime reading being the Tibetan Buddhist classic, *The Life of Milarepa*.[94] In his work he pursued a transcendent dimension that is at the heart of modernist art, a spiritual impulse expressed through abstraction. There is now a growing body of art-historical scholarship which recognises the intimate relationship between modernism in fine art and the spiritual. For a long time, however, such ideas were taboo, particularly in Europe and the US after WW2.

Maurice Tuchman, curator of the Los Angeles Museum of Art's exhibition *The Spiritual in Art: Abstract Painting 1890-1985* (and editor of the exhibition catalogue by the same name) tells us that the pioneering studies of Sixten Ringbom in the 1970s started a re-evaluation of secular assumptions around art, and that 'by the late 1970s numerous scholars had taken up the question of artists' interest in mysticism and the occult.'[95] Many of those scholars contributed to the Tuchman catalogue, including art historian Linda Dalrymple Henderson, whose interests lie in the fourth dimension and its impact on abstract art through the writings of Minkowsky, Einstein, Bragdon and the mystical Russian philosopher P.D. Ouspensky.[96]

In 1986 the biographer of art historian Ananda Coomaraswamy, Roger Lipsey, published the first systematic account of the spiritual in twentieth-century art,[97] drawing as much from an understanding of Eastern spirituality as Western religion. In 1992 Professor Mike Tucker at Brighton University published *Dreaming With Open Eyes: The Shamanic Spirit in Twentieth-Century Art & Culture*,[98] followed by an introduction to a retrospective exhibition in 1993 of the works of Scottish born painter Alan Davie that brought out his links to shamanism.[99] In 1995 Frances Stonor Saunders, drawing on such material, presented the case for the spiritual origins of modernism in a Channel Four documentary called *Hidden Hands*, commissioned by art critic Waldemar Januszczak.[100] Tuchman, in his 1986 catalogue essay, traces the fluctuating fortunes of the spiritual critique in modern art. Apparently the influences of esoteric groups like Theosophy, Anthroposophy, Mazdaznan and Gurdjieff/Bennett/Ouspensky on Mondrian, Kandinsky, Malevich and others was well reflected in art histories up to the 1930s.[101] In the 1930s and 40s, however, the association of mystical and esoteric beliefs with the Nazis – who it was believed drew on Theosophy to support the theory of Aryan supremacy – led to an increasing suspicion regarding the spiritual in general, and so the word became an unhelpful association for an artist, particularly in the US. Alfred Barr, director of the Museum of Modern Art in New York, took art history in a different direction,

ignoring the obvious spiritual influences on abstraction and focussing instead on aesthetic formalisms as a genealogy of influence, or
on the *process* of painting. Art critic Clement Greenberg inherited
and extended this approach in respect of the American Abstract
Expressionists, and for decades since then art history has reflected
this strictly secular emphasis. The *Hidden Hands* programme set out
to debunk the rationalist view of modern art, drawing on extensive
material showing the origins of abstract art in esoteric and mystical
thinking.

In 1995 art historian Peg Weiss published *Kandinsky and Old
Russia: Artist as Ethnographer and Shaman.*[102] This work seems to
have been written and researched quite independently of Tucker's
analysis of shamanism in twentieth-century arts and culture.
1995 also saw the hosting of a panel session, *The Subjugation of the
Spiritual in Art*, by the College Art Association in Texas, leading to
the publication of essays edited by Dawn Perlmutter and Debra
Koppman entitled *Reclaiming the Spiritual in Art.*[103] In 1999 the Tate
Britain gallery presented *The Spiritual in Twentieth-Century Art*, a
lecture series by art historian Sarah O'Brien Twohig, and in 2000
John Golding published *Paths to the Absolute*, which explicitly
recognises the spiritual influences on Mondrian, Malevich,
Kandinsky, Pollock, Newman, Rothko and Still, while avoiding
overtly spiritual language.[104] In 2001 the group Poeisis presented
The S Word discussion forum at the Institute of Contemporary Art
in London, bringing art, science and the spiritual together, through
thinkers like Don Cupitt (Sea of Faith) Satish Kumar (editor of the
nature and spirituality journal *Resurgence*), Margaret Boden (writer
on AI and creativity) and Rupert Sheldrake (radical biologist). In
2002 Lynn Gamwell published *Exploring the Invisible: Art, Science
and the Spiritual*, which brings out the important third strand
– science – and its relation to art and the esoteric.[105] The year 2004
saw American video artist Bill Viola's *The Passions* exhibition at the
National Gallery, raising questions about the relationship between
the spiritual and the emotional.

Viola's exhibition was accompanied by a catalogue and an
exhibition guide. The catalogue is edited by John Walsh, director
of the J. Paul Getty Museum, and in his introduction we approach
Viola's work through art-criticism-as-spiritual-literacy, pandering
little to secular assumptions. It is an easy discussion of the world's
religious and mystical traditions as Viola draws on them, a spiritual
literacy clearly shared by Walsh and Viola. Walsh records that Viola
'broke with the prevailing social ideals of art in the 1970s,' quoting

Viola: 'For me, the shift from ideas about social perfection to the idea of self-perfection was a big turning point.' Walsh continues: 'The shift resulted in part from Viola's study of ancient Hindu scriptures and its ideal of perfecting the self, which, transmitted through Buddhism, had become the focus of the Zen thought and personal experience that has informed his work.'[106] The *exhibition guide*, on the other hand, prepared by the National Gallery, made no assumptions of spiritual literacy in the British art-going public: it adopted the neutral art-historical tone of the classicist. Classicism is certainly a valid critical perspective on Viola's show, but that safely puts questions of the spirit within the dead world of the (presecular) past instead of the living and urgent (postsecular) present. Viola himself clearly wants to foster an open spiritual literacy in his public: he instructed the National Gallery to stock not just his exhibition catalogue and closely related publications at the checkout, but also a veritable cherry-picking of the world's spiritual literature.[107]

Anish Kapoor is an internationally-renowned artist – his huge stainless steel 'doughnut', for example, was commissioned by Chicago for its Millennium Park, but he shares with Viola a spirituality that is present in his work if one is aware of the visual clues necessary for such a reading. Kapoor was born in Bombay in 1954 of an Indian father and a Jewish mother. These facts speak not just to a richness of cultural heritage, but also to a lineage of spiritual impulse belonging to two of the root religions of the world. In Kapoor's *1000 Names* series of 1979-80 we can spot the play of Hindu religious festival in the pigment powders and the Judaic in the interest in the *names* (of God). We also discern the secular heritage of architectural and biomorphic form: the organic shapes are not those of shamanism but of cultures that have built great temples and stared down microscopes. Kapoor read C.G. Jung while at Hornsey and Chelsea schools of art in London, and was drawn to the alchemical obsessions of Marcel Duchamp, often credited as the founding artist of modernism. 'Alchemical' is a useful clue: it may be used as a shorthand in art criticism for a discrete range of form and purpose, with their roots in the pebbles, sticks and creatures of the shamanic world but abstracted through agrarian polytheistic cultures into esoteric tradition. In fact Kapoor's work draws forth a criticism that stretches itself over an array of spiritual heritages, a criticism as 'spiritual literacy' perhaps, but in that awkward juxtaposition to the intensely secular mainstream so often shown. Two commentators on Kapoor demonstrate this: Germano Celant,[108] originator of the term 'Arte Povera' and curator of the New York Guggenheim, and

Homi K. Bhabha, leading postcolonial theorist, born into a Parsi community in Bombay (Parsi being the community of contemporary Zoroastrians, that religion living in the mid-point between East and West).[109] Central to the discussion of Kapoor in both cases is the idea of the *void*, a way of referring to the transcendent goal of the *via negativa* mystic.[110]

All the scholars of the spiritual in art make reference to the American Abstract Expressionism of such artists as Jackson Pollock and Mark Rothko. In both cases the transcendent concept of the void, articulated in the Western tradition as the Divine Darkness or the Cloud of Unknowing, or in the East as *nirvana* or *shunyata* (emptiness), finds visual expression. The Rothko room at the Tate (housing a series of his most sombre colour-field paintings) had long been the most visible cultural icon of transcendence, and the work is also one of the most popular in modern art for theologians. The modern art gallery has to some extent replaced the church as a natural place to visit on a Sunday, and the Rothko room seems to consistently evoke in its audience a mood of deep reflection. At the same time, art historians have explored the shamanic influences on Pollock and Rothko, and Peg Weiss has shown that Kandinsky was an ethnographer exposed to shamanic cultures even before he was a painter.

Jackson Pollock read esoteric works like Blavatsky's *Secret Doctrine* when young, and attended lectures by Jiddu Krishnamurti: his instinctive search for a language of interiority had found inspiration in these sources. Later, suffering from bouts of alcoholism and violence, Pollock entered into psychoanalysis. Joseph Henderson, Pollock's Jungian analyst in the late 1930s, persuaded Pollock to search into his unconscious and to learn from Native American art. He did so on the basis of two of Jung's dictums: that all genuine art originates in the unconscious, and that colonising people inherit the racial memory of the natives they displace – the latter implying to Henderson that native imagery was *already* in Pollock's unconscious.[111] In fact Pollock had been exposed to the Native American spirit as a child, and through the twelve volume set of the *Annual Report of the Bureau of American Enthnology*, that he had bought. These influences show explicitly in paintings like *Guardians of the Secret* (1943) and *Totem Lesson I* and *II* (1944/45).

Art historian Roger Lipsey provides an insight into the artists' movement between the material and the spiritual – on what it means to have an 'eye for art' – drawing on a letter from the Trappist monk and religious author Thomas Merton. Lipsey recalls the Sufi distinction between 'eyes of flesh', drawn to the material world, and 'eyes of fire', directed to the eternal world.

> Eyes of flesh perceive the world and mankind as densely material; in such eyes life is a losing struggle for permanence, although sometimes full of beauty. Eyes of flesh acutely perceive details of time, place, person, action and ideas, but in relation to one another rather than to anything beyond them.
>
> Eyes of fire perceive each thing as the outer sign of an inner fact, or the local sign of a distant power. For such eyes nothing is lonely matter, all things are caught up in a mysterious, ultimately divine whole that challenges understanding over a lifetime. Eyes of flesh focus on the thing itself, eyes of fire on facts but still more intently on their participation in a larger meaning by which they are raised.
>
> Merton's brief reflections evoke the idea that *eyes for art* strike a balance between these sensibilities. They are at one and the same time eyes of flesh and eyes of fire.[112]

Lipsey's definition of the *eyes for art* is nothing short of a restatement of the *via positiva* Neoplatonist ideal of the Italian Renaissance, implying that the artist lives between the poles of the divine *void* on the one hand and the profusely contingent materiality of the embodied life on the other. It is no accident that Rothko drew on both Krishnamurti and shamanic traditions: it is the same confluence that brings Buddhism and shamanism into such close relationships all over the Far East.

Film

While modern art has been theorised by scholars in relation to a wide variety of religious thought, including Eastern and the shamanic, the spiritual in film has received the scholarly attention of more conventionally theological tradition. Film lies between art and writing: it is a visual medium intimately bound up with human dialogue, and hence makes much more concrete reference to the Western location of its tradition than does abstract art or music. Mike Tucker's *Dreaming With Open Eyes* is one of the few works that treats film outside of a monotheist context.[113] Yet within the huge output of Western and Eastern filmmaking one can find a portrayal of almost every spiritual impulse as articulated in the Two-Fold Model of Spiritual Difference. Tucker admirably points out shamanic elements in many films, but uses the term in too broad a way, as a general poetics of the spiritual. The shamanic is engagingly visualised in

Kurusawa's *Dersu Uzula* (1975) and *Rashômon* (1950), for example, but there is also an undercurrent of deeply Buddhist compassion in his work, as in his best-known film *Seven Samurai* (1954). In contrast Robert Bresson's *Diary of a Country Priest* (1951) is a deeply spiritual work, but has nothing of the shamanic: instead we glimpse the heart of Christian transcendent piety, pitted against the merciless secularism of post-war France.

There is effectively a canon of arthouse filmmakers who engage with the spiritual, including Bresson, Dreyer, Bergman, Tarkovsky, and Kurusawa. Other filmmakers are known for occasional deeply spiritual works, including Pier Paulo Pasolini who has provoked the conundrum: how is it that a Marxist, atheist homosexual has made the Jesus film most widely recognised as the best, *The Gospel According to St. Matthew* (1964)? Even the Pope of that day, bound as he was to regard Pasolini as representing everything vile, debauched and decadent in the modern world, acknowledged it as a masterpiece. But the remarkable feature of film is that the spiritual emerges within it in the most popular and unlikely places, beyond either approval or censure from the Pope, or comment from a secular world. While films abound that peddle titillatory pseudo-occultisms, such as *The Exorcist* (1973) or *The Da Vinci Code* (2006) – and Hitchcock's entire oeuvre can be also analysed from this viewpoint – a film like M. Night Shyalaman's *The Sixth Sense* (1999) deals in a remarkably thoughtful way with the presence of spirits. Independent filmmaker Jim Jarmusch engages with Native American spirituality in a quite uncompromising way in *Dead Man* (1995), and with Japanese samurai spirituality in *Ghost Dog: The Way of the Samurai* (1999). Even mainstream actor and filmmaker Kevin Costner sensitively portrays the shamanic basis of Native American spiritual life in *Dances with Wolves* (1990), despite his typically antinomian self-absorption.

The Novel

Where one might construct a short list of films which arguably convey a postsecular sensibility, perhaps even the beginning of a canon despite their hugely varied cultural locations, novels are more problematic. We saw in *Secularism* that Sartre's *Nausea*, almost the blueprint for the twentieth-century novel of alienation, contained within it an inverted mysticism born out of Sartre's experience with mescaline. Aldous Huxley's novels, emerging from similar experiences, are as resolutely pro-mysticism as Sartre's are anti-mysticism, but appear to literary tradition as poor stuff in comparison. Chaim Potok's *The Chosen* explores the tension between secular and orthodox Judaism, but its parameters are drawn along the old Enlightenment battle-lines. Carlos Castaneda's novels of esoteric shamanism spoke mostly to the New Age. Robert Pirsig's *Zen and the Art of Motorcycle Maintenance*, and *Lila: An Inquiry into Morals* are more mainstream and perhaps approach the postsecular via metaphysics with a hint of New Age.

We saw that John Updike's *Terrorist* was a great deal more sympathetic to religion than the short dramatisation of the last days of Muhammad Atta by Martin Amis. It was suggested that Updike's classless American nihilism is more open to the question of religion, which the British middle-class smugness of Amis and McEwan dismiss along the lines of a modern-day distaste for 'enthusiasm'.

Tina Beattie considers Ian McEwan as 'offering perhaps the best examples of what we might call new atheist literature.'[114] She is intrigued by Hitchens' praise of McEwan. In *The Portable Atheist* Hitchens says: 'A novelist who has worked luminously on the frontier that separates the ordinary from the mystical, Ian McEwan has even less patience than Joseph Conrad with the silly invocation of the supernatural.'[115] Hitchens repeats this in *God is Not Great* when he concludes with a remark on McEwan that his 'body of fiction shows an extraordinary ability to elucidate the numinous without conceding anything to the supernatural.'[116] Presumably Hitchens uses the terms 'luminous', and even 'numinous', to indicate some literary aesthetic he detects surrounding moments of dramatic tension in the novels. But, as we saw, McEwan introduces such irruptions into his ordered middle-class world in order that its very rationality should triumph over disorder. What *would* make them numinous would be if Perowne in *Saturday* was moved to investigate Islam sympathetically (as Updike's novel *Terrorist* does), or if Rose was moved by Parry to discover a latent devotional religiosity in himself: one that was genuine where Parry's was false and hysterical. We can say the same of Lodge's novel *Thinks . . .* : what if Messenger had found in Helen Reed a religion so luminous as to adequately challenge his neuroscientific materialism? What if Taylor's antistructure could erupt within the structure of middle-class life and actually bring something of eternity with it?

In Pirsig's *Lila* this opposition of rationalist structure against religious anti-structure is called the opposition of the 'static' against the 'Dynamic', and is framed in terms that are often, though not exclusively, transcendent. Philip K. Dick's *Valis* is a novel that pursues philosophy and religion even more intensely than *Lila*, the antistructure being a Gnostic-induced madness.[117] This is too small a sample to draw sure conclusions from, but it might well be that the postsecular novel already is a sub-genre within American fiction. If nothing else, *Valis* suggests that the statistics of the American exception are valid: its ordinary American characters, even if sceptical, are inclined to dispute within the domain of religion without embarrassment.

Music: Taverner, Cage, Jenkins and Numan

We have noted that many of the new atheists, while disparaging of biblical scripture when it comes to content, seem to be in thrall to its style. In other words, many of them wish somehow to retain it as culture, even when it is disposed of as revelation. One can put this down to a general cultural conservatism found in the new atheists, but there might also be another factor at work: the status of the 'Word' in the Western mind. Perhaps this is why the novel is not as hospitable a ground to the postsecular as is fine art or cinema, which draw on the visual. In music we have a form that may be without any referential basis at all – a purely formal art that speaks in some mysterious way to the emotions – or there may be lyrics, in which case we can examine these for postsecular sentiment. Or, if musicians happen to also write, we might detect a postsecular sensibility there that would be otherwise hard to reverse engineer from the music.

As with the novel, the field of contemporary music is so vast that only a haphazard selection can be made here: we will briefly look at Sir John Taverner, John Cage, Karl Jenkins and Gary Numan. All of them deal with religious themes in their music. The question we pursue is: to what extent might one argue that their engagement with religious themes is *postsecular* rather than presecular, i.e. that it involves some form of critique of religion or spirituality? Taverner, Cage and Jenkins are composers whose religious themes roam across the world's religions, so in that sense they are already good candidates, on the premise that religious pluralism is a postsecular phenomenon. Numan, on the other hand, in his so-called 'atheist' albums, rages against the specifics of Christianity, making him a less likely candidate at first glance.

Taverner's religious affiliation appears to be to Orthodox Christianity, but he has also been involved in Sufism and several of his works are settings for the poetry of Perennialist/Sufi spiritual teacher Fritjof Schuon (Taverner's brother is a committed Sufi). Cage, on the other hand, leans further Eastward with an interest in Indian and Buddhist religions; in addition his music may rely on aleatory constructions from Taoist I-Ching sources. Jenkins, classically trained, was known in his early career for his jazz work, contributing to ensembles such as Nucleus and Soft Machine. His later works are orchestral, and in *Requiem*, for example, he draws both on Christian liturgy and Zen haikus. In the music of Taverner and Jenkins one has to ask how much of it is presecular in its classical structuring and sonorities, and how much of it owes to modernity, including the use of electronic sounds and recording techniques, and to the more machine-like and metronomic timekeeping of popular music.

Gary Numan's music, as mentioned earlier, is based in his early success as dystopian sci-fi electronic pioneer, which transmutes in his later career into a heavily anti-religious oeuvre in a style known as 'Dark Wave'. The bridge between science fiction themes and religion in his music is, according to sleeve notes to his album *Sacrifice*, Von Daniken's *Chariots of the Gods?* book series. (It could just as well be *Valis*, a reminder that science-fiction has long engaged with religious themes.) The location of Numan in pop music as opposed to orchestral composition might lead the cultural conservative such as McEwan's Henry Perowne to dismiss the music as the 'three chord trick', which is how Perowne indulgently accommodates his son's blues playing. But the sonorities and plangencies of Numan's electronic style give enormous energy to his rage against religion, the themes of which were apparent to a small degree in his early work, but are most notable in *Sacrifice* (1994), *Exile* (1997), *Pure* (2000) and *Jagged* (2006). It is clear from this list that only one of these albums post-dates 9/11, so his atheism – if that is what it is – is not triggered by that event, as with many of the new atheists considered earlier. What makes Numan's music potentially postsecular rather than secular is that the question of religion should generate such anger in him, and that, on closer examination, his lyrics suggest a rage just as much at its failure to *be* a religion to him, as a rage against its known tyrannies. This is not the casual atheism of Marx and Foucault; it is not the Monty Python atheism of the Footlights generation; and it is not the vituperative atheism of Dawkins and Crick: it is a rage against *loss*. In the rage of Numan, one might suggest, there is potentially more religion than in the polite 'North Oxford' theism of so many of the new defenders of faith.

In listening first to Numan's *Pure*, and then to Taverner's *Schuon Lieder*, one is struck by the palpable religious intensity in both. But they arise in quite different musical traditions, Numan's richly layered but metronomic electronic soundscapes contrasting vividly with Taverner's conventional purity of avant-garde acoustic dissonances and rubato. Numan's religious intensity arises in the breakdown of the 'buffered self': his sacrilege is as convincingly religious as Taverner's sanctity, but has the energy of the antinomian rather than tradition.

Postsecularism and the Arts

Brancusi, Pollock, Pirsig, Cage, Shyalaman and Jarmusch (to pick just a few examples) represent a potentially postsecular engagement with spirituality, because their work arises out of a secular freedom from the Church. Artists are nothing like philosophers, theologians or scientists. Their 'eyes for art' (or music, cinema, or literature) are antinomian, so not bound to church tradition; non-literal, so not bound to the plodding ratiocination of the philosopher; and find in the material world that which the scientist denies: an intimation of the whole, or of eternity. They have 'eyes of fire'. Or ears. Artists are maddeningly immediate in their perceptions; they neither can nor want to explain the chain of reasoning that brings about their insight. They are often drunk, irresponsible, and reckless. Pasolini well represents the life of an artist: his work is chaotic and unpredictable; his murder at the hands of an outraged gay prostitute gruesome. Equally appalling is the image of Rothko lying in a colour-field of his own blood after committing suicide. No church-sanctioned costume drama of the life of Jesus has ever reached the heights of Pasolini's version, but almost any costume drama treatment of St. Francis of Assisi is better than Pasolini's bizarre attempt in *Uccelacci e Uccellini* (1966).

The spiritual abounds in the Western arts of the twentieth century, but is everywhere hemmed in by the two opposing cultural forces of traditional religion and atheist secularism. It is neither a coherent voice of spirituality against conservative religion, or against dismissive secularism, because it is so thinly interspersed within a cultural production mostly indifferent to questions of the spirit. But it is possible in each field to collect together works that represent a creative critical engagement with those questions. An effort comparable to that of the scholars of the spiritual in art, dedicated to the whole of Western cultural production, would yield a rich and diverse canon of the spiritual. Such an effort would be characteristically postsecular, as it requires the secular revolutions in freedom of thought to make it possible.

But the forces of secularism within cultural production are very strong, infiltrated from one angle by socialist humanism, and from another by reductionist science (its influence growing as that of Marxism wanes). Dennett, for example, says of music: 'The comparison of religion to music is particularly useful here, since music is another natural phenomenon that has been ably studied by scholars for hundreds of years but is only just beginning to be an object of the sort of scientific study I am recommending.'[118] What Dennett is after is a scientific study, from a Darwinist perspective, of the question: *why* does music exist? By declaring music and religion to be 'natural phenomena' they fall under the purview of science, it seems. The fact that music is beautiful to us, as Dennett puts it, is a 'perfectly good biological question.' But what evades reductionist thinkers like Dennett is the issue of what would we do with the answer? There is certainly no harm in asking the question that Dennett poses, and we might wish him luck in his investigation, but neither the question nor the answer, in the case of either music or religion, even begins to capture the *essence* of those domains.

What is missing in the Darwinist account, to return to Gould's non-overlapping magisteria, is that scientific questions address scientific problems, religious questions address religious problems and artistic questions address artistic – that is, broadly speaking, *aesthetic* – problems. When we approach cultural productions such as fine art, cinema, the novel and music with the question of their secularity or postsecularity, we are asking a religious question about the aesthetic domain. This is legitimate, as long as we recognise that *in the first instance* Brancusi is a sculptor, Tarkovsky is a filmmaker, Dick is a novelist, and Taverner a composer. So we ask religious questions of their work after first acknowledging their art as art. If we ask scientific questions about any domain of cultural production, we must do the same, and realise in both cases that the answers are not necessarily of the slightest interest to artist, filmmaker, novelist or musician. In saying this we begin perhaps to spell out what NOMA looks like in practice: it doesn't prevent the asking of any question across the boundaries of a magisterium, but it denies that any one magisterium can truly illuminate or explicate another.

Chapter 12:
Postsecularism and Postmodernism

It was suggested earlier that the contemporary mind is largely modern as opposed to postmodern, and that postmodernism, to the extent that it pursues a sceptical deconstruction of all systems of thought, cannot offer the 'hermeneutics of trust' that is necessary for religion. However, there are interesting and important exceptions.

John D. Caputo, a Derridean scholar, represents a strand of postmodern thought deeply engaged with the spiritual. His short book *On Religion* not only contemplates postmodernism, but also postsecularism as an emerging term. Remarkably, he represents not just a postsecular engagement with religion, but stands amongst the few great intellectual Christians of the West to show a markedly *bhakti* orientation, placing him in the company of Augustine, Pascal, and Kierkegaard.[119] In an email dialogue with philosopher Edith Wyschogrod, Caputo writes the following:

> In just the past year we have seen two books edited by English theologians – one entitled *The Postmodern God*, the other *Post-Secular Philosophy* – that have pressed the claim that 'postmodern' must be understood to mean or at least to include 'postsecular', that the delimitation of the claims of Enlightenment rationalism must also involve the delimitation of Enlightenment secularism. A critical stance toward modernism goes hand in hand with a critical stance toward secularism. In France, Jacques Derrida's most recent work has taken a turn toward what he calls 'religion without religion', that is, to a thinking that involves a certain repetition of basic religious structures, most notably the 'messianic'. . . . As these thinkers have been arguing, it seems that God is making a comeback.[120]

Is 'God' making a comeback via postmodernism? Is postmodernism assisting in the 'twilight of atheism' as McGrath puts it? At the very least, as Caputo says, 'a critical stance toward modernism goes hand in hand with a critical stance toward secularism.' We saw in *Secularism* that the 'linguistic turn' in the hands of theologian Don Cupitt was a mixed blessing for the spiritual life, but at least did not work to its overthrow. Postmodernism can be summed up by its most useful generalisation to date, from Francois Lyotard: Postmodernism is an incredulity towards metanarratives.[121]

A metanarrative, or grand narrative, is a monolithic, hierarchical, authoritarian system of thought and injunction which dismisses those not served by the dominant culture, e.g. women, gays, ethnic minorities. Postmodernism proposes that we have been guilty of phallocentrism, logocentrism, chronocentrism, and many other 'centrisms' – underlying and unprovable assumptions that we make because we are white middle-class European males. To some this attack on the hidden assumptions of the modernist project is welcome, while others point out that postmodernists are largely white middle-class European males drawing fat university salaries. As pointed out earlier, to some extent postmodernism is a 'hermeneutics of suspicion', a stance that promises a critical approach to a subject such as spirituality, but one that could also scoff at the position of trust at the heart of the spiritual life. Postmodernism is a large field indeed, but here we look at just two interesting cases: the relation of thought between Emmanuel Levinas and Jacques Derrida, and the 'Radical Orthodoxy'.

Levinas and Derrida

Three texts form a conversation between Levinas and Derrida: Levinas's book *Totality and Infinity*, Derrida's essay 'Violence and Metaphysics', and Levinas's essay 'God and Philosophy'. These two philosophers understand Husserl and Heidegger as their 'Masters', though they both in one way or another reject their illustrious predecessors.

Levinas (1905-1995) writes from a distinctly Judaic perspective, which is at the heart of the difference between him and Derrida. In addition to the works intended for a general philosophical public, such as *Totality and Infinity*, Levinas was also a Talmudic scholar and published works in this field. His extensive familiarity with the German phenomenologists and their French inheritors (Sartre and Merleau-Ponty) makes phenomenology his starting point. He introduces new concerns into this discourse, however, centred around the notion of the 'other'. Levinas is influenced in this by Martin Buber, but also by a reading of Descartes which is unusually sympathetic.

Judaic tradition, with no obligation to clarify itself to the outside world, is marked by levels of codification in which the meanings of texts are available only through other texts, or through the personal teachings of a Rabbi. Although one may not want to push this metaphor too hard, Judaism unlike Hellenism can be seen as feminine, dark and moist, while Greek thought is masculine, luminous and dry. In comparison to the Christian 'God' – the relation with whom is based on love – the Jewish 'God' is much more a 'person' with whom one has a discussion, a debate, or even an argument. The Jewish 'God' is always referred to as 'thou', a form of address that encompasses the contradiction of 'God' as both 'other' and remote, and intimate and involved. But, in Jewish thought there also exists the profoundly anti-anthropomorphic tendency which contradicts all 'conversation'.

With these remarks we can turn to *Totality and Infinity* which Levinas subtitled 'An Essay on Exteriority'. The three terms, 'totality', 'infinity' and 'exteriority' are the central concern of the book: totality standing for structures of thought that 'totalise' understanding into power-structures of violence; infinity for open-ended potential in the relation with the 'other', and exteriority for the fact that the 'other' is always outside one's own horizons. What gradually emerges from Levinas's great text is the ancient Judaic wariness of the Greek impulse to bring being into light, logic and clarity. Exactly the quality that the West has admired in the Greek foundation of civilisation, the rational light of lucid discourse, is here shown to be suspect. Set against the contradictory, open-ended, secretive Judaic relationship with 'God', the Greek impulse is seen as 'totalising', sealed within the sameness of being, cut off from the great 'Other' of 'God', and ultimately violent.

The connection between the philosophy of being – ontology – and violence is bizarre. In *Secularism* the Greek spiritual impulse was characterised as polytheistic in its popular expression, and transcendent *jnani* in the spiritual genius of Pythagoras, Heraclitus and Socrates, leading on to Plotinus and the Neoplatonic tradition. In Socrates, inheritor of Pythagoras, Heraclitus, and the Eleatic tradition, there is no trace of the personal 'God'. For Levinas this is incomprehensible:

> This primacy of the same was Socrates' teaching: to receive nothing of the Other but what is in me, as though from all eternity I was in possession of what comes to me from the outside – to receive nothing, or to be free. Freedom does not resemble the capricious spontaneity of free will; its ultimate meaning lies in this permanence in the same, which is reason.[122]

This short passage conveys the somewhat oblique style of Levinas's writing, but the message is clear: he cannot conceive of the idea that the ultimate in Man lies within him 'from all eternity' – it has to come from exteriority, from 'God'. Levinas would be quite baffled by Buddhism or the great *jnani* strands in Hinduism, which posit respectively that 'all beings have Buddha-nature' and that 'Atman is Brahman' (the soul *is* 'God'). Neither would Levinas be comfortable with the entire apophatic Christian mystical tradition (the negative theology), or the Plotinian 'One'. However, we can learn much from Levinas's misreading of the Greek mind, and in this instance we pursue his text to reveal why 'ontology' and 'violence' are related or conflated by him. The key to this association lies in his phrase 'permanence of the same'. He says that this is nothing else than *reason*.

But why should reason be the villain? Surely in the Socratic dialogues we find reason elucidated through an equivalent to the very core of Judaic religiosity, discourse? But, as another great Jew, Sir Karl Popper, has pointed out, the Socratic dialogues are manipulative, and, in Plato's *Republic*, they lead directly to a world that is fascist and eugenicist.[123] Is there, then, a simple line from Greek ontology – the philosophy of being – through Plato via his 'Republic' into fascism, and hence through its modern vengeance on the Jew, the Holocaust, directly into the sorrow of Levinas? Although this argument may have some merit, it is too easy an answer, too historical. Levinas has scented out something more subtle about Greek rationality, the light and clarity which it brings to bear on being. This light and clarity begins with the ontological tradition of the Eleatic philosophers who stated the doctrine that 'all is Being'. Levinas's critique of Heidegger is also based in this 'primacy of the same', the Eleatic notion that nothing exists that stands either in contrast or in contradiction to Being. Levinas sees this as a ploy to reduce the other, to deny them freedom by placing one's own freedom over and above ethics, the ethics that begins by placing the other first. For Levinas the 'primacy of the same . . . marks the direction of and defines the whole of Western philosophy.'[124] The following passage gives us a clue as to how ontology leads to violence in his mind:

> Ontology as first philosophy is a philosophy of power. It issues in the State and in the non-violence of the totality, without securing itself against the violence from which this non-violence lives, and which appears in the tyranny of the State. Truth, which should reconcile persons, here exists anonymously. Universality presents itself as impersonal; and this is another inhumanity.[125]

Is the 'State' here Plato's fascist Republic? Or is it any state, such as the Jews had been denied possession of for such a large part of their history? Levinas avoids such direct references, just has he avoids making any direct link between Heideggerian ontology and Heidegger's Nazi sympathies. In fact the above passage is typical of Levinas's style, definitely non-Greek, for why, in his argument that totality is violence, would he first introduce the 'non-violence of totality'? In order to catch his moods we have to approach Levinas less by a rationalism that trips over such seeming contradictions and more by intuition. This way the colour of his writing gradually becomes clear: he is suspicious of philosophy itself.

This becomes more obvious as he elucidates what stands over and against totality, and as its remedy: *infinity* as the essential quality of the 'other'. Levinas introduces the section titled 'Transcendence as the Idea of Infinity' by saying: 'But the idea of infinity is exceptional in that its *ideatum* surpasses its idea, whereas for the things the total coincidence of their "objective" and "formal" realities is not precluded; we could conceivably have accounted for all the ideas other than that of Infinity by ourselves.' He is saying that the very idea of infinity comes from outside ourselves, from an exteriority, or: 'Infinity is characteristic of a transcendent being as transcendent; the infinite is absolutely other.' There can be no doubt that the 'absolutely other' is 'God' for Levinas, but what makes *Totality and Infinity* so delightful is that he is ambiguous about this throughout: the other may also be another human being. At times one is convinced that Levinas is talking about another person, at other times that he is talking about the Judaic 'God'. His manner of speaking, however, ensures that we do not read the text as Judaic theology, but as philosophy, though not 'Greek' philosophy. For Levinas, 'Greek' philosophy lacks ecstasy:

> The schema of theory in which metaphysics was found distinguished theory from all ecstatic behaviour. Theory excludes the implantation of the knowing being in the known being, the entering into the Beyond by ecstasy. It remains knowledge, relationship. To be sure, representation does not constitute the primordial relation with being. It is nonetheless privileged, precisely as the possibility of recalling the separation of the I. And to have substituted for the magical communion of species and the confusion of distinct orders a spiritual relation in which beings remain at their post but communicate among themselves will have been the imperishable merit of the 'admirable Greek people' and the very institution of philosophy.[126]

A little later we can see again how Levinas wants to do more than philosophy: 'But to think what does not have the lineaments of an object is in reality to do more or do better than think.' This perhaps is the crux of Levinas's objection to ontology and the Greek manner of philosophy: it is mere thinking. This sets him apart from Heidegger, and one could say from the whole Western tradition, yet at the same time Levinas is still 'doing' philosophy. But let us return to the idea of infinity. Levinas finds this in the 'other' – whether 'God' or a person is left in continual vagueness – but we are left in no doubt that 'conversation' is the key to this, and not in the manner of the Socratic dialogue. This conversation is to 'receive the Other beyond the capacity of the I', it is to contemplate the face of the other, it brings me 'more than I contain'. The 'face' for Levinas is crucial, and also the asymmetry of one's standing in respect of the face of the other, which makes totalisation an impossibility. Above all the allowing of the face of the other is the primary ethical act, which places the being and needs of the other over and above one's own freedom: 'In positing the relation with the Other as ethical, one surmounts a difficulty that would be inevitable if, contrary to Descartes, philosophy started from a *cogito* that would posit itself absolutely independently of the Other.'[127]

Levinas has found in Descartes a sympathetic language of the infinite. *Secularism argues* that the modern secular mind has eviscerated Descartes' thinking by bracketing out his references to 'God' (or assuming publishing prudence); in contrast Levinas has taken this to be central to him:

> Descartes, better than an idealist or a realist, discovers a relation with a total alterity irreducible to interiority, which nevertheless does not do violence to interiority – a receptivity without passivity, a relation between freedoms.
>
> The last paragraph of the Third Meditation brings us to a relation with infinity in thought which overflows thought and becomes a personal relation. Contemplation turns to admiration, adoration, and joy.[128]

Levinas then quotes the paragraph from the Third Meditation, in which Descartes says 'my awareness of the infinite must therefore be in some way prior to my awareness of the finite, that is to say, my awareness of God must be prior to that of myself.'

Levinas continues: 'To us this paragraph appears to be not a stylistic ornament or a prudent hommage to religion, but the expression of this transformation of the idea of infinity conveyed by knowledge into Majesty approached as a face.' In this last comment Levinas is rescuing Descartes for the spiritual life, from philosophy, just as was done earlier in denying the secular assumption that this is a mere 'prudent hommage' to the religious authorities of his day. However, Levinas has read Descartes as a theist; we have read him as a *jnani*: the differences in emphasis merely illuminate Descartes from different angles.

Levinas also *reads into* Descartes' account the metaphor of the 'face' . . . but then, why not? *Totality and Infinity* is not an easy book, representing as it does an attempt to obey the religious impulse through the language of philosophy rather than theology. It is rich and complex, partisan in its theism, implacable in its opposition to the philosophy of 'mere thinking', pluralist in its intention, often contradictory, but always a surprise.

Derrida's Critique of Levinas

We turn now to a brief consideration of Jacques Derrida's philosophy, and in particular to his response to *Totality and Infinity* in the long essay 'Violence and Metaphysics'. One might think that Derrida would be in complete accord with the goals that Levinas set himself in *Totality and Infinity*, even if not the detail. (We would, of course, be asking the impossible for one philosopher simply to agree with another – that is not their vocation.) But Derrida's response to Levinas is complex and hard to pin down even by the levels of ellipsis and circumlocution characteristic of postmodern writing. We are not attempting to understand his response in terms of philosophy at all, but to see if there is an impulse behind it, and the rest of his work, that can invigorate the spiritual life.

Derrida begins the essay with a quote from Matthew Arnold, the Victorian poet and literary and social critic, which reminds us that Western culture is pulled between the points of influence of the Hellenic and the Hebraic. He then states quite clearly that philosophy is 'Greek' and 'it would not be possible to philosophize, or to speak philosophically, outside of this medium,' and that the 'ethical is not only dissociated from metaphysics but coordinated with something other than itself, a previous and more radical function.'[129] Derrida is setting the stage for the assessment of Levinas by making sure that philosophy is Greek, and, what is more, that Husserl and Heidegger not only belong to that tradition, 'are Greek', but that the project of Heidegger was to invigorate thinking itself – for too long a time desiccated – by a return to the 'Greek element'. Derrida says: 'It is at this level that the thought of Emmanuel Levinas can make us tremble.'[130] Derrida then frames the questions that Levinas raises for him, or for philosophy, in terms of this return to the Greek source. The first part of his question is to do with this return and the question of violence implicit in the Eleatic 'light'.

A thought which, without philology and solely by remaining faithful to the immediate, but buried nudity of experience itself, seeks to liberate itself from the Greek domination of the Same and One (other names for the light of Being and of the phenomenon) as if from oppression itself – an oppression certainly comparable to none other in the world, an ontological or transcendental oppression, but also the origin or alibi of all oppression in the world.[131]

Derrida speaks as if he were Marx, who made out that *religion* was effectively the origin or alibi of all oppression. But Marx was attacking the Judeo-Christian or Hebraic heritage; why on earth should Derrida attack the Greek mind? Perhaps it is a confusion between metaphysics and religion. He concludes his brief summary of the Levinasian project as follows:

This thought calls upon the ethical relationship – a nonviolent relationship to the infinite as infinitely other, to the Other – as the only one capable of opening the space of transcendence and of liberating metaphysics. And does so without the supporting ethics and metaphysics by anything other than themselves, and without making them flow into other streams at their source.[132]

Derrida is pointing out one of the remarkable qualities of *Totality and Infinity* – that it does not directly draw on theology or mysticism, and in particular not on 'messianic eschatology'. In other words, Levinas painstakingly creates a new language that is fresh, original, and seems to live outside both philosophy and theology. But this is also the problem for Derrida. He seems torn between admiration for the work, and the instinctive feeling that a Western philosopher should not to step outside of the 'language of the Greeks'.

With these opening remarks out of the way, Derrida proceeds to his analysis with a section titled 'The Violence of Light'. His discussion as philosophy is not our direct concern here, but what is plain is an extensive engagement with issues of religion, as we see in phrases like 'messianic eschatology', 'the Face of God' and 'negative theology', and in references to Nicholas of Cusa and Meister Eckhart. There is a well-documented interest of Derrida's in the negative theology, so it is notable that in the short passage on Eckhart we find this point: 'This negative theology is still a theology and, in its literality at least, it is concerned with liberating and acknowledging the ineffable transcendence of an infinite existent.'[133] The 'God' of Eckhart is closer to the non-theistic 'One' of Plotinus than to the cataphatic 'God' of mainstream Christianity, or to the Judaic 'God' of Levinas' inheritance, and hence has some appeal to Derrida. If he could only step outside the hermetically sealed bubble of Western thought then a Buddhist 'negative theology' would give him better leverage on Levinas, but the fact is that Derrida is resisting even the step outside the Greek bubble. His point is that in Levinas 'when the thought of Being goes beyond ontic determinations it is not a negative theology, nor even a negative ontology.' In other words we cannot avoid the face of 'God'.

Derrida continues his meditation on Levinas, probing all the places where he finds Levinas to be 'the enemy of thought'. But towards the end Derrida, although possibly in admiration of Levinas and possibly wishing it really were possible to step philosophically outside of the Greek source, turns back to that source. He quotes an unnamed Greek: 'If one has to philosophize, one has to philosophize; if one does not have to philosophize, one has to philosophize (to say and to think it). One always has to philosophize.'[134] Derrida finishes his essay on the theme with which it began, that we live between the Jewish and Greek minds, quoting James Joyce in *Ulysses*: 'Jewgreek is greekjew. Extremes meet.' [135]

Levinas's Response to Derrida

How in turn does Levinas read Derrida's 'Violence and Metaphysics'? Levinas's 1975 essay 'God and Philosophy' answers this question by starting with Derrida's point 'Not to philosophize is still to philosophize.' Levinas's opening remarks are telling:

> The philosophical discourse of the West claims the amplitude of an all-encompassing structure or of an ultimate comprehension. It compels every other discourse to justify itself before philosophy.
>
> Rational theology accepts this vassalage. If for the benefit of religion, it reserves a domain from the authority of philosophy, one will know that this domain will have been recognized to be philosophically unverifiable.[136]

There is a typical Levinasian illogic to this statement: if rational theology *really* accepts vassalage before philosophy, then how can it reserve a domain from this authority? In this simple contradiction we have the heart and soul of the Judaic outlook – an almost Hindu fluidity of category – against the clarity of the Greek. For Levinas to speak on that which really concerns him, he doesn't need or want Aristotle's law of the excluded middle. In a simple opening remark he has put the poor Greek in his place, confined to mere logic. And from this more expansive and generous position Levinas can include the Greek as well. To hesitatingly return to a metaphor used earlier, whenever does male logic stand a chance against female logic? The Judaic will always triumph in this context, until philosophy rediscovers the illogic at the heart of the Greek mind, i.e. in Pythagoras, Heraclitus and the 'real' Socrates, as against the logic of the Eleatics, Plato and Aristotle.

Levinas has new insights for us in 'God and Philosophy', including a delightful new metaphor, that of insomnia, a state of unintentional wakefulness. Having worked around such themes he closes the essay with a direct refutation of Derrida: 'Not to philosophize would not be "to philosophize still," nor to succumb to opinion.'[137] Derrida as a 'Greek' dares not really step outside of philosophy (although he was born a Jew); Levinas as a 'Jew' moves freely between the Hebraic and the Hellenic, a movement that confounds Derrida.

This conversation reinforces again how much the Western mind lives in the creative tension between the Hellenic and Hebraic influences. From a postsecular point of view it retrieves what has been lost for so long: that it has a *religious* tension in its origins. It also, however, shows how postmodern philosophy and theology live untouched by so many other postsecular influences: the new physics, consciousness studies, transpersonal psychology, the New Age, nature mysticism and the arts. By the same token the obscurity of postmodern language prevents wider impact of its ideas. We look now at how a specifically *Christian* theology deals with the Hebraic/Hellenic impasse through deconstruction.

The Radical Orthodoxy

The 'Radical Orthodoxy' is a form of theology deeply indebted to postmodern philosophy, and originates with a group of Cambridge thinkers. Three of its principal architects, John Milbank, Catherine Pickstock, and Graham Ward have edited a collection of essays called *Radical Orthodoxy*,[138] which has been the subject of much debate within Christianity. Amongst the 'radical theologians' we can also include Don Cupitt, Rowan Williams (the Archbishop of Canterbury), and other Cambridge alumni including Philip Blond. Their aim, in drawing so heavily on postmodernism, is quite natural: to end the stifling compromises that Christian thought has had to make with modernist secularism. Hence it is 'radical' because of its

adoption of postmodernism, but 'orthodox' because, under the prolix ramblings of its adopted postmodern literary style, it can re-assert
the Christian fundamentals that the Age of Reason denied it. Tina
Beattie mentions such postmodern strategies but suggests that they
are not postmodern enough, particularly when it comes to feminism
and post-colonialism.[139]

R.R. Reno, writing in the journal *First Things* ('The Journal of
Religion and Public Life'), is sympathetic to both the critical project
of Radical Orthodoxy and its constructive project. Reno believes that
'Milbank et al. use the prevailing vocabulary and verbal techniques
of cultural and literary studies to expose the dark emptiness of
secular postmodernism, hoisting it on its own petard.'[140] He sees that
this critique leads to the constructive side of the project, one which
will supersede the secular.

But why does Reno think that the Radical Orthodoxy ultimately
fails? On the positive side he suggests that it counters the 'dark emptiness' of secular postmodernism by replacing the Nietzschean vision
of violence, the will-to-power, with the Augustinian and Neoplatonist
vision of peace on earth. Reno finds, however, that the Radical Orthodoxy, in its use of postmodernist tools to attack modernism, does not
complete the Augustinian project: it simply does not dare go that
far back. Instead, Reno finds that the Radical Orthodoxy manages
to rewind modernism only as far back as Hegel and Kant. In other
words, it does not achieve the orthodoxy that it proclaims.

From the postsecular point of view the Radical Orthodoxy and
such criticisms of it raise a number of questions, principally: how
do presecular religions attempt the renewal of the spiritual life in
a secular context? The use of deconstruction to reveal modernism's
basis in violence, and hence to oppose that with the spiritual peace of
the Augustinian vision, is one possible strategy: to say that if power
ultimately lies only with humanity then violence is the foundation
of the social order; in contrast, if power ultimately lies with the love
of God then peace is the foundation of the social order. Kant and
Hegel had, for Reno, removed the essential reality of 'God' and Jesus
from the Christian message, so on that basis the Radical Orthodoxy
must fail: it doesn't go far back enough. From a postsecular point of
view the question of 'rewinding' modernism does not arise: one can
neither negate modernism as a whole, or merely rewind as far back
as Kant (if that indeed be a fair assessment of the Radical Orthodoxy).
The essential dilemma remains for Christianity: its roots are absolutist and non-pluralist.

In the intersection of philosophy and theology the term 'postsecular' occurs again in the 2004 debate between the German philosopher Jürgen Habermas and the German theologian Joseph Raztinger. The two men were invited to represent the poles in the secular/religious debate, not long before Ratzinger was elected Pope Benedict XVI. While both men are interested in the term, there is little articulation within their discussion of its wider implications.[141]

Blond on Levinas

We can examine these issues and at the same time return to our discussion of Levinas and Derrida: we do this by examining Philip Blond's essay 'Emmanual Levinas: God and Phenomenology'. The essay is in the book he has edited, *Post-Secular Philosophy*, which also includes essays by Rowan Williams, John Milbank and Graham Ward. Blond's essay is rich with traces of the problematic history of religion in the West, reflecting tensions both between Christianity and secularism, and Christianity and non-Christian religion. Blond's text is an example of what Reno describes as the use of deconstruction to attack both modernism and postmodernism, though it has to be said that Blond does not use the Derridean language in the same way as, for example, Rowan Williams. In fact, he finishes the essay with its most endearing prose: a hymnic and rhapsodic account of the Christian vision from his own point of view, one that is cataphatic.

Blond argues against phenomenology in general in the first part of his essay and Levinas in particular in the second. His argument against *Totality and Infinity* is quite different from Derrida's: unlike Derrida, who merely *suspects* Levinas of doing theology, Blond assumes from the start that he is doing so, but of the wrong sort. Blond's attack on phenomenology is firstly an attack on a secular 'science' as he sees it, one that does not predicate 'God' at the out-set of its inquiry. Descartes, effectively carrying out a precursor to the phenomenological enquiry, has yielded us a profound *jnani* discourse, recognised neither by the Church nor secular culture. Blonde's rejection of phenemonology is not that surprising, but his attack on Levinas has a less obvious source, though recognisable in the Church's historical intolerance to 'minor difference'. He says that the decisive issue is 'the deemed congruence of interest between alterity and God.'[142] For Blond, the Levinasian language of 'God' is not the right language; he finds surprising the general acceptance of it by Christianity. He also attacks what he sees as a Gnostic or Manichaean opposition that Levinas draws between 'God' and the world. Blond calls this opposition *idolatrous*. From a *via positiva* perspective (or cataphatic perspective in the Christian tradition) we can sympathise with Blond. The secular world, having drawn the distinction between 'God' and the world, rejects the 'God' half of the equation; Levinas appears to reject the world half. Hence, in our terminology, Levinas appears to Blond as an advocate of the *via negativa*. What must appear bizarre to both the secular and postsecular viewpoint is Blond's use of the term *idolatrous* to describe this position. Idolatry means to worship idols, things, material objects, but here it means to reject the world. Clearly he is using the term, not in any useful way of rejecting the *via negativa*, but simply as the most damning or pejorative term he can lay his hands on. Not only does he use it eight times in all in his essay, but a *further fifteen times* in his editorial introduction to *Post-Secular Philosophy*. While Blond's exposition of his own cataphatic spiritual vision is delightful and endearing, his attack on Levinas is an embarrassing reminder of the 'totalising' character of Christianity, epitomised in his incontinent and incongruous deployment of the term 'idolatrous'.

It is here that the Radical Orthodoxy is caught between two opposing forces: its desire to use postmodernism to attack the modern and move beyond it towards its conception of the postsecular, and its desire to simply revert to the presecular. Contrary to both Blond and Derrida, Levinas's *Totality and Infinity* is of great merit; firstly contra Blond because its postmodern theology epitomises the best interpenetration of secular thought with presecular spirituality, and secondly contra Derrida because it 'reserves a domain from the authority of philosophy.' *Totality and Infinity* preserves the *secular* ethical imperative, while creating a text of spiritual nuance and adventure, precisely because Levinas instantiates the mystery of the 'other', a mystery preserved through the Judaic genius of never naming 'God'. To dismiss *Totality and Infinity* as idolatrous is to also miss a tremendous opportunity: to allow Levinas to end the great misfortune of Western religious tradition, the proscription against idolatry. We saw in *Secularism* how the Judaic destruction of rival religions on the grounds that idolatry was an abomination inadvertently set the pattern for much later monotheistic persecution. Levinas, in his attack on 'totality', and in so far as he might be taken to represent the Judaic tradition in its own attempt to enter the postsecular world, heals the ancient wounds. For Derrida to dismiss Levinas because he wants to preserve a region of human experience from the rationalising power of 'Greek' philosophy is regrettable but understandable, but for Blond to dismiss him for doing the 'wrong' kind of theology is merely embarrassing.

The various elements of postmodernism – phenomenology, deconstruction and the linguistic turn – provide a rich context of thought wherein the fortunes of the spiritual life are buffeted but perhaps subtly reinforced. Above all postmodernism overcomes the blanket rejection of the spiritual life. The vastly prolix nature of its writings makes a deeper acquaintance difficult, and when a tradition almost as verbose – theology – deploys postmodern language, it may seem impenetrable. But to the extent that postmodernism is a hermeneutics of suspicion it stands against religion, which *has* to be a hermeneutics of trust, however 'trust' might be interpreted. Postmodern theology, as the Levinas-Derrida debate makes clear, is a meeting of the Hebraic and the Hellenic. But here lies the real problem: this 'meeting of opposites', as James Joyce says, is still too small a world to properly account for the fullness of the spiritual life. Without the Hindu concept of *jnani*, and its Buddhist instantiations for example, Greek spirituality remains impossible to comprehend. Without the Hindu concept of *bhakti*, and its expression in the mystical thought of Europe, the Middle East and India, the Christian mind is impossible to comprehend. Postmodernism on its own fails as a project of *spiritual* pluralism because it is adamantly 'Greek', resistant to the Hebraic, largely ignorant of the East, and often suspicious of what needs to be trusted: existence itself.

Postmodernism, the New Debate and NOMA

There appears to be no pattern to the way that the new atheism debate intersects with postmodernism: proponents on both sides of the argument may or may not consider it significant. Scientists like Dawkins are inclined to dismiss it – in his case, as we saw, as 'Francophonyism' – and are likely to cite the Sokal incident as proof of the its intellectual bankruptcy.[143] Dennett says with obvious regret: 'In fact, one of the few serious differences between the natural sciences and the humanities is that all too many thinkers in the humanities have decided that the postmodernists are right. . . .'[144] Victor Stenger's position is a little more subtle. He is keen to show that science is provisional in its findings and its theories only a model of the universe, but adds: 'Having read this, please do not assume that the doctrine of *postmodernism* is being promoted here.' He concludes: 'While we might consider science another "cultural narrative", it differs from other cultural narratives because of its superior power, utility, and universality.'[145] While these positions are broadly dismissive of postmodernism, we saw that Michel Onfray castigates such atheists for *not* having adopted a postmodern stance. The new defenders of faith are equally divided, though overall perhaps more sympathetic: McGrath, for example, devoting a significant section of *The Twilight of Atheism* to exploring it, states 'postmodernity seriously undermines the plausibility of atheism. . . .'[146] Likewise, Tina Beattie's *The New Atheists* comes close to adopting the 'cultural narrative' view of science, and is broadly sympathetic to postmodernism. Francis Collins, on the other hand, clearly finds that his commitment to the Moral Law of C.S. Lewis 'is in serious conflict with the current postmodernist philosophy. . . .'[147]

But McGrath is right to suggest that postmodernism opens the door to religion again, by casting doubt on the 'grand narratives' of modernity, and seeking instead the uncertainty of multiple narratives and conversations. It is no friend to the religion of *authority*, which is why Collins sees it in conflict to his version of religion, but its insistence on pluralism makes it more hospitable ground to NOMA than modernism. Still, one could argue that while modernism with its assumed grand narrative of science rules NOMA out, postmodernism takes it too far. We saw with the work of Ferrer in transpersonal psychology that he had leapt from the single spiritual goal of the perennialists to an infinity of spiritual goals – a postmodern strategy of thought which is so open as to be barely useful.

Chapter 13:
Postsecularism and Feminism

What contemporary cultural force is best placed to make an egress from the Greek philosophical / Hebraic theological confine, even if between them they have so far apparently made immense the horizon of Western thought? A so-called immensity that is merely the Western bubble of thought when viewed from the East? Feminism, perhaps. Deconstruction might have as its goal the overthrow of all power structures in Western thought, but, as it is mostly written by well-salaried white *male* university lecturers, it turns within too narrow a circle, as Beattie points out. And the new atheism debate, from this perspective, is just the perennial old stag fight. Feminist thought is inherently more likely to open up the Western tradition, even if it has to start with male intellectual tools, such as anthropology, theology and postmodernism, which it inherits from that tradition.

For anyone intensely engaged with the spiritual life and viewing monotheism from the outside, it is as plain as day, stunningly obvious in fact, that its male 'God' is a *male* invention. The deep-seated problem of anthropomorphism within the 'God' religions was discussed in *Secularism*, without pointing out the awkward tendency to see 'God' not just as a human, but as a *male* human. Monotheism suffers this inability to encompass the female and the male equally, because it has only one 'God'. Popular Buddhism, Hinduism, Taoism and Shinto may have become just as embedded within patriarchal power structures, but can more easily adapt to women's liberation as modernism prevails because of their multiplicity of deities, male and female. 'Real' Buddhism has no god or gods at all, so, apart from the occasional misogyny in the Buddha's thinking there is nothing essentially masculine in it. Monotheism, however, is stymied.

Women's liberation is a project begun in the Enlightenment, and, by the time of its real achievements in the middle-late twentieth century, it had become intimately associated with atheist secular culture. Susan Budd and Susan Jacoby, as women writers on the emergence of secularism in the UK and US respectively, rightly devote much space to women's emancipation and the relation of that fight with the fight against religious authority. Jacoby's devastating exposure of the resistance that religion in America posed to every step of progress in the abolition of slavery and the establishment of civil liberties also details its resistance to women's rights.[148]

Simone De Beauvoir

Simone de Beauvoir's 1949 study of women's subjugation, *The Second Sex*, was one of the key books in promoting awareness of feminism within a wide and international audience. Placed as it was in the French context of Existentialist and Marxist philosophy, it shared with Sartre's work a casual dismissal of the spiritual. Her feminist assessment of Christianity is hard to argue with, however:

> Christian ideology has contributed no little to the oppression of woman. Doubtless there is in the Gospel a breath of charity that extends to women as to lepers; . . . it seemed obvious that the wife should be totally subordinated to her husband: through St. Paul the Jewish tradition, savagely anti-feminist, was affirmed.[149]

In the 1940s, when de Beauvoir was researching her study on women, she only had access to the male-dominated anthropology of her day through writers like James George Frazer and Claude Lévi-Strauss. Just as Freud and Jung too readily drew conclusions from an anthropology that projected the values of white male Hellenic / Hebraic culture onto indigenous peoples, de Beauvoir perhaps too quickly concludes that the 'Golden Age of Woman is only a myth.'[150] She is persuaded that 'Public or simply social authority always belongs to men,' quoting Lévi-Strauss. She accepts that matrilineal societies existed, but that the 'Goddess' merely represents that other pole of the male subjugation of women: his elevation of her onto a pedestal for worship, the confirmation of her as totally 'other'. As we shall see, contemporary feminist scholarship challenges this.

Like Sartre, de Beauvoir 'read the mystics', drawing similar secular conclusions from her study. Like Cupitt she believes that the devotional mysticism of women like Teresa of Avila cannot be just as much a male phenomenon. She says: 'To be sure, there have also been men who burned with that flame, but they are rare and their fervour is of a highly refined intellectual cast . . .'[151] As a confirmed secularist de Beauvoir would have had no reason to look more deeply into this issue: if she had she would have found in Richard Rolle and St. John of the Cross male devotional mystics using the same anti-intellectual language of mystical eroticism as the women. If she had looked at Sufi and Hindu male devotional mystics, she would not have been able to assert that their fervour was in any way intellectual. In our terminology that domain belongs to the *jnani* mystic. De Beauvoir finds in the female Christian mystics only an image of female subjugation, colluded with through narcissistic attention seeking. This is quite understandable from the feminist secular perspective: there is within the secular mind no concept of the *bhakti via negativa* as a genuine domain of human experience and expression. It is the whole medieval context of religious self-abnegation that is repellent to the modern mind, understood only as an internalised form of the prevailing oppression of both men and women of that time.

While de Beauvoir rejects spirituality and organised religion, her intellectual boundaries are still set by the twin forces of the Hebraic and Hellenic. In religion it is the Judeo-Christian tradition that she rejects, without awareness of the possibilities of a broader religious enquiry. As a thinker and philosopher, however, she is less able to see how the Hellenic pervades her assumptions. In her discussion of the role and status of the mother, for example, she indirectly asserts the Existentialist claim that 'existence precedes essence': it is the mother that provides existence to the boy-child, whose challenge is then to come into consciousness and freedom. But for de Beauvoir pregnancy is not a 'project' that the mother has control over like the creative artist, who shapes at the same time the work of art and his or her own personal essence and destiny: for the mother there is always the possibility of a deformed child. De Beauvoir says: 'she gives expression to this uncertainty in two contradictory fantasies: every mother entertains the idea that her child will be a hero, thus showing her wonderment at the thought of engendering a being with consciousness and freedom; but she is also in dread of giving birth to a defective or a monster, because she is aware of the frightening hazards of the flesh – and this embryo dwelling in her is only flesh.'[152] In this passage de Beauvoir repeats the secular assumption that the embryo is mere flesh: a contradiction of all the spiritual traditions of the world which recognise that the child, prior to language and experience, is also a spirit-being. More than this, it is assumed by de Beauvoir that the child is male, and that a woman should subscribe to the hero-myth, in which her only validation is in the vicarious, reflected light of the hero as son, husband or father.

This is a Greek idea, which, we suggest, emerged with the destruction of the Goddess religions: the hero as armoured, solitary, aggressive and male. His values are derived from the horizon of possibilities between the heroic and the hubristic, between success and failure, and which appear to be at the core of the Western secular world. In the Existentialist variant, the male hero starts as mere fleshly existence produced by the blind biological process of pregnancy, and must fight his way to essence. The Greek hero acknowledges the woman only as the source of his fleshly existence, or as the booty of conquest, or, if inclined to the arts and poetry, as the Muse. The latter is Robert Graves' vision of the 'eternal feminine' in his desire to reclaim the lost Goddess religions, not for women, but for the male poet.[153]

To sum up: de Beauvoir's feminism is secularised, Hellenistic, anti-Abrahamic, and framed by understandings of women in antiquity largely constructed by the male tradition.

Merlin Stone and Feminist Archaeology

Recent feminist archaeology and anthropology is beginning to challenge the male white conception of early cultures, the vision framed by men like Frazer, Lévi-Strauss and Graves, a vision outside of which de Beauvoir was unable to step. One of the best accounts of feminist scholarship struggling against the assumptions of the male Hebraic / Hellenic worldview is provided by Merlin Stone in her introduction to *When God was a Woman*. The research leading up to its publication in 1976 made her comment: 'It is shocking to realize how little has been written about the female deities who were worshipped in the most ancient periods of human existence and exasperating to then confront the fact that even the material there has been almost totally ignored in popular literature and general education.' The artefacts of Goddess cultures, those that were not destroyed by monotheist religions in their vicious crusades against idolatry, 'have been dug out of the ground only to be reburied in obscure archaeological texts, carefully shelved away in the exclusively protected stacks of university and museum libraries.'[154] It is the male adherents of the Judeo-Christian tradition, she asserts, that pooh-pooh the female deities and practices, resorting to linguistic tricks to describe them, such as 'fertility cults', 'ritual prostitutes', and 'virgin harlots'. Double standards ruled, such as the use of capitals for male 'Gods' and lower case for 'goddesses'. She says: 'Within descriptions of long-buried cities and temples, academic authors wrote of the sexually active Goddess as "improper", "unbearably aggressive", or "embarrassingly void of morals", while male deities who raped or seduced legendary women or nymphs were described as "playful", or even admirably "virile".[155] Although Stone only blames the male Hebraic for these male-centred 'morals', it is surely also the male Hellenic myth that makes it solely the male heroic privilege to initiate sexual relations, and to complete them in the mode of conquest.

It is Stone's assessment of the destruction of Goddess religion by the Hebrews that is the most devastating, showing for example that the male authors of the Old Testament used the derogatory image of Israel as 'harlot' to condemn the worship of other gods. Stone's reading of the Old Testament book of Hosea suggests that when 'God' told Hosea 'to take unto thee a wife of whoredoms and children of whoredoms' it means a woman worshipping another god . . . or goddess. Stone assumes that Gomer, the woman that Hosea chooses, is a 'sacred woman of the temple'. 'God' tells Hosea later on (Hosea 4:10-14):

> For they will eat, and never be satisfied, resort to prostitutes and never have children, for they have abandoned the Lord to give themselves to immorality.
>
> Wine, old and new, steals my people's wits; they ask advice from a piece of wood and accept the guidance of the diviner's wand; for a spirit of promiscuity has led them astray and they are unfaithful to their God.
>
> They sacrifice on mountaintops and burn offerings on the hills, under oak and poplar and the terebinth's pleasant shade. That is why your daughters turn to prostitution and your sons' brides commit adultery. I shall not punish your daughters for becoming prostitutes or your sons' brides for their adultery, because your men resort to whores and sacrifice with temple prostitutes.[156]

To the secular mind these are the deluded ravings of an Old Testament prophet, but it begins to make more sense once one realises that all references to 'whoring' mean worship of other gods. The Revised English Bible assumes that Gomer is 'unchaste' but the King James version, when it says 'a wife of whoredoms and children of whoredoms,' may well mean that she is a devotee of another deity and descendent of such devotees. 'Sacrifice with temple prostitutes' could be interpreted literally, or it might be a reference to devotion to a female deity. As there are only ambiguous and translation-dependent references to goddesses in the Old Testament, we might be left in doubt, but Stone shows that the archaeological evidence from the land of Canaan is overwhelming: it had been for thousands of years a place of goddess-worship. Once this is understood, the countless references in the Old Testament to the priests of Baal and the priestesses of Asherah (the female deity), and the injunction to slaughter them, becomes clear. The overthrow of idolatrous polytheism is as much a destruction of the old female deities as it is of the old male ones. It is also the overthrow of the old nature religions, with their roots in shamanic culture, as made clear by the repeated reference to 'groves', 'poles', 'mountaintops' and trees. Indeed the use of the terms 'pole', 'stock', 'piece of wood' and so on are references to trees or branches, or Frazer's 'golden bough', all of which strike horror into the later Christian soul: Joan of Arc was questioned mercilessly by her Inquisitors about a certain tree in her village, and accused of possessing a mandrake (a root with supposed magical properties). All this would be baffling if we did not read it as a historically reinforced and culturally irresistible revulsion against the old nature religions and the central role that women played in them.

In 1991 Anne Baring and Jules Cashford published *The Myth of the Goddess: Evolution of an Image*, which gave further archaeological evidence for the brutal emergence of the male 'God' in the Judaic religion. They say: 'In every major archaeological excavation in Palestine female figures have been found, dating to between 2000 BCE and 600 BCE.'[157] This tallies well with Karen Armstrong's thesis that monotheism was only finally established by about 600 BCE, and that the Hebrews engaged in something like 800 years of struggle to abandon their earlier gods and goddesses. The deity we now just refer to as 'God' was originally a tribal warrior god of the Canaanite people called *Elohim*. Baring and Cashford cite biblical scholar Raphael Patai who makes the point that despite the concept of 'God' as beyond gender, the Hebrew language renders him male:

> When a pronoun is used to refer to God, it is the masculine 'He'; when a verb describes that he did something or an adjective qualifies him, they appear in the masculine form (in Hebrew there are male and female forms for verbs and adjectives). Thus, every verbal statement about God conveys the idea that he was masculine.... No subsequent teaching about the aphysical, incomprehensible or transcendent nature of the deity could eradicate this early mental image of the masculine God....[158]

Those of the *jnani* persuasion, right up to the time of David Hume, continued to resist the anthropomorphism of 'God' (though objections to his masculinity are more recent) while for the *bhakti*, or even for the ordinarily pious Christian, masculine anthropomorphism has always been a natural way of speaking. Languages with two genders, including Hebrew, always assign the male gender to 'God'. But even in a language with a third, neutral, gender, such as German, the same is true: 'Das Gott' is as unheard of as 'Die Gott'.

According to Baring and Cashford male deities prior to monotheism were sons, lovers and consorts to female deities, as Elohim probably was to the goddess Asherah in the Canaanite religion. The eradication of the goddess from Judaism took many centuries, and involved a male re-writing of Jewish history, but its legacy was to make late-Victorian Western scholars dismiss the goddess religions as 'fertility cults' and make difficult the emergence of feminist archaeology and anthropology. However, the Hellenic, just as much as the Hebraic, ensured that the feminine would be marginalised in the West through a parallel process of re-writing its own mythology to favour the masculine.

Just why it should be that cultures, not just in the West, seemed to have universally shifted from Goddess religions to warrior polytheism, or warrior monotheism, is not clear. Some suggest that iron weapons were the cause, or others, like Leonard Shlain, holds that it was due to the emergence of writing.[159] In Marija Gimbutas' extraordinary work, *The Language of the Goddess*, she explores the imagery of early Goddess cultures, but, unlike other scholarship in this area, her book does not pursue a textual argument; rather it revolves around a series of visual themes, profusely illustrated and commented on in short passages. Gimbutas promotes the idea of Goddess cultures as largely lacking in hierarchy and militarism: 'The Goddess-centred art with its striking absence of images of warfare and male domination, reflects a social order in which women as head of clans or queen-priestesses played a central part. Old Europe and Anatolia, as well as Minoan Crete were a gylany.'[160] Gimbutas has adopted the term 'gylany', coined by feminist Riana Eisler from *gy*- from 'woman' and *an*- from *andros*, 'man', and the letter 'l' to link them. A gylany is a peaceful society where men and women rule equally. Critics of Gimbutas think that she has overstated the case for peaceful advanced matriarchies in antiquity, but the strength of her book lies in its visual depictions. It needs to be approached effectively by artists, i.e. those who speak and are sensitive to a visual language, rather than by the male inheritors of the 'Word'. Looking at the huge number of illustrations in the book, one begins to see that Shlain's case is made stronger: the visual language is of the feminine and of nature in its sacred profusion. The fact that monotheism in many of its branches has been destructive of visual representations also lends support to the idea that iconoclasm was part of the suppression of the feminine. The emergence of feminism in the twentieth century and the renewed interest in Goddess religions in the last twenty-five years also coincide with the rapid growth of an intensely visual culture, and the decline of book-reading. Hence the alignment of feminism and an increased reliance on visual culture creates a specific and promising site for postsecularism. The relationship between future feminine spiritualities and a barely-recoverable past is, of course, the subject of much debate.

Starhawk and the Goddess Religions

Merlin Stone writes:

> I am not suggesting a return or revival of the ancient female religion.... I do hold hope, however, that a contemporary consciousness of the once-widespread veneration of the female deity as the wise Creatress of the Universe and all life and civilisation may be used to cut through the many oppressive and falsely founded patriarchal images, stereotypes, customs and laws that were developed as direct reactions to Goddess worship by the leaders of the later male-worshipping religions.[161]

Freud, Jung and de Beauvoir may have rested too many of their arguments on the scholarship of their day in archaeology and anthropology, unaware that those disciplines reflected many un-challenged assumptions of their own Western thought. As the disciplines progress, their arguments look dated. The fact that God-dess scholarship has begun to create the wider consciousness of early feminine religions that Stone is seeking is highly significant for the early twenty-first century. However, the disciplines of archaeology and anthropology will continue to throw up new findings, and in any case the reconstruction of ancient ways of life always contains large amounts of guesswork. In particular the interiority or lived experience of cultures which did not record their thoughts in writing is hard to enter – for that matter even ancient modes of writing can also be impenetrable.

For Starhawk what counts is the contemporary revival of the Goddess religion, mostly under the term 'witchcraft' or just 'craft'. She says: 'Witches, on the whole, are interested in discussions of our history. There are now conferences, magazines, articles, and panels at the American Academy of Religions on the subject. But that interest is separate from any sense that the validity of our spiritual choices depends on documenting their origins, their antiquity, or their provenance.'[162]

Starhawk was born as Miriam Simos in 1951, of Jewish parentage.

Her book *The Spiral Dance: A Rebirth of the Ancient Religion of the Great Goddess* was published in 1979, and has run into several editions since then. Her presence, listed as a 'witch' on the staff of radical theologian Matthew Fox's Institute for Culture and Creation Spirituality, was one of the causes for the attention of the 'Pope's Rottweiler', the then-Cardinal Ratzinger. Fox's attempts to bring about religious change within his Roman Catholic tradition have not been well received by the authorities, but his *jnani via positiva* orientation and focus on the natural world are both contemporary and appropriate to women's spirituality.

Starhawk herself has evolved in her thinking since the first publication of *The Spiral Dance*, being now more open to ideas from the East, and to Nature. She says: 'A few years ago, while meditating in – where else? – my garden, I received this message: "You're teaching too much meditation and not enough observation." '[163] Although she had defended Nature and 'had often gone to jail defending her' – for example in connection with non-violent direct action to save redwoods – she found that a deeper connection was needed. For Starhawk 'observation' includes both the scientific tradition (started with Leonardo da Vinci) and the way of the shaman or nature mystic who spends time with nature as a core spiritual practice. Women in the ancient Goddess religions, as far as we can tell, shared with the earlier shamanic systems the veneration of Nature. Whether Starhawk represents a *return* to the Goddess tradition or simply an expression of a modality of the spirit that is *a priori* part of our inner landscape does not matter. It is the equal weight given to each and every authentic modality of the spirit that is only made possible by the secular world, and which the Roman Catholic Church so unfortunately resists. Starhawk sums up very simply a difference between her religion and that of Christianity: 'The world is not a flawed creation, not something from which we must escape, not in need of salvation or redemption.'[164] In the global history of religion it seems that very few *men* have been able to say this – certainly not in monotheism.

Luce Irigaray

Feminism, growing up amongst other secular battles against religious conservatism, was a largely secular movement, as the work of de Beauvoir illustrates. But by the turn of the twenty-first century, perhaps because women had won many freedoms that had been an unconscionably long time coming, the question of spirituality and religion opened up again. While Hebraic 'religion' and Greek 'metaphysics' were male inventions, 'spirituality' could perhaps be more neutral; more than that, the secular world did not feed a hunger felt by the feminine spirit perhaps more keenly than by the masculine. In the re-opening of questions of the spirit, very different strategies present themselves to feminist thinkers than to males for whom the masculine 'God' is to one degree or another still palatable. For traditional feminist theologians there is always the possibility of some linguistic wrigglings on the part of the Church regarding the male 'God', and ordination of women priests as a first step in the Anglican community held out the promise of slow, but sure reform. More radical feminist theologians, however, are insisting on a re-writing of 'God' as 'Goddess', a strategy that can work to some degree in California, but not currently, for example, in Israel.

While postmodernism is a largely male enclave, there have in fact been a number of significant feminist thinkers within the movement. They have generally drawn on the same Marxist and psychoanalytical theories that Deleuze and Guattari, for example, have done. Luce Irigaray is remarkable, however, for re-evaluating the spiritual despite the atheist legacies of Marx and Freud within postmodernism. Both Derrida and Irigaray turned in their later writings to the question of religion, but their approaches have been radically different. Derrida and his followers have effectively re-opened the *via negativa* tradition of the West, the negative theology, at a time when the *via positiva*, since Aquinas, has become an unstoppable force. Irigaray, in contrast, has turned to the East and to the body, bringing her effectively into an alliance with Starhawk rather than Teresa of Avila.

Irigaray's 1999 book *Between East and West: from Singularity to Community* is an extraordinary work for a Continental postmodernist. Its title alone is both a rebuke to the insularity of the 'Greek' mode of philosophy, and to the solitary male. Instead of a merely Western outlook it draws on the Yoga tradition of Patanjali, and instead of the male 'singularity' it focuses on the relational. From Freud and Lacan to Deleuze and Guattari, the Oedipal myth is foundational: Irigaray steps outside of it by focussing on the East, the body, the breath, and the relationship between male and female. Her revolution against her teachers Lacan and Derrida is complete. In the introduction she says:

> Does not deconstruction, including through its recourse to innumerable linguistic ruses, remain trapped in a secular manner of know-how, and does it not imprison reason itself, . . . leading to a nihilistic madness as the ultimate Promethean gesture?[165]

She approves of the core motivation of deconstruction – which as we saw earlier was justice – but believes that one cannot 'break chains, reopen prisons, unveil lies and illusions' without recourse to the element of life itself, and in particular 'the first and last gesture of the natural and spiritual life: to breathe by oneself.'[166] Her accusation is at heart that philosophy has become ungrounded, cut off from the body and from relationship. She has particularly harsh words for Schopenhauer, finding his famously misogynist *Essay on Women* quite in keeping with the larger thesis that philosophy is a matter of death, and, for Irigaray, absolute patriarchy.[167]

Irigaray visited India in 1984 and studied yoga there, including *pranayama*, the spiritual practice of breathing. She was much impressed by what seemed to her to be the honoured remnants of an ancient Goddess culture, present in what she calls the 'aboriginal feminine'. She is not blind to the problems within India and its religions, saying: 'To be sure, there are in India tensions between feminine aboriginal cultures and patriarchal Aryan cultures. It is significant that Western philosophy recovers only the most Aryan elements of the Indian tradition.'[168] This is partly a North-South divide in India: the more ancient Dravidian culture was pushed to the south by warrior invasions far in the past. Irigaray's instincts and scholarship on such issues are born out by the work of academics such as J.J. Clarke[169] and David Loy,[170] who have made a life-long study of the relationship of the philosophies of East and West. Her emphasis on the breath is quite outside such scholarship however, and despite some rather imaginative and unfounded leaps in her thinking it connects her more to ancient practices like yoga, the Buddha's 'mindfulness of breathing', and to the thinking of ecologists like David Abram. But it is not clear, for example, why Irigary states that men and women breathe differently: to those who work with the psychotherapeutic possibilities of the breath it would be obvious that on the whole men and women breathe equally badly. (Irigaray does in fact point out that we breathe badly but does not elaborate.)[171] It is also obvious in the therapeutic situation that much pathology lies with the breath: the work of pioneering psychologist Wilhelm Reich has led generations of therapists to understand poor breathing as body armouring against the potential treachery of sexual desire. This is not mentioned by Irigaray.

Whatever the shortcomings of detail in her account of the breath, her work is nevertheless an astonishing opening within postmodernism to ideas of the East and of the body. As a French feminist she emphasises sexual difference (American feminists on the whole have focussed on equality), and is intrigued that yoga has understood since ancient times the bodily and spiritual differences between men and women. It is again perhaps a sign of the confidence that feminism has attained that the question of difference can be opened up again. Sexual difference, just like spiritual difference, can be comfortably explored only if the perceived or proposed dichotomies do not privilege one of the pairing over the other. She says, for example, that the Western tradition has privileged speech over life, and suggests that the breath is the meeting place of the two. Perhaps her most intriguing contribution is not much more than an aside: the reference to the possibility of an *accomplished interiority*.[172] She clearly understands this as the goal of the spiritual life, a goal not possible within the realm of a philosophy that privileges speech, the written word, and propositional logic. This simple but very meaningful phrase – an accomplished interiority – sums up what the reductionist worldview denies. At the same time Irigaray is clear, as in the subtitle of her book, that this accomplished interiority is not the pursuit of singularity, but of community. Marxist certainty that we are only social beings also pursues the goal of community, but founders because it focuses solely on the material circumstances of a person.

We can conclude that where feminism and spirituality come together we have a uniquely postsecular framing of thought. Feminism, or more broadly the equal role of women in all aspects of public and private life, is one of the genuine triumphs of secularism. Feminist scholars of the spiritual life bring out in their work the stark contrast between the presecular and the postsecular, particularly when presecular monotheism is pitted against the potential of postsecular spirituality. Where the Radical Orthodoxy wants to turn the clock back and potentially makes possible all the discredited monotheist traditions of misogyny, feminist spiritualities are rightly watchful against such retrenchment. Postsecular feminist spirituality does much more than guard against old prejudices, however – it also offers a re-assertion of an ancient modality of the spirit, and explores genuinely new ones.

Reflections and Conclusions

The contexts examined for postsecular leanings in Part Three are not an exhaustive list, nor within the categories so far can we be exhaustive: literature, for example, including the novel and poetry, represents a huge field to survey. Likewise in popular music, a field of similar proportion that needs thorough investigation to find material like Numan's anguished atheism which lives on the cusp of religiosity, and which is not simply a continuation of presecular musical genres and themes. In the field of medical practice there is some considerable interest in spirituality and health, and in business 'organisational spirituality' attracts conference attendance and funding from a wide range of medium sized companies and multinationals. News broadcasting has also undergone a change, within Britain at least, in terms of new sensitivities towards religion, as a recent House of Commons Select Committee report has discovered.[1]

One way of thinking about each of these varied postsecular contexts is as a 'social imaginary' as Charles Taylor defines the term. He thinks of this as 'something broader and deeper than the intellectual schemes people may entertain when they think about social reality . . .'[2] This is because the intellectual schemes – for example postmodernism – may belong only to a select few, whereas the social imaginary is widely inclusive. When we talk about 'social imaginaries' in the plural we begin talking about *sub-cultures*, and it is these that the postsecular contexts described above represent. Perhaps the largest postsecular subculture is, after all, the New Age, because it has an influence on such fields as transpersonal psychology, consciousness studies, literature and so on. But postsecularism is not coterminous with the New Age, because we find it in fields such as postmodernism and many sectors of the creative arts which are viscerally opposed to New Age ideas. Let us sum up the postsecular contexts so far.

The new physics has provoked many thinkers who have expounded from it the physics-supports-mysticism thesis. While some accept this uncritically others have sharpened the debate, creating an engagement between science and religion that is radically new. We saw that Ken Wilber has suggested in *Quantum Questions* that the thesis of physics-supports-mysticism is thrown into question by examining the writings of the quantum scientists themselves. These and other scientists, including John Polkinghorne, reflect on the relationship between science and the spiritual at a deeply informed and critical level. This is postsecular, rather than New Age, because they don't hold *a priori* assumptions concerning the future development of humankind; they are not prey to naïve Hegelianism, but pursue a proper science of *attempting* to distinguish between proven and unproven hypotheses, and the implications of these for the spiritual life.

In Consciousness Studies we have discovered a discipline deeply divided between the arch-reductionists of neuroscience, and those open to questions of the spirit. Those who broadly accept Chalmer's insistence on the 'hard problem' of consciousness allow for a dialogue between science and mysticism, in particular some of the profound Buddhist insights into consciousness. This debate has all the hallmarks of postsecular thinking. True, the field can also be prone to New Age assumptions and some very confused thinking, represented for example by the film *What the Bleep Do We Know* (2004), where the reductionist biochemistry of Candace Pert is somehow assumed to demonstrate feel-good New Age mysticism.[3] Despite this, however, the opening up of the question of consciousness and its possible relationship to religious thought of the ages is typically postsecular. It was simply not possible in the heyday of positivism.

In Transpersonal Psychology we have again a field that is quintessentially postsecular, but at the same time prone to New Age encroachments. In fact the clinical practitioners of transpersonal psychology are not that likely to find support for the founding principle of the New Age (imminent global transformation of consciousness) because many of their clients are generally struggling to become even normally well. What is postsecular about transpersonal psychotherapeutic interventions is that – in complete contradistinction to Freud – the question of the spiritual development of the client is foregrounded. Is the crisis a psychological one or a spiritual one? The key debate within transpersonal theory is around the issue of the 'transpersonal self', a debate intimately bound up with the spiritual question of transcendence.

Clearly the concept of the 'deep' New Age as evidence for postsecularism is most susceptible to challenge. But the argument here is that open, critical thinking has to cut two ways: New Age assumptions about the future are hypotheses that are often unprovable, and perhaps largely unfounded. But it is as unscientific to dismiss them out of hand as it is to assume their truth. Let the experiment run its course, and in the meantime let the hardest of Enlightenment insights rule: to say that we don't yet know. If we identify the 'deep' New Age with thinkers like Wilber, and with the overlap with the new physics, consciousness studies and transpersonal theory, then we have critical debates that engage with far-reaching questions of the spirit.

In Ecology and Nature Mysticism we have sober thinkers far removed from the New Age, more inclined to predict global catastrophe than impending utopia. The thought of the nature mystics, emerging in the mid-nineteenth century, has a particular and early location in postsecularism, being a simultaneous rejection of Church religion and refusal to succumb to secular reductionism. Ecology as a scientific discipline is, of course, secular in its mechanistic conception, but as it segues into ecosophy, it increasingly adopts the language of the 'whole' – it deploys the language of the mystic.

The creative arts represent a different postsecularism again – mostly opposed to anodyne New Age sentiment and more likely to explore the darker and more threatening aspects of the human psyche. The arts are Janus-faced: bitterly against Church authority on the one hand, yet often abandoning the key secular shibboleth of anti-spirituality on the other. As the wounded shamans of contemporary society, artists are expected to lead lives of irrationality and intensity, perhaps as the antidote in our 'two Cultures' society to the bleakness of reductionist science and technology. In Charles Taylor's terms they provide the 'anti-structure' in a world where social structure now mimics the 'exceptionless natural laws' of physics. The arts have licence to be spiritual if that serves their purpose, and hence represent a postsecularism active throughout the twentieth century and into the twenty-first.

In postmodernism we have the sphere of thought most removed from the New Age. Its hallmark is sophistication and convolution, where the New Age is naïve and direct: postmodernism permits the spiritual through its sophistry where the New Age does through naivety. Much of postmodernism may inherit the secular dismissal of the spiritual, but we have seen that some of its key thinkers use its deconstructive methods to re-open those questions. Above all, it gives license to adopt a critical stance towards modernity and secularism, though sometimes used as we have seen by old religion to *regress* rather than to be truly postsecular.

Finally, in feminism, with perhaps the most serious investment in getting rid of all vestiges of patriarchal religion, we have seen an opening up to questions of the spirit in a particularly radical way. While there are plenty of feminist thinkers still attacking old religion, we have suggested that women possibly mourn the loss of the spiritual life more than men (to which church attendance attests). As feminist scholars tackle questions of religion and explore the archaeology of Goddess cultures, they provide an enormous counterweight to the narrow patriarchal traditions of the past: they represent perhaps a key potential for postsecularism.

'If you are my answer, then I must have asked the wrong question', sings Gary Numan. The question of whether 'God' exists or not is the wrong question, because it does no useful work. Dennett quotes an old saw: 'Philosophy is questions that may never be answered. Religion is answers that may never be questioned.'[4] 'God' was an answer that could not be questioned in monotheism, but it is now a question with no useful answer. How could it have a useful answer within a social imaginary that now includes Buddhism and other non-Western systems of thought? But the various postsecular contexts that we have considered pose questions of the spirit, the very pursuit of which represents a renewed engagement with the spiritual life. The spiritual landscape after secularism reframes questions of the spirit, and re-energises them.

When we ask why 9/11 should apparently have engendered such a large-scale public debate on religion it seems that the issue of religious extremism is not a sufficient explanation. In addition, there was a head of steam built up since the 1970s in which 'permission' to think about spirituality and religion had slowly leaked into the social imaginary. If we couple this with the new sensitivity to religion, epitomised in Martin Amis's remark that he was no longer permitted to disparage any one religion, so he would disparage them all, then we can understand why McGrath and other new defenders of faith have found public voice again. So, if we ask where the growing sense of 'permission' to debate religion came from, it seems to have two sources: firstly the kind of postsecular contexts discussed in Part Three, perhaps initiated by Wilber's early books and *The Tao of Physics*, and secondly by the encounter with resurgent Islam. Postsecularism arises from the breaking down of the mutual ignorance pact or secular-religious détente, given impetus by 9/11.

The Western Détente

The word 'détente' is French for loosening or relaxing, and was applied in the Cold War when it appeared that tensions could be de-escalated between the superpowers. It has come to mean more generally a relationship between two groups that are endemically hostile to each other, or hold utterly incompatible worldviews, where the two parties enter into a pact to effectively tolerate each other but make no final attempt to settle the argument. There may be no violence, but no exchange of ideas can take place in détente either. This well describes the relationship between old religion and secularism: each was confined to its domain, and each seemed grateful that it did not have to examine its unfounded assumptions. The shibboleths of old religion were effectively guaranteed to old religion as were the shibboleths of secularism to the secular world. The challenge posed by Voltaire and the Enlightenment had in reality been ducked. The secular world, up to the recent new atheism debate, mostly did not criticise the Bible, but ignored it.

The standoff or détente between old religion and secularism left two incompatible worlds: the arid reductionist playground of secularism and the intellectual and cultural ghetto of old religion. The New Age was pursued oblivious to both.

The secular tradition of thought, and the University teaching of philosophy, portrays the Enlightenment philosophers shorn of their spiritual insights. David Hume is a good example: he was assumed atheist in his day, and is still assumed to be one by such eminent thinkers as Isaiah Berlin. However, even as a first approximation, this is false, and derives from confusing *anticlericalism* with atheism. Hume was writing against clericalism – the stranglehold on thought and action of Church tradition – and also what was known in those days as *enthusiasm*. It is proposed here that to really rethink the Enlightenment a more radical analysis is needed than is provided by commentators to date, an analysis based on the concepts of *bhakti* and *jnani*, devotional and non-devotional religiosity. Most of the Enlightenment thinkers were either nascent or fully-developed *jnanis*, i.e. they were guided by a non-devotional spiritual impulse which manifested itself in an anti-anthropomorphic stance: they pushed for a deity shorn of human attributes. Hume does this, and in his stance against *enthusiasm*, shows another typical *jnani* trait: a distaste for religious emotionality. Criticism of the predominant religiosity of the day it may have been, but atheism it was not.

We saw in *Secularism* that Blaise Pascal was an exception amongst Enlightenment literati: his instincts were more *bhakti* – devotional

– and he most usefully gave us the terminology by which to describe the deity which Hume and the other *jnani* thinkers (and Antony Flew) acknowledged: the 'God of the philosophers'. As a broad generalisation this can be called a Deist principle, bound up with the Argument from Design, which Hume quite explicitly signs up to. It is that Deism which held the promise of an Enlightenment religion – one in which 'God' could be conceived of in much more abstract terms (such as the Plotinian 'One', Hume's 'Mind', or Hegel's 'Spirit') – but which foundered on Darwinism, and was quietly and with great relief buried both by the Christian world and the secular one. From there the détente described above has emerged, one which allowed both sides to abandon the difficult project of mutual comprehension.

But the most promising aspect of the new atheism debate, remarked upon earlier, is that both sides are reading within the domains of their opponents with an appetite not seen since the Enlightenment: religionists are reading science and atheists are reading religion. The motives at this stage are not necessarily postsecular, being more often the desire to construct negative arguments, but the possibility remains that this debate, being energised in a way not seen for centuries, will improve mutual understanding rather than reinforce the old hostilities. As we saw, John Humphrys perhaps leads the debate in this respect, being at the same time unconvinced that the new atheists are right – suspicious as he is of their dogmatic shrillness – and yet quite capable of detecting intolerance and dogmatism in old religion. Most usefully he observes that the British public have lost their *reticence* in respect of religion. The American public may never have been so reticent perhaps (the 'American exception'?), but the new debate is just as galvanising there.

Postsecularism and the Hidden Challenge to Extremism

The new atheists are mounting an obvious and highly visible challenge to extreme religion. Both sides of the new atheism debate agree to condemn religious violence, but they disagree on how to tackle it. *Viscerally*, the more fanatical of the new atheists want to end religious extremism by ending religion itself, even though in more rational moments they admit that this is a hopeless prospect. Nevertheless they carry the torch of anti-extremism. Suggestions of a symmetry of fanaticism between the sides are exaggerated, because atheists are not violent, but the rhetoric on both sides can be as immoderate. C.S. Lewis in *Mere Christianity*, the book that has influenced so many new defenders of faith, and which is quoted by Hitchens, says that if witches existed they probably ought to be hanged as 'filthy quislings'.[5] (Sadly Francis Collins, as a disciple of Lewis, seems unable to condemn this proposition.)[6] Sam Harris, by chance, uses the same intransigent language when he says: 'many believers have taken refuge in Stephen J. Gould's quisling formulation of "nonoverlapping magisteria..." '.[7] To use the term 'quisling', meaning traitor, is extreme, and is just the kind of language which a sharp commentator like Humphrys picks up on, and which motivates his rejection of its author's views.

But will the challenge posed by extreme atheists work? It might confirm in some what they already know, and will help others to become more vociferous in what was a lazy secularism. Some will join the Secular Society of Great Britain or the Council for Secular Humanism in America. But, to the extent that the new atheists want to end religious extremism by ending religion itself, such an approach is bound to fail. In the cases of the most uncompromising subscribers to what is called here the 'Black Mass Fallacy' there seems to be a belief that by ending religion *all* extremism will be ended. The more moderate atheists do agree, however reluctantly, that it is the job of moderate religion to curb extreme religion. This is also the position of the new defenders of faith, and is best summed up by Keith Ward's insistence that religions have the resources within them to do this. Yet Harris is right to some degree, at least, to say that religious moderation is the product of secular knowledge and scriptural ignorance. For religion to put its house in order it clearly needs help from the secular world but the secular world needs to acknowledge that religious violence is not just violence *by* religion but also *against* religion. The majority of the faithful are wounded in their faith by the violence of the few.

But religion cannot accept help from the secular world while the legacy of the mutual ignorance pact exists. The secular world largely lost the intellectual tools by which to approach religion, Marx, for example, having comprehensively discredited them for all of left-leaning Western thought. If postsecularism really emerges as a coherent framework of thought, then it is placed to achieve just what moderate atheists and the new defenders of faith are seeking: a means to provide or strengthen the resources within religion to purge itself of extremism. Postsecularism as we have described it is not, however, an easy option for either side, and so represents a challenge to extreme thought in religion *and* in atheism. To the extent that postsecularism is only just emerging as an option, it is a *hidden* challenge. Let us see how this challenge could work out in practice by returning to Dawkins and his unwoven rainbow.

The Violence of Category Reduction

It was suggested earlier that the argument between science and religion is a mistake of categories, where Dawkins and creationists each deny the categories of the other (though it is much harder within the contemporary social imaginary to credibly deny the category of science). To deny a category is to dismiss it as illusion or irrelevant. When Queen Victoria refused her ministers' request to outlaw lesbianism, she was replacing the potential violence of legal persecution of a sexual minority with a violence that denied their very existence. Lesbians were spared prosecution but were denied a legitimate social category. When Dawkins say that religion is a 'know nothing' and 'no contest' domain of human endeavour, he is inflicting a category denial (violence of the second kind), though his humanist ethics would recoil at the banning of religion and prosecution of its adherents (violence of the first kind). Harris, more alarmingly, *does* contemplate violence of the first kind. Dawkins explicitly rejects Stephen Jay Gould's concept of Non Overlapping Magisteria (NOMA), reasoning that religion is not a valid magisterium or category because it does not offer explanations that match those of science.

'Religion' is a cathected word, as the discussion in *Secularism* of the 'spiritual wounds of the West' has shown, and one cannot rehabilitate it by fiat. Nevertheless, the Two-Fold Model shows religion – or spirituality if one prefers that word – to be vastly more than monotheism, to be a magisterium that requires extensive travel deep into its hinterland rather than petulant stone-throwing at a single narrow border. Gould's NOMA is the intellectually more generous position, because it respects a domain of human experience and endeavour not familiar to the outsider. To reject religion as a magisterium on the basis of its worst outcomes – well documented and lamentable as they are – is as absurd as rejecting science on the basis of its worst outcomes.

The Abrahamic fundamentalist and those pursuing scientism make the same mistake: they believe that all of human experience, knowledge and endeavour must fall within a *single* category. This is a monoculture of the mind that is in itself a kind of mild autism, a desire for certainty, a desire to deny the unknown. It is found in the brittle intellects of highly intelligent and educated people, and also in the ignorant and stupid. In more technical terms we can describe this as *epistemological monism* – that is, the belief that there is only one kind of knowledge or knowing. Its converse is epistemological pluralism, its corollary a methodological pluralism – and Gould's concept of NOMA is an elegant starting point for its articulation. The word 'magisterium' naturally conjures up a domain worthy of respect, even if we know little of its workings, and suggests a set of geopolitical metaphors. Those that live in one magisterium who speak about another should do so out of respect for its inhabitants and customs, and above all should do so out of a *knowledge* of the other domain. The positive aspect of the new atheism debate appears to be a growing effort to acquire knowledge of the other's magisterium.

Dawkins' hero is Isaac Newton: the founder of modern science, or rather physics. The phenomenally predictive accuracy of physics is due to its phenomenally narrow domain of enquiry, as Polkinghorne points out. Galileo set this out: a questioning of the behaviour of lifeless matter in terms of its primary qualities, which are mass, length and time. The magisterium of science is defined by this narrow remit, put beautifully and succinctly by Descartes as the domain of 'extended stuff'. But mind, consciousness, love, beauty and ethics – for starters – do not belong to that domain, and are not within the remit of science, a domain that Newton set aside after his seminal work in order to concentrate on the domain of esoteric religion. Religious, spiritual and mystical experiences are not in the domain of science: these two magisteria lived separately and with equal weight in Newton, as they do today in Polkinghorne. The range of human experience that lies outside of science is vast compared to what lies within it, hence an attempt to reduce human experience to the single magisterium of science is a form of far-reaching violence. The love that dare not speak its name is silenced by science: that is oppression.

Two Cultures – Three Magisteria
While there is a regrettable historical basis for the antagonism between science and religion, where Dawkins has gone much further is in his attempt to deny the magisterium known in the Two Cultures debate as the 'arts'. We saw that in his book *Unweaving the Rainbow* Dawkins takes a series of nineteenth-century poets and attempts to arrogate their achievements to the domain of science, effectively performing a second category reduction. Having denied the category of religion he now arrogates the category of 'poetry' to science. The absurdity of his position on the arts illustrates the absurdity of his position on religion.

Dawkins clearly feels the beauty of a rainbow or the flora and fauna which are the subjects of his zoological training, and in the Romantic poets he finds a kindred spirit. But he is pained by Keats' insistence that the Newtonian understanding of the rainbow 'unweaves' it – destroys its mystery – and by Yeats' dismissal of science as the 'opium of the suburbs'. The rainbow serves in fact as a poignant symbol of secularism: it was the subject of the *experimentum crucis* which Michael White believes dates the birth of modern science. We can look at Dawkins' arguments around it, and show that he has confused two very different aesthetics, *neither* of which have their origins in science. Aesthetics, which deals with the gestalt of wholes, cannot have a mechanical basis in matter, in the mass, length and time of the parts. Dawkins' argument, in a nutshell, is that the physics of the rainbow does not detract from its beauty and mystery; on the contrary, an understanding of the science adds to it. But his conclusion is absurd: he says that because science adds to the beauty of the rainbow, it shows that poetry *derives* from science.

Dawkins says that 'word for word, I wish I had written the following famous quatrain . . .' referring to William Blake's poem *Auguries of Innocence*:

> To see the world in a grain of sand
> And heaven in a wild flower
> Hold infinity in the palm of your hand
> And eternity in an hour.

Dawkins reproduces these lines in a crucial early chapter of *Unweaving the Rainbow* where he deals with the poets. He follows Blake's poem with this statement:

> The stanza can be read as all about science, all about standing in the moving spotlight, about taming space and time, about the very large built from the quantum graininess of the very small, a lone flower as a miniature of all of evolution. The impulse to awe, reverence and wonder which led Blake to mysticism (and lesser figures to paranormal superstition as we shall see) are precisely those that lead others of us to science.[8]

Just about every sentiment expressed in this passage is based on a reductionist misconception, except that Blake shares with Dawkins an initial 'impulse to awe, reverence and wonder'. From that initial state the two minds – and magisteria – diverge radically. At least Dawkins admits that the initial inspiration is outside of science, but the key difference between the mystic and the scientist, or between the religious mind and the scientific mind, lies in the issue of *explanation*. Dawkins responds to the grain of sand and the wild flower by pursuing the question of mechanism: how does the flower arise from the mineral substratum of an Earth originally presumed inanimate? To pursue the science of the sand and flower is to pursue the part – ever smaller parts receding to DNA and quantum particle. In Leibniz's *Monadology* such a quest has only an arbitrary terminating point as 'explanation': for Dawkins it is the gene. But to pursue the part is to lose the whole – which Leibniz understood keenly as a man who dedicated his life to multiple magisteria, including both science and religion. When Dawkins wrings his hands over Blake's comparison of science to 'an iron scourge over Albion / Reasonings like vast Serpents Infold around my limbs . . .' he entirely misses the point. 'Reasonings' are well visualised as serpents infolding around one's limbs because they remove the self from the immediate presence of the sand and flower and propel one into the mental cage of fevered ratiocination. This world of logical deduction, based on the close observation of nature, has its own aesthetics of course, but it is of a completely different order to that of the poetical and mystical. Newton forced the first Astronomer Royal, John Flamsteed, to endlessly squint up the great telescope in Greenwich at the stars to gather data, but that gaze was narrowed, purposeful and always serving the *part* – not the *whole*. Did Flamsteed ever take a break on a summer's night and fling himself on the grass by the Royal Observatory, look up, and just absorb the heavens – as a *whole*? If so, he would have shifted into the realm of the poet and the mystic.

When Blake talks about seeing the world in a grain of sand, he is recapitulating the entire Neoplatonist and Renaissance tradition of the microcosm. This is a perception that is not just *beyond* ratiocination, it is one that actively *requires* the suspension of rational part-processing language-based 'Reasonings', in favour of the immediate, unmediated, apperception of the whole. Such apperception steps outside of time and location, hence Blake's instinctive use of the terms 'infinity' and 'eternity'. There is *no* possible translation of these terms when used in their mystical sense into the domain of space and time as used by a scientist: Descartes understood this as well as Blake. For Dawkins to say that Blake's poem is about 'taming space and time' is to make a category mistake of the first order – one that almost defines the secular mind. Blake was untameable, and wished to tame nothing, least of all the mysteries of time and space. 'Explanations' would merely profane what Blake held to be sacred.

Dawkins says that Blake's rejection of science is a 'waste of poetic talent'. He follows with: 'It is my thesis that poets could better use the inspiration provided by science and that at the same time scientists must reach out to the constituency that I am identifying with, for

want of a better word, poets.' [9] One can only shudder at the idea of
scientists 'reaching out' in a Dawkins-like manner to the domain of
poetry, i.e. the arts (as we saw, Dennett attempts this through meme
theory). For Dawkins 'reaching out' appears to consist of providing a
small list of suitable topics – those in science – and an embargo on all
those that (rightfully) question the arrogance of scientism. Dawkins
says that monotheism should not dictate to Einstein the manner of
his spirituality.[10] Bravo. But science should live by the same principle;
it should not dictate to Blake, or to the arts in general, their subject
matter or opinions.

But we need to proceed a little more slowly: we are not dealing
with a 'Two Cultures' debate as is David Lodge's novel *Thinks . . . ,*
but rather with three magisteria: science, religion and the arts.
As a starting point Gould's NOMA is important, because it gives
each domain its dignity and integrity: no one domain should be
compromised or co-opted by any other. But what happens along the
boundaries *is* interesting, and Dawkins forces us to take this seriously.
He is starting with a feeling – a feeling, note – of awe and wonder.
More specifically this arises, he says, in contemplation of the natural
world, and is heightened by a knowledge of science. But it does not
start from science. So, the question is raised: in which domain or
magisterium does a feeling of awe and wonder, a cosmo-theophany,
properly belong? On the basis of our definition of spirituality as a
profound connectedness, we have proposed that awe and wonder
properly belong to the domain of religion. When confronted with
the 'grandeur of life' – whether in a situated specific rainbow over
a rain-swept meadow, or in the reading of Newton's *Optics* – one
experiences an expansion of self that gives rise to awe and wonder.
This expansiveness is paradoxical: it both makes the self small and
vast – all at the same time. Hence this feeling is powerful, knocks one
out of self-absorbedness, and connects one to the greater scheme of
things. *Profound connectedness* is a movement to the whole, not the
part. A movement to the whole is religion, a movement to the part is
science. One is holistic, the other atomistic.

Religion is not the exclusive domain of literalist Abrahamic
monotheism; awe and wonder arise across the very varied
hinterlands of the spiritual life, a landscape mapped out with the
Two-Fold Model of Spiritual Difference. Awe and wonder as a
religious or spiritual experience might belong to either a *bhakti* or
a *jnani* modality of the spirit, though, we will suggest, where Blake
and Dawkins are concerned it becomes a *jnani* impulse. Dawkins and
Einstein both say that such an impulse lies behind science, or behind

the human strivings that eventually reveal the laws of science, but they cannot show that it is *within* science, or co-opt it to science. The impulse to awe and wonder might lie along the boundaries between science and religion, but as it moves towards the different heartlands of those domains, it becomes an utterly different phenomenon. If we imagine, in this geopolitical metaphor, that the arts represent a third territory, then awe and wonder move from its boundary with religion in a yet different way: its manifestation is *creativity*.

The Two-Fold Model lets us hone this argument further, through the polarity of *via positiva* and *via negativa*. Awe and wonder might arise in the renunciative *via negativa* traditions of Christianity and Buddhism, for example, but they make no natural move to either the arts or science. In Christianity it becomes the *jnani fascinans tremendum* of Otto, or it might become the impetus to a *bhakti via negativa* mysticism like that of Teresa of Avila. In Buddhism it might become veneration towards the 'three jewels' – Buddha, *dharma*, and *sangha*. But when awe and wonder arise as a *jnani via positiva* impulse, then that impulse may move towards science as with Newton and so many Enlightenment thinkers, or towards the arts, as with Blake and so many Romantic poets and inheritors of the Neo-platonist traditions. But because the Christian tradition is at its core *bhakti via negativa*, and the move to *jnani via positiva* was resisted as Christianity rejected both the Renaissance and the Enlightenment, there is no Christian language to rebut Dawkins. In fact Alister McGrath and Tina Beattie make a good attempt, but, as typically modern Christians they offer only that Augustine and Aquinas demonstrate the rationality of religion.[11] 'Rationality' is the wrong instrument to defend Christianity against science; the failure of the Argument from Design makes that clear. The Two-Fold Model, on the other hand, gets right to the heart of the issue.

Let us return to the rainbow again. Dawkins quotes from Leonardo da Vinci, Wordsworth, Coleridge, and Ruskin on the subject of rainbows, laying down the challenge that science adds to our appreciation of the rainbow, in the face of Keats' or Blake's or D.H. Lawrence's insistence that 'cold philosophy' makes all her 'charms fly'. We saw in chapter ten, 'Postsecularism and Nature', that Arne Naess provides the best clue to the sense of awe and wonder that Nature inspires when he talks about the specific sense of place that, say, a mountain or rock gives to experience. Dawkins chose a passage from Wordsworth which was the poet's response to a *specific* rainbow, in a *specific* place (in the Lake District). It was framed by wind and cloud; beyond that we have to imagine the totality of the experience including a myriad other sensations. What Newton did in his *experimentum crucis* was to abstract from the rainbow that which could be measured: he brought colour from its place in sense perception into the scientific world of number. In doing so he not only extracted what was universal out of what was particular in each rainbow – for the poet and mystic at least, and perhaps we could also say for every child – but also developed the theory of its *mechanism*. It is precisely the mechanism of the rainbow which Dawkins believes should invoke awe and wonder in us. Yes, there is undoubtedly an aesthetic response to scientific explanations of natural phenomena like the rainbow, a kind of aesthetic that might also be a response to an elegant game of chess, or to the circuitous solving of an apparently intractable crime. But, as already pointed out, these explanations require a sequence of reasoning. One can see a rainbow, made specific by its location (across water under lowering autumn clouds, or perhaps segmented by the complex industrial architecture of an oil refinery), and then rehearse the scientific chain of reasoning that tells the story of its mechanism. The poet and mystic engage in the first manner. According to Dawkins (and he draws on physicist Richard Feynman in support) the scientist immeasurably expands the 'merely' mystical or poetic appreciation by engaging in the second. The mystic is propelled to a direct experience of eternity, the poet to words that might capture that feeling – and the scientist to a mental rehearsal of Newton's *experimentum crucis*. But the wonder in the initial revelation grows the weaker with repetition: as noted, it quickly joins all other explanations in the 'dull catalogue of common things'.

The real problem with the scientific response to the rainbow is that it can only ever be a rehearsal. What makes this response utterly different to the mystical or poetic response is that it is an exchange of the unknown, immediate, and unexpected, for the *known*. When the fox turns to look into one's eyes – unexpectedly, heart-stoppingly – one's boundaries are dissolved, the buffered self becomes for a brief instant porous again, *if and only if* ratiocination of any kind is stilled. (Though by all means ratiocinate after the event; all things in their proper place.) The sudden sense of awe and wonder of the situated specific rainbow is a rush of feeling to the heart and mind; the recapitulation of the laws of reflection, refraction, density, electromagnetic spectrum and the science of human perceptual systems is a retreat from the unknown to the known. The great *jnani* spiritual teacher of the twentieth century, Jiddu Krishnamurti, characterised the meditative state as *freedom from the known*.[12]

(Dionysius, father of the great Western tradition of unknowing, gave us *agnosia* as the equivalent.) It is the unknown which kindles awe and wonder, but Dawkins' science does exactly what Keats complains of: it unweaves the rainbow into a process, a mechanism.

We saw that Dawkins asks: 'Could anyone seriously suggest that it *spoils* it to be told what is going on inside all those thousands of falling, sparkling, reflecting and refracting populations of raindrops?'[13] 'Spoil' is perhaps not quite right: 'substitute' is better. Dawkins substitutes the aesthetic of scientific explanation for the aesthetic of the wild, dangerous, unknowable moment of awe that natural phenomena trigger in the mystical and poetic mind. But each rainbow occurs in a *different* setting, its locatedness makes each experience of the rainbow unique, and that includes even the mood of the person who perceives it. But how many times can one be moved by the *same* scientific explanation? Or the *same* audacious chess opening? Or the *same* account of an intractable crime finally solved? These are aesthetics of a different order, not conflatable to the mystical or poetic, and belonging to radically different magisteria. Yes, the magisterium of science is vast and magnificent, and Dawkins can take us on an exhilarating journey from the rainbow through the Fraunhofer lines in its spectrum to atomic theory and quantum mechanics. All very good, but this is an aesthetic that is ratiocinative, not sensual, unterminating in the Leibnizian sense, but finished in another sense: how can one add to the visible spectrum or the periodic table or the human genome? Once discovered they belong to the realm of the known, while the world of the mystic and the poet is not bounded in this fashion. And, as Blake says, the bounded is loathed by its possessor. The mystics do not need an ever bigger cyclotron or radio telescope to explore the boundaries of the unknown; they contemplate the natural, sacred, and subjective worlds at first hand, unmediated by instruments.

'Knowledge' in Different Magisteria

This brings us back to Dawkins' key accusation: that the 'knowledge' provided by religion is bogus. We saw in *Secularism* that Augustine was exercised by this question in respect of his former religion, Manichaeism, and one can suggest that Augustine's reflections on this provide a defining statement as to the nature of religion itself. Augustine says: 'But who asked that any Manichee should write about science as well as religion, when we can learn our duty to God without a knowledge of these things?' He goes on to say of his brother Christian : '[I] think it no harm to him that he does not know the true facts about material things, provided that he holds no beliefs unworthy of you, O Lord, who are the Creator of them all.' We don't need to believe in 'God' to understand the principle here. Onfray didn't need to believe in 'God' to feel a deep respect for his Muslim desert guide.

The creationists who Dawkins does battle with are misguided to challenge modern science from the position of biblical literalism, but they are the true inheritors of Augustine's statement, which, in the domain of religion, is not foolishness but a profound wisdom. If we take this passage from Augustine's *Confessions* and interpret it in a non-literal and non-realist way with respect to 'God', then it simply asserts priorities in the spiritual life. To hold a theistic belief in the 'Creator' may simply be another way of expressing awe and wonder at creation; to have faith is infinitely more important than mere mechanistic knowledge. Dawkins *simply cannot show* that it does harm to a Christian to hold that creation began four thousand years ago rather than four billion years ago. The meadow, the mountain, the gathering storm clouds, the rainbow: these are only known in the moment. The *fascinans tremendum* arises on the spot, comes from nowhere, is a movement from the known to the unknown, and – in the magisterium of religion – the plodding ratiocinative rehearsal of the science of the rainbow is irrelevant. How could the date of the Earth's origin matter a jot in such a moment?

To attack Darwinism from the position of biblical literalism is a form of ignorance. To attack religion from the position of scientific reductionism is also a form of ignorance. Dawkins' *Guardian* article just four days after 9/11 was titled 'Religion's misguided missiles'. His analysis was predictable: because religion teaches that there is life after death, the suicide bomber can be motivated to any kind of atrocity. He says that the promise of paradise in the after-life might tempt young men to kill themselves. 'Would they fall for it?' he asks. 'Yes, testosterone-sodden young men too unattractive to get a woman in this world might be desperate enough to go for 72 virgins in the next.' His anger is understandable, but his article is an insult to Islam, to religion in general, and probably to the attractiveness of the young men he is talking about. He concludes: 'To fill a world with religion, or religions of the Abrahamic kind, is like littering the streets with loaded guns. Do not be surprised if they are used.' But what about atomic weapons? If the world is filled with science, is that not like littering the streets with loaded guns? Weapons of war accumulate in arsenals, and guns litter the cities of America, because the ballistics of Leonardo, Galileo and Newton, and the chemistry of Lavoisier, Priestley and Nobel make them effective. Do the devastated cities of Hiroshima and Nagasaki not show that science also leads to slaughter? What about Chernobyl and the thousands of farmers across Europe with contaminated livestock? To err is to be human, and it may yet be that errors committed in the name of science will prove far more deadly than errors committed in the name of religion. But the errors don't invalidate the magisterium: they call for the deeper application of intelligence to the magisterium. A much deeper application of scientific intelligence is called for to solve the world's problems: Dawkins rightly insists on better scientific education. A deeper application of religious intelligence is perhaps even more urgent, but to insult religion is to make it *more* dangerous, not less, by placing it beyond intelligent debate. Spiritual education on the scale of scientific education is called for. A spiritual literacy is urgently needed in Western culture to match its scientific literacy. Dawkins demands a considerable scientific imagination in order to engage with his 'Mount Improbable'; a religious imagination of the same order is needed to engage with religion.

A Scientific Culture is an Autistic Culture
The secular world is largely in agreement with Dawkins on religion: it denies it as a valid magisterium. There are even signs that the secular world might abandon the magisterium of the *arts* to science, which is plainly what Dawkins is calling for. In David Lodge's *Thinks* . . . the female protagonist Helen, representing the arts, is seduced and abandoned by the male protagonist Messenger, representing science. Lodge is clearly against the move by science to co-opt the arts, but the very attention he gives to the cognitive sciences strengthens their cultural reach. Cognitive science and neurology are the glittering snakes in whose glare the rabbits of art and poetry are, it seems, transfixed. The neurologising of self is more than the unweaving of the rainbow, it is the unweaving of entire inner world of love, intuition, experience and connectedness: the very world that Lodge believes to be the domain of poetry and literature. But that domain needs the bulwark of the spiritual, a renewed spirituality more potent than the tired Roman Catholicism that Helen draws on, which is insufficient as counterweight to Messenger's predatory sexuality – and predatory reductionism. In the cold light of secularism poetry has to deny its spiritual source. A contemporary disenchanted culture has two powerful sources: Marxism (on the wane) and scientism (on the march). Marx said that religion was the illusory happiness of the people: he was wrong, as the collapse of communism and the

revival of religion in Russia shows. Religious happiness is what the profound connectedness of the spiritual life provides, whether in its inward manifestation as meditation and prayer, or in its outward manifestation in the life of the *sangha* and in compassion and charity for others.

Dawkins' selfish gene is a thrilling story, but it does not account for *what it is like to be me*. It does not account for lived experience, indeed there is no direct experiential correlate to 'gene'; its appearance on computer screens is merely a visualisation of the end-result of a thought process, a digital representation of a model originally built out of sticks by Watson and Crick. It may 'explain' everything, but it means nothing, because it is a story at the wrong level of hierarchy. One may thrill at the story of the selfish gene, as one does at chess played by a grand master, or at a murder mystery. But one shuts the book ... and *lives*. No genes there. Likewise neurons and peptides: the story is thrilling, and it evokes an aesthetic ratiocinative response in the intellect, but neurons and peptides are not part of *experience*. There is no experiential correlate of neuron and peptide; they are not part of *what it is like to be* a human being. Damasio, as all reductionists must do, denies Descartes his *res cogitans*, the domain of unextended mind, soul, love, thought and feeling. 'Damasio's Error' – as characterised here – is the desire to 'to move the spirit from its nowhere pedestal to a somewhere place' – perhaps the defining error of contemporary scientism. It is meta-science, not science. This error is to deny Chalmer's 'hard problem' of personal conscious experience. Its cultural repercussion is a retreat to anything that can replace it: Prozac, cocaine ... or even science as the 'opium of the suburbs'. Science unweaves not just the rainbow but the Self: its personal lived experience and its sacred cosmic dimension are reduced to quarks or chemistry. In return the secular world hands out 'Reasonings like vast Serpents' that 'Infold' around our limbs, and in the stark terror of this meaninglessness we are offered sex, cocooned physical security, murder mysteries, and if we feel a little nauseous, then Prozac can make us 'better than well'.

Conclusions

A hidden challenge might seem a contradiction in terms, but really it means a quiet refusal of extremes. If postsecularism is to present itself as a coherent intellectual framework from which extremism in religion can be challenged, it will need to find a voice beyond the occasional use of the term, as for example in Caputo's or Taylor's work. It has been shown that postsecularism is not the same as postmodernism, the New Age, or the religious left, but has some common ground with each. It is not postmodernism, although postmodernism is pluralist, because postsecularism prefers a 'hermeneutics of trust' over a 'hermeneutics of suspicion'. It is not the New Age, although the New Age is open to questions of the spirit, because postsecularism pursues critical enquiry. It is not the religious left, although the religious left is just as dispersed, because postsecularism finds both monotheism and Marxism inadequate starting points. It is a thread that runs through much of moderate religion, though it has no necessary indebtedness to old religion. It is not quite the 'nova' of Charles Taylor, because it is not religion by other means: it is *explicitly* spiritual, without subterfuge. Like 'ecosophy', postsecularism is a speculative coinage; there may be multiple postsecularisms like Naess's conception of multiple ecosophies. One postsecularism might adhere to NOMA, while another might prefer the hierarchical formulations of the Leibniz-Koestler-Wilber tradition.

For postsecularism to develop and gain cultural momentum, the scientism of recent times will need to abate: we need to undo 'Damasio's Error'. There is an appetite for this. Charles Taylor speaks of the heroism of the modern misanthropic stance, saying 'The heroism consists in continuing to live in the face of the perceived meaninglessness and worthlessness of life.'[14] But increasingly this heroic misanthropy appears strained, as shown by commentators like John Humphrys, who notice the new loss of reticence over questions of the spirit. Heroic misanthropy is not just uncomfortable, but actually not heroic at all: merely a cultural autism, the narcissism of self-sufficiency.

This volume begins a collecting together of what is dispersed: a renewed openness to questions of the spirit, appearing in widely differing cultural contexts or social imaginaries. It is an advocacy of the spiritual life, and an encouragement to further gather the postsecular diaspora of thought into a coherent framework, which quietly undoes both extremism in religion and the atheist reaction to it.

References

Introduction (pages 5-7)

1. Amis, Martin, *The Second Plane: September 11, 2001-2007*, London: Jonathan Cape, 2008, p. x

Part One: Towards a Postsecular Sensibility (pages 9-47)

1. This was the conclusion of *Secularism*.
2. Flew, Antony, *There is a God: How the World's Most Notorious Atheist Changed His Mind*, New York: HarperOne, 2007, p. xvi
3. Humphrys, John, *In God We Doubt: Confessions of a Failed Atheist*, London: Hodder & Stoughton, 2007, p. 298
4. Humphrys, John, *In God We Doubt: Confessions of a Failed Atheist*, London: Hodder & Stoughton, 2007, p. 186
5. Taylor, Charles, *A Secular Age*, Cambridge, MA and London: The Belknap Press of Harvard University Press, 2007, p. 331
6. Taylor, Charles, *A Secular Age*, Cambridge, MA and London: The Belknap Press of Harvard University Press, 2007, p. 439
7. Taylor, Charles, *A Secular Age*, Cambridge, MA and London: The Belknap Press of Harvard University Press, 2007, p. 729
8. Nanamoli, Bhikku and Bhodi, Bhikku, *The Middle Length Discourses of the Buddha: A New Translation of the Majjhima Nikaya*, Boston: Wisdom Publications, 1995, p. 260
9. Taylor, Charles, *A Secular Age*, Cambridge, MA and London: The Belknap Press of Harvard University Press, 2007, p. 15
10. Tillich, Paul, *Dynamics of Faith*, New York: Harper Torchbooks, 1957, p. 1
11. King, Mike, *Secularism: The Hidden Origins of Disbelief*, Cambridge: James Clarke & Co., 2007, section 5.1
12. Beattie, Tina, *The New Atheists: The Twilight of Reason & The War on Religion*, London: Darton, Longman and Todd, 2007, p. 10
13. King, Mike, *Secularism: The Hidden Origins of Disbelief*, Cambridge: James Clarke & Co., 2007, ch. 2
14. Chadwick, Owen, *The Secularization of the European Mind in the Nineteenth Century*, Cambridge: Cambridge University Press, 1975, p. 164

15. King, Mike, *Secularism: The Hidden Origins of Disbelief*, Cambridge: James Clarke & Co., 2007, p. 18

16. Dawkins, Richard, *The God Delusion*, London: Black Swan, 2007, p. 78

17. Dennett, Daniel C., *Breaking the Spell: Religion as a Natural Phenomenon*, London: Penguin Books, 2007, p. 30

18. Dennett, Daniel C., *Breaking the Spell: Religion as a Natural Phenomenon*, London: Penguin Books, 2007, p. 120

19. Grayling, A.C., *Against All Gods: Six Polemics on Religion and an Essay on Kindliness*, London: Oberon Books, 2007, p. 31

20. Dennett, Daniel C., *Breaking the Spell: Religion as a Natural Phenomenon*, London: Penguin Books, 2007, p. 71

21. Wilber, Ken, *The Marriage of Sense and Soul*, Dublin: Gateway, 1998, pp. 17-20

22. Watson, Peter, *A Terrible Beauty: The People and Ideas that Shaped the Modern Mind*, London: Phoenix, 2000, p. 20

23. Cited in Lodge, David, *Consciousness and the Novel*, London: Secker and Warburg, 2002, p. 16

24. Flew, Antony, *There is a God: How the World's Most Notorious Atheist Changed His Mind*, New York: HarperOne, 2007, p. xix

25. Ricoeur, Paul, *Freud and Philosophy: An Essay on Interpretation*, New Haven, CT and London: Yale University Press, 1970, p. 32

26. Kramnick, Isaac (ed.), *The Portable Enlightenment Reader*, London: Penguin, 1995, p. 26

27. Dawkins, Richard, *The God Delusion*, London: Black Swan, 2007, p. 388

28. Wolpert, Lewis, *The Unnatural Nature of Science*, London: Faber, 1992

29. The full discussion of this is in: King, Mike, *Secularism: The Hidden Origins of Disbelief*, Cambridge: James Clarke & Co., 2007, pp. 45-89

30. Taylor, Charles, *A Secular Age*, Cambridge, MA and London: The Belknap Press of Harvard University Press, 2007, p. 311

31. Taylor, Charles, *A Secular Age*, Cambridge, MA and London: The Belknap Press of Harvard University Press, 2007, p. 314

32. King, Mike, *Secularism: The Hidden Origins of Disbelief*, Cambridge: James Clarke & Co., 2007, pp. 113-117

33. King, Mike, *Secularism: The Hidden Origins of Disbelief*, Cambridge: James Clarke & Co., 2007, p. 272

34. King, Mike, *Secularism: The Hidden Origins of Disbelief*, Cambridge: James Clarke & Co., 2007, p. 38

35. Beattie, Tina, *The New Atheists: The Twilight of Reason & The War on Religion*, London: Darton, Longman and Todd, 2007, p. 45

36. McGrath, Alister, *The Dawkins Delusion?: Atheist Fundamentalism and the Denial of the Divine*, London: SPCK, 2007, p. 33

37. Bruce, Steve, *God is Dead: Secularization in the West*, Oxford: Blackwell, 2002, p. 2

38. Bruce, Steve, *God is Dead: Secularization in the West*, Oxford: Blackwell, 2002, p. 39

39. Bruce, Steve, *God is Dead: Secularization in the West*, Oxford: Blackwell, 2002, p. 3

40. Bruce, Steve, *God is Dead: Secularization in the West*, Oxford: Blackwell,

2002, p. 43

41. Bruce, Steve, *God is Dead: Secularization in the West*, Oxford: Blackwell, 2002, p. 74

42. Bruce, Steve, *God is Dead: Secularization in the West*, Oxford: Blackwell, 2002, p. 219

43. Taylor, Charles, *A Secular Age*, Cambridge, MA and London: The Belknap Press of Harvard University Press, 2007, p. 530

44. Bruce, Steve, *God is Dead: Secularization in the West*, Oxford: Blackwell, 2002, p. 116

45. Martin, David, *On Secularization: Towards a Revised General Theory*, Aldershot: Ashgate, 2005, p. 3

46. Martin, David, *On Secularization: Towards a Revised General Theory*, Aldershot: Ashgate, 2005, p. 75

47. Martin, David, *On Secularization: Towards a Revised General Theory*, Aldershot: Ashgate, 2005, p. 89

48. Martin, David, *On Secularization: Towards a Revised General Theory*, Aldershot: Ashgate, 2005, p. 19

49. Bruce, Steve, *God is Dead: Secularization in the West*, Oxford: Blackwell, 2002, p. 107

50. Bruce, Steve, *God is Dead: Secularization in the West*, Oxford: Blackwell, 2002, p. 230

51. Martin, David, *On Secularization: Towards a Revised General Theory*, Aldershot: Ashgate, 2005, p. 123

52. Martin, David, *On Secularization: Towards a Revised General Theory*, Aldershot: Ashgate, 2005, p. 59

53. Taylor, Charles, *A Secular Age*, Cambridge, MA and London: The Belknap Press of Harvard University Press, 2007, p. 19

54. Taylor, Charles, *A Secular Age*, Cambridge, MA and London: The Belknap Press of Harvard University Press, 2007, p. 38

55. Taylor, Charles, *A Secular Age*, Cambridge, MA and London: The Belknap Press of Harvard University Press, 2007, p. 40

56. Taylor, Charles, *A Secular Age*, Cambridge, MA and London: The Belknap Press of Harvard University Press, 2007, p. 49

57. Bruce, Steve, *God is Dead: Secularization in the West*, Oxford: Blackwell, 2002, p. 51

58. Taylor, Charles, *A Secular Age*, Cambridge, MA and London: The Belknap Press of Harvard University Press, 2007, p. 80

59. Smith, Graeme, *A Short History of Secularism*, London, New York: I.B. Tauris & Co. Ltd, 2007, p. 1

60. Bruce, Steve, *God is Dead: Secularization in the West*, Oxford: Blackwell, 2002, p. 47

61. Smith, Graeme, *A Short History of Secularism*, London, New York: I.B. Tauris & Co. Ltd, 2007, p. 190

62. King, Mike, *Secularism: The Hidden Origins of Disbelief*, Cambridge: James Clarke & Co., 2007, section 5.1

63. Bucke, R.M., *Cosmic Consciousness: A Study in the Evolution of the Human Mind*, London: Olympia Press, 1972, p. 71

64. Russell, Bertrand, *Mysticism and Logic*, London: George Allen and

Unwin, 1963, p. 15

65. Russell, Bertrand, *Mysticism and Logic*, London: George Allen and Unwin, 1963, p. 16

66. Varghese gives this as the reference: Russell, Bertrand, *The Autobiography of Bertrand Russell*, London: George Allen and Unwin, 1967, p. 146

67. Flew, Antony, *There is a God: How the World's Most Notorious Atheist Changed His Mind*, New York: HarperOne, 2007, p. xxi

68. Harris, Sam, *The End of Faith: Religion, Terror, and the Future of Reason*, London: The Free Press, 2006, p. 39

69. Beattie, Tina, *The New Atheists: The Twilight of Reason & The War on Religion*, London: Darton, Longman and Todd, 2007, p. 130

70. King, Mike, *Secularism: The Hidden Origins of Disbelief*, Cambridge: James Clarke & Co., 2007, pp. 30-31

71. Steiner, R., *The Course of My Life*, New York: Anthroposophic Press, 1986, ch. 11

72. Bruce, Steve, *God is Dead: Secularization in the West*, Oxford: Blackwell, 2002, p. 98

73. Lutyens, M., *The Life and Death of Krishnamurti*, London: Rider, 1991, p. 92

74. See for example pages 306, 361, 365, 366, 367, and 701 in Taylor, Charles, *A Secular Age*, Cambridge, MA and London: The Belknap Press of Harvard University Press, 2007

75. King, Mike, *Secularism: The Hidden Origins of Disbelief*, Cambridge: James Clarke & Co., 2007, p. 95

76. Mesibov, Gary B., Shea, Victoria and Adams, Lynn W., *Understanding Asperger Syndrome and High Functioning Autism*, New York, Boston, Dordrecht, London and Moscow: Kluwer Academic/Plenum Publishers, 2001, p. 3

77. Mesibov, Gary B., Shea, Victoria and Adams, Lynn W., *Understanding Asperger Syndrome and High Functioning Autism*, New York, Boston, Dordrecht, London and Moscow: Kluwer Academic/Plenum Publishers, 2001, p. 6

78. Schopler, Eric and Mesibov, Gary B. (eds.), *High-functioning Individuals with Autism*, New York and London: Plenum Press, 1992, p. 23

79. Haddon, Mark, *The Curious Incident of the Dog in the Night-Time*, London: Definitions, 2004

80. Williams, Andrew, '60 SECONDS: Gary Numan', *Metro*, 6 November 2006

81. Elder, Jennifer, *Different Like Me: My Book of Autism Heroes*, London and Philadelphia, PA: Jessica Kingsley Publishers, 2006

82. Taylor, Charles, *A Secular Age*, Cambridge, MA and London: The Belknap Press of Harvard University Press, 2007, p. 534

Part 2: Postsecularism and the New Atheism Debate (pages 49-121)

1. King, Mike, *Secularism: The Hidden Origins of Disbelief*, Cambridge: James Clarke & Co., 2007, p. 101

2. Dawkins, Richard, *The God Delusion*, London: Black Swan, 2007, p. 33

3. Dawkins, Richard, *The God Delusion*, London: Black Swan, 2007, p. 41

4. Dawkins, Richard, *The God Delusion*, London: Black Swan, 2007, p. 183
5. Dawkins, Richard, *The God Delusion*, London: Black Swan, 2007, p. 81
6. Humphrys, John, *In God We Doubt: Confessions of a Failed Atheist*, London: Hodder & Stoughton, 2007, p. 197
7. Dawkins, Richard, *The God Delusion*, London: Black Swan, 2007, p. 323
8. Dawkins, Richard, *The God Delusion*, London: Black Swan, 2007, p. 181
9. Dawkins, Richard, *The God Delusion*, London: Black Swan, 2007, p. 342
10. Dawkins, Richard, *The Selfish Gene*, Oxford and New York: Oxford University Press, 1992, p. 192
11. Harris, Sam, *The End of Faith: Religion, Terror, and the Future of Reason*, London: The Free Press, 2006, p. 14
12. Harris, Sam, *The End of Faith: Religion, Terror, and the Future of Reason*, London: The Free Press, 2006, p. 40
13. Harris, Sam, *The End of Faith: Religion, Terror, and the Future of Reason*, London: The Free Press, 2006, p. 43
14. Harris, Sam, *The End of Faith: Religion, Terror, and the Future of Reason*, London: The Free Press, 2006, p. 15
15. Harris, Sam, *The End of Faith: Religion, Terror, and the Future of Reason*, London: The Free Press, 2006, p. 18
16. Harris, Sam, *The End of Faith: Religion, Terror, and the Future of Reason*, London: The Free Press, 2006, p. 21
17. Harris, Sam, *The End of Faith: Religion, Terror, and the Future of Reason*, London: The Free Press, 2006, p. 23
18. Hitchens, Christopher, *God is Not Great: How Religion Poisons Everything*, New York and Boston: Twelve, 2007, p. 153
19. Hitchens, Christopher, *The Portable Atheist: Essential Readings for the Nonbeliever*, London: Da Capo Press, 2007, p. xiv
20. Hitchens, Christopher, *God is Not Great: How Religion Poisons Everything*, New York and Boston: Twelve, 2007, p. 195
21. Hitchens, Christopher, *God is Not Great: How Religion Poisons Everything*, New York and Boston: Twelve, 2007, p. 4
22. Shlain, Leonard, *Art and Physics: Parallel Visions in Space, Time and Light*, New York: Quill William Morrow, 1991, p. 74
23. Hitchens, Christopher, *God is Not Great: How Religion Poisons Everything*, New York and Boston: Twelve, 2007, p. 52
24. Hitchens, Christopher, *God is Not Great: How Religion Poisons Everything*, New York and Boston: Twelve, 2007, p. 117
25. Hitchens, Christopher, *God is Not Great: How Religion Poisons Everything*, New York and Boston: Twelve, 2007, p. 119
26. Taylor, Charles, *A Secular Age*, Cambridge, MA and London: The Belknap Press of Harvard University Press, 2007, p. 651
27. Hitchens, Christopher, *God is Not Great: How Religion Poisons Everything*, New York and Boston: Twelve, 2007, p. 120
28. Hitchens, Christopher, *God is Not Great: How Religion Poisons Everything*, New York and Boston: Twelve, 2007, p. 107
29. Hitchens, Christopher, *God is Not Great: How Religion Poisons Everything*, New York and Boston: Twelve, 2007, p. 133
30. Hitchens, Christopher, *God is Not Great: How Religion Poisons Everything*,

New York and Boston: Twelve, 2007, p. 200

31. Hitchens, Christopher, *God is Not Great: How Religion Poisons Everything,* New York and Boston: Twelve, 2007, p. 199

32. Taylor, Charles, *A Secular Age,* Cambridge, MA and London: The Belknap Press of Harvard University Press, 2007, p. 529

33. Hitchens, Christopher, *God is Not Great: How Religion Poisons Everything,* New York and Boston: Twelve, 2007, p. 230

34. Hitchens, Christopher, *God is Not Great: How Religion Poisons Everything,* New York and Boston: Twelve, 2007, p. 282

35. Dennett, Daniel C., *Breaking the Spell: Religion as a Natural Phenomenon,* London: Penguin Books, 2007, p. 9

36. Dennett, Daniel C., *Breaking the Spell: Religion as a Natural Phenomenon,* London: Penguin Books, 2007, p. 253

37. Dennett, Daniel C., *Breaking the Spell: Religion as a Natural Phenomenon,* London: Penguin Books, 2007, p. 17

38. Dennett, Daniel C., *Breaking the Spell: Religion as a Natural Phenomenon,* London: Penguin Books, 2007, p. 259

39. Dennett, Daniel C., *Breaking the Spell: Religion as a Natural Phenomenon,* London: Penguin Books, 2007, p. 10

40. Dennett, Daniel C., *Breaking the Spell: Religion as a Natural Phenomenon,* London: Penguin Books, 2007, p. 198

41. Dennett, Daniel C., *Breaking the Spell: Religion as a Natural Phenomenon,* London: Penguin Books, 2007, p. 206

42. King, Mike, *Secularism: The Hidden Origins of Disbelief,* Cambridge: James Clarke & Co., 2007, p. 276

43. Dennett, Daniel C., *Breaking the Spell: Religion as a Natural Phenomenon,* London: Penguin Books, 2007, p. 71

44. Dennett, Daniel C., *Breaking the Spell: Religion as a Natural Phenomenon,* London: Penguin Books, 2007, p. 341

45. Pirsig, Robert M., *Lila: An Enquiry into Morals,* London: Black Swan, 1991, p. 182

46. Stenger, Victor J., *God, the Failed Hypothesis: How Science Shows That God Does Not Exist,* New York: Prometheus Books, 2007, p. 17

47. Stenger, Victor J., *God, the Failed Hypothesis: How Science Shows That God Does Not Exist,* New York: Prometheus Books, 2007, p. 148

48. Stenger, Victor J., *God, the Failed Hypothesis: How Science Shows That God Does Not Exist,* New York: Prometheus Books, 2007, p. 164

49. Stenger, Victor J., *God, the Failed Hypothesis: How Science Shows That God Does Not Exist,* New York: Prometheus Books, 2007, p. 170

50. Stenger, Victor J., *God, the Failed Hypothesis: How Science Shows That God Does Not Exist,* New York: Prometheus Books, 2007, p. 234

51. Weinberg, Steven, 'Free People From Superstition', *Freethought Today,* vol. 17, no. 3, April 2000

52. Glanz, James, 'Physicist Ponders God, Truth and "a Final Theory"', *The New York Times,* January 25, 2000

53. Weinberg, Steven, 'What about God', in Hitchens, Christopher (ed.), *The Portable Atheist: Essential Readings for the Nonbeliever,* London: Da Capo Press, 2007, p. 375

54. Weinberg, Steven, 'What about God', in Hitchens, Christopher (ed.), *The Portable Atheist: Essential Readings for the Nonbeliever*, London: Da Capo Press, 2007, p. 376
55. Weinberg, Steven, 'What about God', in Hitchens, Christopher (ed.), *The Portable Atheist: Essential Readings for the Nonbeliever*, London: Da Capo Press, 2007, p. 369
56. Weinberg, Steven, 'What about God', in Hitchens, Christopher (ed.), *The Portable Atheist: Essential Readings for the Nonbeliever*, London: Da Capo Press, 2007, p. 366
57. Weinberg, Steven, 'What about God', in Hitchens, Christopher (ed.), *The Portable Atheist: Essential Readings for the Nonbeliever*, London: Da Capo Press, 2007, p. 372
58. Onfray, Michel, *In Defence of Atheism: The Case against Christianity, Judaism and Islam*, London: Serpent's Tail, 2007, p. 213
59. Onfray, Michel, *In Defence of Atheism: The Case against Christianity, Judaism and Islam*, London: Serpent's Tail, 2007, p. 4
60. Onfray, Michel, *In Defence of Atheism: The Case against Christianity, Judaism and Islam*, London: Serpent's Tail, 2007, p. 46
61. Onfray, Michel, *In Defence of Atheism: The Case against Christianity, Judaism and Islam*, London: Serpent's Tail, 2007, p. 25
62. Onfray, Michel, *In Defence of Atheism: The Case against Christianity, Judaism and Islam*, London: Serpent's Tail, 2007, p. xiv
63. Grayling, A.C., *Against All Gods: Six Polemics on Religion and an Essay on Kindliness*, London: Oberon Books, 2007, p. 7
64. Grayling, A.C., *Against All Gods: Six Polemics on Religion and an Essay on Kindliness*, London: Oberon Books, 2007, p. 13
65. Grayling, A.C., *Against All Gods: Six Polemics on Religion and an Essay on Kindliness*, London: Oberon Books, 2007, p. 9
66. Amis, Martin, *The Second Plane: September 11, 2001-2007*, London: Jonathan Cape, 2008, p. 12
67. Amis, Martin, *The Second Plane: September 11, 2001-2007*, London: Jonathan Cape, 2008, p. 12
68. Amis, Martin, *The Second Plane: September 11, 2001-2007*, London: Jonathan Cape, 2008, p. 15
69. Amis, Martin, *The Second Plane: September 11, 2001-2007*, London: Jonathan Cape, 2008, p. 14
70. Amis, Martin, *The Second Plane: September 11, 2001-2007*, London: Jonathan Cape, 2008, p. 25
71. Amis, Martin, *The Second Plane: September 11, 2001-2007*, London: Jonathan Cape, 2008, p. 92
72. Amis, Martin, *The Second Plane: September 11, 2001-2007*, London: Jonathan Cape, 2008, p. 193
73. McEwan, Ian, 'End of World Blues', in Hitchens, Christopher (ed.), *The Portable Atheist: Essential Readings for the Nonbeliever*, London: Da Capo Press, 2007, p. 364
74. McEwan, Ian, 'End of World Blues', in Hitchens, Christopher (ed.), *The Portable Atheist: Essential Readings for the Nonbeliever*, London: Da Capo Press, 2007, p. 365

75.McEwan, Ian, *Saturday*, London: Jonathan Cape, 2005, p. 4

76.McEwan, Ian, *Saturday*, London: Jonathan Cape, 2005, p. 17

77.McEwan, Ian, *Saturday*, London: Jonathan Cape, 2005, p. 124

78.McEwan, Ian, *Saturday*, London: Jonathan Cape, 2005, p. 55

79.McEwan, Ian, *Enduring Love*, London: Vintage, 1998, p. 66

80.Taylor, Charles, *A Secular Age*, Cambridge, MA and London: The Belknap Press of Harvard University Press, 2007, p. 365

81.Bloom, Allan, *The Closing of the American Mind: How Higher Education has Failed Democracy and Impoverished the Souls of Today's Students*, London: Penguin, 1987, p. 155

82.Updike, John, 'From *Roger's Version'* in Hitchens, Christopher (ed.), *The Portable Atheist: Essential Readings for the Nonbeliever*, London: Da Capo Press, 2007, p. 245

83.Updike, John, *Self-Consciousness: Memoirs*, London: Penguin, 1990, ch. 4

84.Amis, Martin, *The Second Plane: September 11, 2001-2007*, London: Jonathan Cape, 2008, p. 101

85.Meacham, Steve, 'The shed where God died', *Sydney Morning Herald*, 13 December 2003

86.McGrath, Alister, *The Dawkins Delusion?: Atheist Fundamentalism and the Denial of the Divine*, London: SPCK, 2007, p. xiii

87.Dawkins, Richard, *The God Delusion*, London: Black Swan, 2007, p. 320

88.McGrath, Alister, *The Dawkins Delusion?: Atheist Fundamentalism and the Denial of the Divine*, London: SPCK, 2007, p. 8

89.McGrath, Alister, *The Dawkins Delusion?: Atheist Fundamentalism and the Denial of the Divine*, London: SPCK, 2007, p. 10

90.McGrath, Alister, *The Dawkins Delusion?: Atheist Fundamentalism and the Denial of the Divine*, London: SPCK, 2007, p. 15

91.McGrath, Alister, *The Dawkins Delusion?: Atheist Fundamentalism and the Denial of the Divine*, London: SPCK, 2007, p. 19

92.McGrath, Alister, *Dawkins' God: Genes, Memes, and the Meaning of Life*, Oxford and Victoria: Blackwell, 2005, p. 6

93.McGrath, Alister, *The Dawkins Delusion?: Atheist Fundamentalism and the Denial of the Divine*, London: SPCK, 2007, p. 40

94.McGrath, Alister, *The Dawkins Delusion?: Atheist Fundamentalism and the Denial of the Divine*, London: SPCK, 2007, p. 25

95.Ward, Keith, *Is Religion Dangerous?*, Oxford: Lion, 2006, p. 16

96.Ward, Keith, *Is Religion Dangerous?*, Oxford: Lion, 2006, p. 8

97.Ward, Keith, *Is Religion Dangerous?*, Oxford: Lion, 2006, p. 9

98.Ward, Keith, *Is Religion Dangerous?*, Oxford: Lion, 2006, p. 10

99.Ward, Keith, *Is Religion Dangerous?*, Oxford: Lion, 2006, p. 26

100.Ward, Keith, *Is Religion Dangerous?*, Oxford: Lion, 2006, p. 38

101. Ward, Keith, *Is Religion Dangerous?*, Oxford: Lion, 2006, p. 110

102. Ward, Keith, *Is Religion Dangerous?*, Oxford: Lion, 2006, p. 114

103. Ward, Keith, *Is Religion Dangerous?*, Oxford: Lion, 2006, p. 112

104. Ward, Keith, *Is Religion Dangerous?*, Oxford: Lion, 2006, p. 113

105. Ward, Keith, *Is Religion Dangerous?*, Oxford: Lion, 2006, p. 180

106. Dawkins, Richard, 'Richard Swinburne's *Is There a God?*', *The Sunday Times*, 4 February 1996

107. Swinburne, Richard, *The Existence of God* (2nd Ed.), Oxford: Clarendon Press, 2004, p. 184

108. Lennox, John, *God's Undertaker: Has Science Buried God*, Oxford: Lion, 2007, p. 12

109. Lennox, John, *God's Undertaker: Has Science Buried God*, Oxford: Lion, 2007, p. 77

110. Lennox, John, *God's Undertaker: Has Science Buried God*, Oxford: Lion, 2007, p. 110

111. Stenger, Victor J., *God, the Failed Hypothesis: How Science Shows That God Does Not Exist*, New York: Prometheus Books, 2007, p. 55

112. Stenger, Victor J., *God, the Failed Hypothesis: How Science Shows That God Does Not Exist*, New York: Prometheus Books, 2007, p. 58

113. Dawkins, Richard, *Climbing Mount Improbable*, London: Penguin Books, 2006, p. 127

114. Lennox, John, *God's Undertaker: Has Science Buried God*, Oxford: Lion, 2007, p. 150

115. Stenger, Victor J., *God, the Failed Hypothesis: How Science Shows That God Does Not Exist*, New York: Prometheus Books, 2007, p. 66

116. See for example King, Mike, 'Programmed Graphics in Computer Art and Animation', in *Leonardo*, vol. 28, no. 2, 1995, pp. 113-121 and King, Mike, 'Computers and Modern Art: Digital Art Museum', in Candy, Linda and Edmonds, Ernest (eds.), *Creativity and Cognition 2002*, Proceedings of the 4th Creativity and Cognition Conference, Loughborough University, New York: ACM Press, 2002, pp. 88-94

117. Lennox, John, *God's Undertaker: Has Science Buried God*, Oxford: Lion, 2007, p. 49

118. Lennox, John, *God's Undertaker: Has Science Buried God*, Oxford: Lion, 2007, p. 149

119. Lennox, John, *God's Undertaker: Has Science Buried God*, Oxford: Lion, 2007, p. 169

120. Collins, Francis, *The Language of God: A Scientist Presents Evidence for Belief*, London: Pocket Books, 2007, p. 2

121. Collins, Francis, *The Language of God: A Scientist Presents Evidence for Belief*, London: Pocket Books, 2007, p. 93

122. Collins, Francis, *The Language of God: A Scientist Presents Evidence for Belief*, London: Pocket Books, 2007, p. 192

123. Dawkins, Richard, *The God Delusion*, London: Black Swan, 2007, pp. 158-159

124. Collins, Francis, *The Language of God: A Scientist Presents Evidence for Belief*, London: Pocket Books, 2007, p. 193

125. Collins, Francis, *The Language of God: A Scientist Presents Evidence for Belief*, London: Pocket Books, 2007, p. 107

126. Collins, Francis, *The Language of God: A Scientist Presents Evidence for Belief*, London: Pocket Books, 2007, p. 5

127. Collins, Francis, *The Language of God: A Scientist Presents Evidence for Belief*, London: Pocket Books, 2007, p. 166

128. Collins, Francis, *The Language of God: A Scientist Presents Evidence for Belief*, London: Pocket Books, 2007, p. 205

129. www.truthdig.com/report/item/20060815_sam_harris_language_ ignorance, last accessed on 9 May 2008

130. Flew, Antony, *There is a God: How the World's Most Notorious Atheist Changed His Mind*, New York: HarperOne, 2007, p. vii

131. Flew, Antony, *There is a God: How the World's Most Notorious Atheist Changed His Mind*, New York: HarperOne, 2007, p. 92

132. Flew, Antony, *There is a God: How the World's Most Notorious Atheist Changed His Mind*, New York: HarperOne, 2007, p. 34

133. Flew, Antony, *There is a God: How the World's Most Notorious Atheist Changed His Mind*, New York: HarperOne, 2007, p. 75

134. Flew, Antony, *There is a God: How the World's Most Notorious Atheist Changed His Mind*, New York: HarperOne, 2007, pp. 75-77

135. Lennox, John, *God's Undertaker: Has Science Buried God*, Oxford: Lion, 2007, p. 155

136. Dawkins, Richard, *The God Delusion*, London: Black Swan, 2007, p. 137

137. Flew, Antony, *There is a God: How the World's Most Notorious Atheist Changed His Mind*, New York: HarperOne, 2007, p. 78

138. Onfray, Michel, *In Defence of Atheism: The Case against Christianity, Judaism and Islam*, London: Serpent's Tail, 2007, p. 139

139. Flew, Antony, *There is a God: How the World's Most Notorious Atheist Changed His Mind*, New York: HarperOne, 2007, p. 187

140. Flew, Antony, *There is a God: How the World's Most Notorious Atheist Changed His Mind*, New York: HarperOne, 2007, p. 188

141. Collins, Francis, *The Language of God: A Scientist Presents Evidence for Belief*, London: Pocket Books, 2007, p. 224

142. Flew, Antony, *There is a God: How the World's Most Notorious Atheist Changed His Mind*, New York: HarperOne, 2007, p. 196

143. Beattie, Tina, *The New Atheists: The Twilight of Reason & The War on Religion*, London: Darton, Longman and Todd, 2007, p. 2

144. Beattie, Tina, *The New Atheists: The Twilight of Reason & The War on Religion*, London: Darton, Longman and Todd, 2007, p. 9

145. Dawkins, Richard, *The God Delusion*, London: Black Swan, 2007, p. 57

146. Beattie, Tina, *The New Atheists: The Twilight of Reason & The War on Religion*, London: Darton, Longman and Todd, 2007, p. 9

147. Beattie, Tina, *The New Atheists: The Twilight of Reason & The War on Religion*, London: Darton, Longman and Todd, 2007, p. 159

148. Wolf, Gary, 'The Church of the Non-Believers', *Wired*, issue 14.11, November 2006

149. Beattie, Tina, *The New Atheists: The Twilight of Reason & The War on Religion*, London: Darton, Longman and Todd, 2007, p. 3

150. Beattie, Tina, *The New Atheists: The Twilight of Reason & The War on Religion*, London: Darton, Longman and Todd, 2007, p. 11

151. Beattie, Tina, *The New Atheists: The Twilight of Reason & The War on Religion*, London: Darton, Longman and Todd, 2007, p. 47

152. Beattie, Tina, *The New Atheists: The Twilight of Reason & The War on Religion*, London: Darton, Longman and Todd, 2007, p. 131

153. Beattie, Tina, *The New Atheists: The Twilight of Reason & The War on*

Religion, London: Darton, Longman and Todd, 2007, p. 153

154. Beattie, Tina, *The New Atheists: The Twilight of Reason & The War on Religion*, London: Darton, Longman and Todd, 2007, p. 89

155. Amis, Martin, *The Second Plane: September 11, 2001-2007*, London: Jonathan Cape, 2008, p. 141

156. Taylor, Charles, *A Secular Age*, Cambridge, MA and London: The Belknap Press of Harvard University Press, 2007, pp. 642-656

157. Humphrys, John, *In God We Doubt: Confessions of a Failed Atheist*, London: Hodder & Stoughton, 2007, p. 66

158. Humphrys, John, *In God We Doubt: Confessions of a Failed Atheist*, London: Hodder & Stoughton, 2007, p. 287

159. Humphrys, John, *In God We Doubt: Confessions of a Failed Atheist*, London: Hodder & Stoughton, 2007, p. 281

160. Quoted in Humphrys, John, *In God We Doubt: Confessions of a Failed Atheist*, London: Hodder & Stoughton, 2007, p. 282

161. Humphrys, John, *In God We Doubt: Confessions of a Failed Atheist*, London: Hodder & Stoughton, 2007, p. 193

162. Humphrys, John, *In God We Doubt: Confessions of a Failed Atheist*, London: Hodder & Stoughton, 2007, p. 189

163. Lorimer, David, *Radical Prince: The Practical Vision of the Prince of Wales*, Edinburgh: Floris Books, 2003, p. 233

164. Damasio, Antonio R., *Descartes' Error: Emotion, Reason and the Human Brain*, London: MacMillan, 1996, p. 252

165. Schrödinger, Erwin, *What is Life?*, Cambridge: Cambridge University Press, 2007, p. 1

166. Ricoeur, Paul, *Freud and Philosophy: An Essay on Interpretation*, New Haven, CT and London: Yale University Press, 1970, p. 3

167. Pirsig, Robert M., *Lila: An Enquiry into Morals*, London: Black Swan, 1991, p. 189

168. Harris, Sam, *The End of Faith: Religion, Terror, and the Future of Reason*, London: The Free Press, 2006, p. 16

169. Schumacher, E.F., *A Guide for the Perplexed*, London: Abacus, 1978

170. Harding, D.E., *The Hierarchy of Heaven and Earth*, Gainesville, FL: University Presses of Florida, 1979

171. Pirsig, Robert M., *Lila: An Enquiry into Morals*, London: Black Swan, 1991, p. 181

172. Benatar, David, 'The Optimism Delusion', *Think*, issue 16, Winter 2008

173. Freke, Timothy, and Gandy, Peter, *The Jesus Mysteries: Was the "Original Jesus" a Pagan God?*, New York: Three Rivers Press, 1999

174. Warraq, Ibn, 'The Koran', in Hitchens, Christopher (ed.), *The Portable Atheist: Essential Readings for the Nonbeliever*, London: Da Capo Press, 2007, p. 394

175. Harris, Sam, *The End of Faith: Religion, Terror, and the Future of Reason*, London: The Free Press, 2006, p. 45

176. Lerner, Michael, *The Left Hand of God: Taking Back our Country from the Religious Right*, New York: HarperSanFrancisco, 2006, p. 3

177. Harris, Sam, *The End of Faith: Religion, Terror, and the Future of Reason*, London: The Free Press, 2006, p. 52

178. Gray, John, *Black Mass: Apocalyptic Religion and the Death of Utopia*, London: Allen Lane, 2007, p. 1

179. Grayling, A.C., 'Through the looking glass', *New Humanist*, vol. 122, issue 4, July/August 2007

180. McEwan, Ian, 'End of the World Blues' in Hitchens, Christopher (ed.), *The Portable Atheist: Essential Readings for the Nonbeliever*, London: Da Capo Press, 2007, p. 355

181. Pullman, Philip, 'Text, lies and videotape', *The Guardian*, 6 November 2004

182. Taylor, Charles, *A Secular Age*, Cambridge, MA and London: The Belknap Press of Harvard University Press, 2007, p. 80

183. Harris, Sam, *The End of Faith: Religion, Terror, and the Future of Reason*, London: The Free Press, 2006, p. 65

184. Harris, Sam, *Letter to a Christian Nation*, New York: Vintage Books, 2008, p. 23

Part Three: Some Postsecular Contexts (pages 123-228)

1. Davies, Paul, *God and the New Physics*, London: Penguin, 1990, p. 8

2. Davies, Paul, *God and the New Physics*, London: Penguin, 1990, p. 100

3. Davies, Paul, *God and the New Physics*, London: Penguin, 1990, p. ix and p. 229

4. Hawking, Stephen, *A Brief History of Time*, London: Guild Publishing, 1988, p. 175

5. Davies, Paul, *God and the New Physics*, London: Penguin, 1990, p. viii and p. ix

6. Wilber, Ken, *Quantum Questions: Mystical Writings of the World's Great Physicists*, Boston and London: Shambhala, 1985, p. ix

7. Zukav, Gary, *The Dancing Wu Li Masters*, London: Fontana, 1979, p. 49

8. Gell-Mann, Murray, *The Quark and the Jaguar*, London: Abacus, 2002, p. 129

9. White, Michael, *Isaac Newton: The Last Sorcerer*, London: Fourth Estate, 1998, p. 233

10. Tacey, David, *The Spirituality Revolution: The Emergence of Contemporary Spirituality*, Hove and New York: Brunner-Routledge, 2004, p. 1

11. Polkinghorne, John, *Reason and Reality: The Relationship between Science and Theology*, London: SPCK, 1991, p. 4

12. Polkinghorne, John, 'The Old One and me', *Times Higher Educational Supplement*, 3 September 1999

13. Hayward, Jeremy, *Shifting World, Changing Mind: Where the Sciences and Buddhism Meet*, Boston and London: Shambhala, 1987, p. 44

14. Schrödinger, Erwin, *What is Life?*, Cambridge: Cambridge University Press, 2007, ch. 1

15. Blackmore, Susan, 'Near-Death Experiences on TV: Why quantum coherence cannot explain the NDE', *Sceptic Magazine*, vol. 17, no. 1, Spring 2004, pp. 8-10

16. Feuerbach, Ludwig, *The Essence of Christianity*, New York: Prometheus Books, 1989, p. 2

17. Chalmers, David J., 'Facing Up to the Problem of Consciousness,' *Journal of Consciousness Studies*, vol. 2, no. 3, 1995, pp. 200-219

18. King, Mike, *Secularism: The Hidden Origins of Disbelief*, Cambridge: James Clarke & Co., 2007, p. 248

19. Pagels, Elaine, *The Gnostic Gospels*, New York: Vintage Books, 1979, (Thomas 13), p. 26

20. Nanamoli, Bhikku and Bhodi, Bhikku, *The Middle Length Discourses of the Buddha: A New Translation of the Majjhima Nikaya*, Boston: Wisdom Publications, 1995, (123.22), p. 983

21. Dennett, Daniel, 'Commentary on Chalmers', *Journal of Consciousness Studies*, vol. 3, no. 1, 1996, pp. 4-6

22. Goswami, Amit, *Self-Aware Universe: How Consciousness Creates the Material World*, New York: Jeremy P. Tarcher, 1993

23. King, Mike, 'Towards a Science of Consciousness 1966: "Tucson II"', in *Digital Creativity*, vol. 8, no. 1, April 1997, pp. 34-35

24. Lodge, David, 'Sense and Sensibility', *The Guardian*, 2 December 2002

25. Nagel, Thomas, 'What is it like to be a bat?' *The Philosophical Review* LXXXIII, 4, October 1974, pp. 435-50

26. Lodge, David, *Thinks...*, London: Penguin, 2001, p. 97

27. Lodge, David, *Consciousness and the Novel*, London: Secker and Warburg, 2002, p. 16

28. Taylor, Charles, *A Secular Age*, Cambridge, MA and London: The Belknap Press of Harvard University Press, 2007, p. 284

29. Jung, C.G., *Memories, Dreams, Reflections*, London: Fontana, 1993, p. 306

30. Maslow, A. *Religions, Values and Peak-Experiences*, Harmondsworth: Penguin Arkana 1970, p. 92

31. Hardy, Jean, *A Psychology with a Soul*, Routledge and Kegan Paul, 1987, p. 15

32. Daniels, Michael, 'The Transpersonal Self: 2. Comparing Seven Psychological Theories', *Transpersonal Psychology Review*, 2002, vol. 6, no. 2, pp. 4-21

33. Wilber, Ken, *Eye of Spirit: An Integral Vision for a World Gone Slightly Mad*, Boston and London: Shambhala, 1998, p. 153

34. Rowan, John, *The Transpersonal*, London: Routledge, 1993, p. 103

35. Wilber, Ken, *The Spectrum of Consciousness* (2nd Ed.), Wheaton, IL, Madras and London: Quest Books (The Theosophical Publishing House), 1993, p. 254

36. Rowan, John, *The Transpersonal*, London: Routledge, 1993, p. 10

37. Wilber, Ken, *Sex, Ecology, Spirituality: The Spirit of Evolution*, Boston and London: Shambhala, 2000, p. 68

38. Wilber, Ken, *Eye of Spirit: An Integral Vision for a World Gone Slightly Mad*, Boston and London: Shambhala, 1998, p. 279

39. Ferrer, Jorge N., *Revisioning Transpersonal Theory: A Participatory Vision of Human Spirituality*, Albany, NY: State University of New York Press, 2002, p. 22

40. Walsch, Neale Donald, *Conversations with God: Book One*, London: Hodder and Stoughton, 1995

41. Heelas, Paul, *The New Age*, Oxford and Malden: Blackwell Publishers,

1996, p. 18

42. Bruce, Steve, *God is Dead: Secularization in the West*, Oxford: Blackwell, 2002, p. 91

43. Bruce, Steve, *God is Dead: Secularization in the West*, Oxford: Blackwell, 2002, p. 105

44. Taylor, Charles, *A Secular Age*, Cambridge, MA and London: The Belknap Press of Harvard University Press, 2007, p. 511

45. Heelas, Paul and Woodhead, Linda, *The Spiritual Revolution: Why Religion is Giving Way to Spirituality*, Oxford: Blackwell Publishing, 2005, p. 45

46. Heelas, Paul, *The New Age*, Oxford and Malden: Blackwell Publishers, 1996, p. 23

47. Bruce, Steve, *God is Dead: Secularization in the West*, Oxford: Blackwell, 2002, p. 105 and 133

48. Heelas, Paul, *The New Age*, Oxford and Malden: Blackwell Publishers, 1996, p. 6

49. Caplan, Mariana, *Halfway Up the Mountain: The Error of Premature Claims of Enlightenment*, Prescott, AZ: Hohm Press, 1999

50. Heelas, Paul, *The New Age*, Oxford and Malden: Blackwell Publishers, 1996, p. 137

51. Ferguson, Marilyn, *The Aquarian Conspiracy: Personal and Social Transformation in Our Time*, New York: G.P. Putnam's Sons, 1987, p. 23

52. Ferguson, Marilyn, *The Aquarian Conspiracy: Personal and Social Transformation in Our Time*, New York: G.P. Putnam's Sons, 1987, p. 70

53. Ferguson, Marilyn, *The Aquarian Conspiracy: Personal and Social Transformation in Our Time*, New York: G.P. Putnam's Sons, 1987, p. 405

54. McTaggart, Lynne, *The Field*, London: Element, 2003

55. Redfield, James, *The Celestine Prophecy: An Adventure*, Bantam, 1994, p. 58

56. Capra, Fritjof, *The Tao of Physics* (3rd Ed.), London: Flamingo, 1992, p. 356

57. *What Is Enlightenment*, issue 26, p. 63

58. *What Is Enlightenment*, issue 26, p. 44

59. Wilber, Ken, *The Marriage of Sense and Soul*, Dublin: Gateway, 1998, p. 113.

60. *What Is Enlightenment*, issue 26, p. 87

61. Wilber, Ken, *The Marriage of Sense and Soul*, Dublin: Gateway, 1998, pp. 17-20

62. Rawlinson, Andrew, *The Book of Enlightened Masters: Western Teachers in Eastern Traditions*, Chicago and La Salle, IL: Open Court, 1997

63. Tacey, David, *The Spirituality Revolution: The Emergence of Contemporary Spirituality*, Hove and New York: Brunner-Routledge, 2004, p. 146

64. Taylor, Charles, *A Secular Age*, Cambridge, MA and London: The Belknap Press of Harvard University Press, 2007, p. 349

65. Scholem, Gershom, *Major Trends in Jewish Mysticism*, New York: Schocken Books, 1995, p. 7

66. Brody, Hugh, *The Other Side of Eden: Hunters, Farmers, and the Shaping of the World*, New York: North Point Press, 2000, p. 70

67. Brody, Hugh, *The Other Side of Eden: Hunters, Farmers, and the Shaping of*

the World, New York: North Point Press, 2000, p. 97

68. Brody, Hugh, *The Other Side of Eden: Hunters, Farmers, and the Shaping of the World*, New York: North Point Press, 2000, p. 118

69. Abram, David, *The Spell of the Sensuous*, New York: Vintage Books, 1997, p. 102

70. Brody, Hugh, *The Other Side of Eden: Hunters, Farmers, and the Shaping of the World*, New York: North Point Press, 2000, p. 228

71. Brody, Hugh, *The Other Side of Eden: Hunters, Farmers, and the Shaping of the World*, New York: North Point Press, 2000, p. 231

72. Brody, Hugh, *The Other Side of Eden: Hunters, Farmers, and the Shaping of the World*, New York: North Point Press, 2000, p. 205

73. Abram, David, *The Spell of the Sensuous*, New York: Vintage Books, 1997, p. 246

74. Cook, Reginald Lansing, 'The Nature Mysticism of Thoreau,' in *The Concord Saunterer*, Middlebury, VT: Middlebury College Press, 1940, p. 9

75. Jefferies, R., *The Story of My Heart*, London: MacMillan St Martin's Press, 1968, p. 30

76. Bucke, R.M., *Walt Whitman*, Philadelphia, PA, 1883, p. 61

77. Naess, Arne (trans. and ed. David Rothenberg), *Ecology, Community and Lifestyle*, Cambridge: Cambridge University Press, 1989, p. 36

78. Naess, Arne (trans. and ed. David Rothenberg), *Ecology, Community and Lifestyle*, Cambridge: Cambridge University Press, 1989, p. 61

79. McEwan, Ian, *Enduring Love*, London: Vintage, 1998, p. 71

80. Muir, John, *My First Summer in the Sierra*, Edinburgh: Canongate Classics, 1988

81. Muir, John, *Letters to a Friend, 1866-1879*, Boston and New York: Houghton Mifflin Company, 1915, (letter of 1873)

82. Kant, Immanuel, *Critique of Judgement*, New York: Hafner Press, 1951, p. 100

83. Naess, Arne (trans. and ed. David Rothenberg), *Ecology, Community and Lifestyle*, Cambridge: Cambridge University Press, 1989, p. 61

84. Dawkins, Richard, *Unweaving the Rainbow*, London: Penguin, 1998, p. 49

85. Dawkins, Richard, *The Selfish Gene*, Oxford and New York: Oxford University Press, 1992, p. 2

86. Dawkins, Richard, *Unweaving the Rainbow*, London: Penguin, 1998, p. 26

87. Dawkins, Richard, *Unweaving the Rainbow*, London: Penguin, 1998, p. 16

88. Einstein, Albert, *The World as I See it*, Citadel Press, 1998, p. 91

89. Dawkins, Richard, *Unweaving the Rainbow*, London: Penguin, 1998, p. xii

90. Dawkins, Richard, *Unweaving the Rainbow*, London: Penguin, 1998, p. 180

91. McFarlane, Robert, 'Call of the Wild', *The Guardian*, 6 December 2003

92. Taylor, Charles, *A Secular Age*, Cambridge, MA and London: The Belknap Press of Harvard University Press, 2007, p. 356

93. Lipsey, Roger, *An Art of Our Own: The Spiritual in Twentieth-Century Art*,

Boston and Shaftesbury: Shambhala, 1988

94. Lipsey, Roger, *An Art of Our Own: The Spiritual in Twentieth-Century Art,* Boston and Shaftesbury: Shambhala, 1988, p. 236

95. Tuchman, Maurice (ed.), *The Spiritual in Art: Abstract Painting 1890-1985,* New York, London and Paris: Abbeville Press Publishers (Los Angeles County Museum of Art), 1986, p. 13

96. Henderson, Linda Dalrymple, *The Fourth Dimension and Non-Euclidean Geometry in Modern Art,* Princeton, NJ: Princeton University Press, 1983

97. Tuchman, Maurice (ed.), *The Spiritual in Art: Abstract Painting 1890-1985,* New York, London and Paris: Abbeville Press Publishers (Los Angeles County Museum of Art), 1986

98. Tucker, Mike, *Dreaming with Open Eyes: The Shamanic in Twentieth Century Art and Culture,* London: Aquarian / HarperSanFrancisco, 1992

99. Tucker, Mike (ed.), *Alan Davie: The Quest for the Miraculous,* Brighton: University of Brighton Gallery (Lund Humphries), 1993

100. Saunder, Frances Stonor, *Hidden Hands,* London: Channel 4 Television, 1995

101. Tuchman, Maurice (ed.), *The Spiritual in Art: Abstract Painting 1890-1985,* New York, London and Paris: Abbeville Press Publishers (Los Angeles County Museum of Art), 1986, p. 17

102. Weiss, Peg, *Kandinsky and Old Russia: The Artist as Ethnographer and Shaman,* New Haven, CT and London: Yale University Press, 1995

103. Perlmutter, Dawn and Koppman, Debra (eds.), *Reclaiming the Spiritual in Art: Contemporary Cross-Cultural Perspectives,* Albany, NY: State University of New York Press, 1999

104. Golding, John, *Paths to the Absolute: Mondrian, Malevich, Kandinsky, Pollock, Newman, Rothko, Still,* Princeton, NJ: Princeton University Press, 2000

105. Gamwell, Lynn, *Exploring the Invisible: Art, Science and the Spiritual,* Princeton, NJ and Oxford: Princeton University Press, 2002

106. Walsh, John (ed.), *Bill Viola: The Passions,* Los Angeles: The J. Paul Getty Museum in association with The National Gallery, London, 2003, p. 25

107. Viola's original booklist in spreadsheet form was kindly provided by the National Gallery, and a copy may be supplied on request.

108. Celant, Germano, *Anish Kapoor,* Milan: Charta, 1998

109. Bhabha, H. and Tazzi, O., *Anish Kapoor,* Berkeley, CA, Los Angeles and London: University of California Press, 1998

110. King, Mike, 'Art and the Postsecular,' *Journal of Visual Art Practice,* February 2004

111. Naifeh, S. and Smith, G.W., *Jackson Pollock: An American Saga,* London: Pimlico, 1992, p. 337

112. Lipsey, Roger, *An Art of Our Own: The Spiritual in Twentieth-Century Art,* Boston and Shaftesbury: Shambhala, 1988, p. 17

113. Another is: Sluyter, Dean, *Cinema Nirvana: Enlightenment Lessons from the Movies,* New York: Three Rivers Press, 2005

114. Beattie, Tina, *The New Atheists: The Twilight of Reason & The War on Religion,* London: Darton, Longman and Todd, 2007, p. 157

115. Hitchens, Christopher (ed.), *The Portable Atheist: Essential Readings for*

the Nonbeliever, London: Da Capo Press, 2007, p. 351

116. Hitchens, Christopher, *God is Not Great: How Religion Poisons Everything*, New York and Boston: Twelve, 2007, p. 286

117. Dick, Philip K., *Valis*, New York: Vintage Books, 1991

118. Dennett, Daniel C., *Breaking the Spell: Religion as a Natural Phenomenon*, London: Penguin Books, 2007, p. 43

119. Caputo, John D., *On Religion*, London and New York: Routledge, 2001

120. www.crosscurrents.org/caputo.htm, last accessed on 24 May 2008

121. Lyotard, Jean-Francois, *The Postmodern Condition: A Report on Knowledge*, Manchester: Manchester University Press, 1984, p. xxiv

122. Levinas, Emmanuel (trans. Alphonso Lingis), *Totality and Infinity*, Pittsburgh, PA: Duquesne University Press, 1969, p. 43

123. Popper, Karl, *The Open Society and Its Enemies, Vol. 1: Plato*, London: Routledge, 1973

124. Levinas, Emmanuel (trans. Alphonso Lingis), *Totality and Infinity*, Pittsburgh, PA: Duquesne University Press, 1969, p. 45

125. Levinas, Emmanuel (trans. Alphonso Lingis), *Totality and Infinity*, Pittsburgh, PA: Duquesne University Press, 1969, p. 46

126. Levinas, Emmanuel (trans. Alphonso Lingis), *Totality and Infinity*, Pittsburgh, PA: Duquesne University Press, 1969, p. 48

127. Levinas, Emmanuel (trans. Alphonso Lingis), *Totality and Infinity*, Pittsburgh, PA: Duquesne University Press, 1969, p. 210

128. Levinas, Emmanuel (trans. Alphonso Lingis), *Totality and Infinity*, Pittsburgh, PA: Duquesne University Press, 1969, p. 212

129. Derrida, Jacques, *Writing and Difference*, London and New York: Routledge, 1978, p. 100

130. Derrida, Jacques, *Writing and Difference*, London and New York: Routledge, 1978, p. 101

131. Derrida, Jacques, *Writing and Difference*, London and New York: Routledge, 1978, p. 102

132. Derrida, Jacques, *Writing and Difference*, London and New York: Routledge, 1978, p. 102

133. Derrida, Jacques, *Writing and Difference*, London and New York: Routledge, 1978, p. 183

134. Derrida, Jacques, *Writing and Difference*, London and New York: Routledge, 1978, p. 191

135. Derrida, Jacques, *Writing and Difference*, London and New York: Routledge, 1978, p. 192

136. Levinas, Emmanuel, 'God and Philosophy' in Hand, Sean (ed.), *The Levinas Reader*, Oxford: Blackwell, 1989, p. 167

137. Levinas, Emmanuel, 'God and Philosophy' in Hand, Sean (ed.), *The Levinas Reader*, Oxford: Blackwell, 1989, p. 186

138. Milbank, John, Pickstock, Catherine and Ward, Graham (eds.), *Radical Orthodoxy: A New Theology*, London: Routledge, 1998

139. Beattie, Tina, *The New Atheists: The Twilight of Reason & The War on Religion*, London: Darton, Longman and Todd, 2007, p. 145

140. Reno, R.R., 'The Radical Orthodoxy Project' in *First Things*, vol. 100, February 2000, pp. 37-44

141. Habermas, Jürgen, and Ratzinger, Joseph, *The Dialectics of Secularization*, San Francisco: Ignatius Press, 2006
142. Blond, Phillip, 'Emmanuel Levinas: God and Phenomenology' in Blond, Phillip (ed.), *Postsecular Philosophy: Between Philosophy and Theology*, London and New York: Routledge, 1988, p. 209
143. Dawkins, Richard, *Unweaving the Rainbow*, London: Penguin, 1998, p. 41
144. Dennett, Daniel C., *Breaking the Spell: Religion as a Natural Phenomenon*, London: Penguin Books, 2007, p. 262
145. Stenger, Victor J., *God, the Failed Hypothesis: How Science Shows That God Does Not Exist*, New York: Prometheus Books, 2007, p. 39
146. McGrath, Alister, *The Twilight of Atheism: The Rise and Fall of Disbelief in the Modern World*, New York, London, Toronto, Sidney and Auckland: Doubleday, 2004, p. 227
147. Collins, Francis, *The Language of God: A Scientist Presents Evidence for Belief*, London: Pocket Books, 2007, p. 24
148. Jacoby, Susan, *Freethinkers: A History of American Secularism*, New York: Metropolitan Books, 2004, p. 194
149. de Beauvoir, Simone, *The Second Sex: A Study of Modern Woman*, London: Jonathan Cape, 1972, p. 120
150. de Beauvoir, Simone, *The Second Sex: A Study of Modern Woman*, London: Jonathan Cape, 1972, p. 96
151. de Beauvoir, Simone, *The Second Sex: A Study of Modern Woman*, London: Jonathan Cape, 1972, p. 633
152. de Beauvoir, Simone, *The Second Sex: A Study of Modern Woman*, London: Jonathan Cape, 1972, p. 468
153. Graves, Robert, *The Greek Myths*, London: Penguin, 1992
154. Stone, Merlin, *When God was a Woman*, Orlando, FL: Harcourt, 1976, p. xvi
155. Stone, Merlin, *When God was a Woman*, Orlando, FL: Harcourt, 1976, p. xx
156. Taken from *the Revised English Bible*.
157. Baring, Anne, and Cashford, Jules, *The Myth of the Goddess: Evolution of an Image*, London: Arkana, 1993, p. 456
158. Baring, Anne, and Cashford, Jules, *The Myth of the Goddess: Evolution of an Image*, London: Arkana, 1993, p. 429
159. Shlain, Leonard, *The Alphabet Versus the Goddess: The Conflict Between Words and Images*, Penguin / Compass, 1998, ch. 1
160. Gimbutas, Marija, *The Language of the Goddess: Unearthing the Hidden Symbols of Western Civilization*, New York: Thames and Hudson, 1989, p. xx
161. Stone, Merlin, *When God was a Woman*, Orlando, FL: Harcourt, 1976, p. xxv
162. Starhawk, *The Spiral Dance: A Rebirth of the Ancient Religion of the Great Goddess*, San Francisco, CA: HarperSanFrancisco, 1999, p. 4
163. Starhawk, *The Spiral Dance: A Rebirth of the Ancient Religion of the Great Goddess*, San Francisco, CA: HarperSanFrancisco, 1999, p. 8
164. Starhawk, *The Spiral Dance: A Rebirth of the Ancient Religion of the Great*

Goddess, San Francisco, CA: HarperSanFrancisco, 1999, p. 49

165. Irigaray, Luce, *Between East and West: From Singularity to Community*, New York: Columbia University Press, 2002, p. 4
166. Irigaray, Luce, *Between East and West: From Singularity to Community*, New York: Columbia University Press, 2002, p. 5
167. Irigaray, Luce, *Between East and West: From Singularity to Community*, New York: Columbia University Press, 2002, p. 23
168. Irigaray, Luce, *Between East and West: From Singularity to Community*, New York: Columbia University Press, 2002, p. 39
169. Clarke, J.J., *Oriental Enlightenment: The Encounter Between Asian and Western Thought*, London and New York: Routledge, 1997
170. Loy, David, *Nonduality: A Study in Comparative Philosophy*, New York: Humanity Books, 1998
171. Irigaray, Luce, *Between East and West: From Singularity to Community*, New York: Columbia University Press, 2002, p. 73
172. Irigaray, Luce, *Between East and West: From Singularity to Community*, New York: Columbia University Press, 2002, p. 37

Reflections and Conclusions (p. 229-247)

1. Select Committee on BBC Charter Review Second Report, Session 2005-2006, available at: www.publications.parliament.uk/pa/ld200506/ldselect/ldbbc/128/12811.htm last accessed 26 May 2008
2. Taylor, Charles, *A Secular Age*, Cambridge, MA and London: The Belknap Press of Harvard University Press, 2007, p. 171
3. King, Mike, *Secularism: The Hidden Origins of Disbelief*, Cambridge: James Clarke & Co., 2007, p. 42
4. Anonymous; quoted in Dennett, Daniel C., *Breaking the Spell: Religion as a Natural Phenomenon*, London: Penguin, 2006, p. 17
5. Lewis, C.S., *Mere Christianity*, Glasgow: Collins, 1989, p. 24
6. Collins, Francis, *The Language of God: A Scientist Presents Evidence for Belief*, London: Pocket Books, 2007, p. 24
7. Harris, Sam, *Letter to a Christian Nation*, New York: Vintage Books, 2008, p. 108
8. Dawkins, Richard, *Unweaving the Rainbow*, London: Penguin, 1998, p. 17
9. Dawkins, Richard, *Unweaving the Rainbow*, London: Penguin, 1998, p. 17
10. Dawkins, Richard, 'God's just too small', *Times Higher Educational Supplement*, 29 October 2004
11. McGrath, Alister, *The Twilight of Atheism: The Rise and Fall of Disbelief in the Modern World*, New York, London, Toronto, Sidney and Auckland: Doubleday, 2004, p. 181
12. Krishanmurti, J., *The Only Revolution*, New York and Evanston, IL: Harper and Row, 1970, p. 123
13. Dawkins, Richard, *Unweaving the Rainbow*, London: Penguin, 1998, p. 49
14. Taylor, Charles, *A Secular Age*, Cambridge, MA and London: The Belknap Press of Harvard University Press, 2007, p. 701

Bibliography

Abram, David, *The Spell of the Sensuous*, New York: Vintage Books, 1997

Amis, Martin, *The Second Plane: September 11, 2001-2007*, London: Jonathan Cape, 2008

Baring, Anne, and Cashford, Jules, *The Myth of the Goddess: Evolution of an Image*, London: Arkana, 1993

Barrow, John D. and Tipler, Frank J., *The Anthropic Cosmological Principle*, Oxford: Clarendon Press, 1986

Beattie, Tina, *The New Atheists: The Twilight of Reason & The War on Religion*, London: Darton, Longman and Todd, 2007

Bhabha, H. and Tazzi, O., *Anish Kapoor*, Berkeley, CA, Los Angeles and London: University of California Press, 1998

Blond, Phillip (ed.), *Post-secular Philosophy: Between Philosophy and Theology*, London and New York: Routledge, 1988

Bloom, Allan, *The Closing of the American Mind: How Higher Education has Failed Democracy and Impoverished the Souls of Today's Students*, London: Penguin, 1987

Bohm, D., *Wholeness and the Implicate Order*, London: Ark Paperbacks (Routledge), 1980

Brody, Hugh, *The Other Side of Eden: Hunters, Farmers, and the Shaping of the World*, New York: North Point Press, 2000

Bruce, Steve, *God is Dead: Secularization in the West*, Oxford: Blackwell, 2002

Bucke, R.M., *Cosmic Consciousness: A Study in the Evolution of the Human Mind*, London: Olympia Press, 1972

Bucke, R.M., *Walt Whitman*, Philadelphia, 1883

Caplan, Mariana, *Halfway Up the Mountain: The Error of Premature Claims of Enlightenment*, Prescott, AZ: Hohm Press, 1999

Capra, Fritjof, *The Tao of Physics* (3rd Ed.), London: Flamingo, 1992

Caputo, John D., *On Religion*, London and New York: Routledge, 2001

Celant, Germano, *Anish Kapoor*, Milan: Charta, 1998

Chadwick, Owen, *The Secularization of the European Mind in the Nineteenth Century*, Cambridge: Cambridge University Press, 1975

Clarke, Chris, *Ways of Knowing: Science and Mysticism Today*, Exeter: Imprint Academic, 2005

Clarke, J.J., *Oriental Enlightenment: The Encounter Between Asian and Western Thought*, London and New York: Routledge, 1997

Collins, Francis, *The Language of God: A Scientist Presents Evidence for Belief*, London: Pocket Books, 2007

Cook, Reginald Lansing, *The Concord Saunterer*, Middlebury, VT: Middlebury College Press, 1940

Damasio, Antonio R., *Descartes' Error: Emotion, Reason and the Human Brain*, London: MacMillan, 1996

Davies, Paul, *God and the New Physics*, London: Penguin, 1990

Dawkins, Richard, *Climbing Mount Improbable*, London: Penguin, 2006

Dawkins, Richard, *The God Delusion*, London: Black Swan, 2007

Dawkins, Richard, *The Selfish Gene*, Oxford and New York: Oxford University Press, 1992

Dawkins, Richard, *Unweaving the Rainbow*, London: Penguin, 1998

de Beauvoir, Simone, *The Second Sex: A Study of Modern Woman*, London: Jonathan Cape, 1972

Dennett, Daniel C., *Breaking the Spell: Religion as a Natural Phenomenon*, London: Penguin Books, 2007

Derrida, Jacques, *Writing and Difference*, London and New York: Routledge, 1978

Dick, Philip K., *Valis*, New York: Vintage Books, 1991

Einstein, Albert, *The World as I See it*, New York: Citadel Press, 1998

Elder, Jennifer, *Different Like Me: My Book of Autism Heroes*, London and Philadelphia, PA: Jessica Kingsley Publishers, 2006

Ferguson, Marilyn, *The Aquarian Conspiracy: Personal and Social Transformation in Our Time*, New York: G.P. Putnam's Sons, 1987

Ferrer, Jorge N., *Revisioning Transpersonal Theory: A Participatory Vision of Human Spirituality*, Albany, NY: State University of New York Press, 2002

Feuerbach, Ludwig, *The Essence of Christianity*, New York: Prometheus Books, 1989

Flew, Antony, *There is a God: How the World's Most Notorious Atheist Changed His Mind*, New York: HarperOne, 2007

Freke, Timothy, and Gandy, Peter, *The Jesus Mysteries: Was the "Original Jesus" a Pagan God?*, New York: Three Rivers Press, 1999

Gamwell, Lynn, *Exploring the Invisible: Art, Science and the Spiritual*, Princeton, NJ: Princeton University Press, 2002

Gell-Mann, Murray, *The Quark and the Jaguar*, London: Abacus, 2002

Gimbutas, Marija, *The Language of the Goddess: Unearthing the Hidden Symbols of Western Civilization*, New York: Thames and Hudson, 1989

Golding, John, *Paths to the Absolute: Mondrian, Malevich, Kandinsky, Pollock, Newman, Rothko, Still*, Princeton, NJ: Princeton University Press, 2000

Goswami, Amit, *Self-Aware Universe: How Consciousness Creates the Material World*, New York: Jeremy P. Tarcher, 1993

Gould, Stephen Jay, *Rocks of Ages*, London: Jonathan Cape, 2001

Graves, Robert, *The Greek Myths*, London: Penguin, 1992

Gray, John, *Black Mass: Apocalyptic Religion and the Death of Utopia*, London: Allen Lane, 2007

Grayling, A.C., *Against All Gods: Six Polemics on Religion and an Essay on Kindliness*, London: Oberon Books, 2007

Habermas, Jürgen, and Ratzinger, Joseph, *The Dialectics of Secularization*, San Francisco: Ignatius Press, 2006

Haddon, Mark, *The Curious Incident of the Dog in the Night-Time*, London: Definitions, 2004

Hand, Sean (ed.), *The Levinas Reader*, Oxford: Blackwell, 1989

Harding, D.E., *The Hierarchy of Heaven and Earth*, Gainesville, FL: University Presses of Florida, 1979

Hardy, Jean, *A Psychology with a Soul*, New York: Routledge and Kegan Paul, 1987

Harris, Sam, *Letter to a Christian Nation*, New York: Vintage Books, 2008

Harris, Sam, *The End of Faith: Religion, Terror, and the Future of Reason*, London: The Free Press, 2006

Hawking, Stephen, *A Brief History of Time*, London: Guild Publishing, 1988

Hayward, Jeremy, *Shifting World, Changing Mind: Where the Sciences and Buddhism Meet*, Boston and London: Shambhala, 1987

Heelas, Paul and Woodhead, Linda, *The Spiritual Revolution: Why Religion is Giving Way to Spirituality*, Oxford: Blackwell Publishing, 2005

Heelas, Paul, *The New Age*, Oxford and Malden: Blackwell Publishers, 1996

Henderson, Linda Dalrymple, *The Fourth Dimension and Non-Euclidean Geometry in Modern Art*, Princeton, NJ: Princeton University Press, 1983

Hitchens, Christopher (ed.), *The Portable Atheist: Essential Readings for the Nonbeliever*, London: Da Capo Press, 2007

Hitchens, Christopher, *God is Not Great: How Religion Poisons Everything*, New York and Boston: Twelve, 2007

Hollick, Malcolm, *The Science of Oneness: A Worldview for the Twenty-First Century*, Ropley: O Books, 2006

Humphrys, John, *In God We Doubt: Confessions of a Failed Atheist*, London: Hodder & Stoughton, 2007

Irigaray, Luce, *Between East and West: From Singularity to Community*, New York: Columbia University Press, 2002

Jacoby, Susan, *Freethinkers: A History of American Secularism*, New York: Metropolitan Books, 2004

James, William, *The Varieties of Religious Experience*, Middlesex: Penguin Books, 1986

Jefferies, R., *The Story of My Heart*, London: MacMillan St Martin's Press, 1968

Jung, C.G., *Memories, Dreams, Reflections*, London: Fontana, 1993

Kant, Immanuel, *Critique of Judgement*, New York: Hafner Press, 1951

King, Mike, *Secularism: The Hidden Origins of Disbelief*, Cambridge: James Clarke & Co., 2007

Kramnick, Isaac (ed.), *The Portable Enlightenment Reader*, London:

Penguin, 1995

Krishanmurti, J., *The Only Revolution*, New York and Evanston, IL: Harper and Row, 1970

Laszlo, Ervin, *Science and the Akashic Field: An Integral Theory of Everything*, Rochester, VT: Inner Traditions, 2004

Lennox, John, *God's Undertaker: Has Science Buried God*, Oxford: Lion, 2007

Lerner, Michael, *The Left Hand of God: Taking Back our Country from the Religious Right*, New York: HarperSanFrancisco, 2006

Levinas, Emmanuel (trans. Lingis, Alphonso), *Totality and Infinity*, Pittsburgh, PA: Duquesne University Press, 1969

Lewis, C.S., *Mere Christianity*, Glasgow: Collins, 1989

Lipsey, Roger, *An Art of Our Own: The Spiritual in Twentieth-Century Art*, Boston and Shaftesbury: Shambhala, 1988

Lodge, David, *Consciousness and the Novel*, London: Secker and Warburg, 2002

Lodge, David, *Thinks...*, London: Penguin, 2001

Lorimer, David, *Radical Prince: The Practical Vision of the Prince of Wales*, Edinburgh: Floris Books, 2003

Loy, David, *Nonduality: A Study in Comparative Philosophy*, New York: Humanity Books, 1998

Lutyens, M., *The Life and Death of Krishnamurti*, London: Rider, 1991

Lyotard, Jean-Francois, *The Postmodern Condition: A Report on Knowledge*, Manchester: Manchester University Press, 1984

Martin, David, *On Secularization: Towards a Revised General Theory*, Aldershot: Ashgate, 2005

Maslow, A., *Religions, Values and Peak-Experiences*, Harmondsworth: Penguin Arkana 1970

McEwan, Ian, *Enduring Love*, London: Vintage, 1998

McEwan, Ian, *Saturday*, London: Jonathan Cape, 2005

McGrath, Alister, *Dawkins' God: Genes, Memes, and the Meaning of Life*, Oxford and Victoria: Blackwell, 2005

McGrath, Alister, *The Dawkins Delusion?: Atheist Fundamentalism and the Denial of the Divine*, London: SPCK, 2007

McGrath, Alister, *The Twilight of Atheism: The Rise and Fall of Disbelief in the Modern World*, New York, London, Toronto, Sidney and Auckland: Doubleday, 2004

McTaggart, Lynne, *The Field*, London: Element, 2003

Mesibov, Gary B., Shea, Victoria and Adams, Lynn W., *Understanding Asperger Syndrome and High Functioning Autism*, New York, Boston, Dordrecht, London and Moscow: Kluwer Academic / Plenum Publishers, 2001

Milbank, John, Pickstock, Catherine and Ward, Graham (eds.), *Radical Orthodoxy: A New Theology*, London: Routledge, 1998

Muir, John, *Letters to a Friend, 1866-1879*, Boston and New York: Houghton Mifflin Company, 1915

Muir, John, *My First Summer in the Sierra*, Edinburgh: Canongate, 1988

Naess, Arne (trans. and ed. Rothenberg, David), *Ecology, Community and Lifestyle*, Cambridge: Cambridge University Press, 1989

Naifeh, S. and Smith, G.W., *Jackson Pollock: An American Saga*, London: Pimlico, 1992

Nanamoli, Bhikku and Bhodi, Bhikku, *The Middle Length Discourses of the Buddha: A New Translation of the Majjhima Nikaya*, Boston: Wisdom Publications, 1995

Onfray, Michel, *In Defence of Atheism: The Case against Christianity, Judaism and Islam*, London: Serpent's Tail, 2007

Pagels, Elaine, *The Gnostic Gospels*, New York: Vintage Books, 1979

Perlmutter, Dawn, and Koppman, Debra (eds.), *Reclaiming the Spiritual in Art: Contemporary Cross-Cultural Perspectives*, Albany, NY: State University of New York Press, 1999

Pirsig, Robert M., *Lila: An Enquiry into Morals*, London: Black Swan, 1991

Polkinghorne, John, *Reason and Reality: The Relationship between Science and Theology*, London: SPCK, 1991

Popper, Karl, *The Open Society and Its Enemies, Vol. 1: Plato*, London: Routledge, 1973

Rawlinson, Andrew, *The Book of Enlightened Masters: Western Teachers in Eastern Traditions*, Chicago and La Salle, IL: Open Court, 1997

Redfield, James, *The Celestine Prophecy: An Adventure*, London: Bantam, 1994

Ricoeur, Paul, *Freud and Philosophy: An Essay on Interpretation*, New Haven, CT and London: Yale University Press, 1970

Rowan, John, *The Transpersonal*, London: Routledge, 1993

Russell, Bertrand, *Mysticism and Logic*, London: George Allen and Unwin, 1963

Saunder, Frances Stonor, *Hidden Hands*, London: Channel 4 Television, 1995

Scholem, Gershom, *Major Trends in Jewish Mysticism*, New York: Schocken Books, 1995

Schopler, Eric and Mesibov, Gary B. (eds.), *High-functioning Individuals with Autism*, New York and London: Plenum Press, 1992

Schrödinger, Erwin, *What is Life?*, Cambridge: Cambridge University Press, 2007

Schumacher, E.F., *A Guide for the Perplexed*, London: Abacus, 1978

Sheldrake, R., *A New Science of Life: The Hypothesis of Formative Causations*, London, Glasgow, Toronto, Sidney and Auckland: Paladin Grafton Books (Collins), 1985

Shlain, Leonard, *Art and Physics: Parallel Visions in Space, Time and Light*, New York: Quill William Morrow, 1991

Shlain, Leonard, *The Alphabet Versus the Goddess: The Conflict Between Words and Images*, Harmondsworth: Penguin / Compass, 1998

Sluyter, Dean, *Cinema Nirvana: Enlightenment Lessons from the Movies*, New York: Three Rivers Press, 2005

Smith, Graeme, *A Short History of Secularism*, London, New York: I.B. Tauris & Co. Ltd, 2007

Starhawk, *The Spiral Dance: A Rebirth of the Ancient Religion of the Great Goddess*, San Francisco, CA: HarperSanFrancisco, 1999

Steiner, R., *The Course of My Life*, New York: Anthroposophic Press, 1986

Stenger, Victor J., *God, the Failed Hypothesis: How Science Shows That God Does Not Exist*, New York: Prometheus Books, 2007

Stone, Merlin, *When God was a Woman*, Orlando, FL: Harcourt, 1976

Swinburne, Richard, *The Existence of God* (2nd Ed.), Oxford: Clarendon Press, 2004

Tacey, David, *The Spirituality Revolution: The Emergence of Contemporary Spirituality*, Hove and New York: Brunner-Routledge, 2004

Taylor, Charles, *A Secular Age*, Cambridge, MA and London: The Belknap Press of Harvard University Press, 2007

Tillich, Paul, *Dynamics of Faith*, New York: Harper Torchbooks, 1957

Tuchman, Maurice (ed.), *The Spiritual in Art: Abstract Painting 1890-1985*, New York, London and Paris: Abbeville Press Publishers (Los Angeles County Museum of Art), 1986

Tucker, Mike (ed.), *Alan Davie: The Quest for the Miraculous*, Brighton: University of Brighton Gallery (Lund Humphries), 1993

Tucker, Mike, *Dreaming with Open Eyes: The Shamanic in Twentieth Century Art and Culture*, London: Aquarian / HarperSanFrancisco, 1992

Updike, John, *Self-Consciousness: Memoirs*, London: Penguin, 1990

Wallace, B. Alan, *Choosing Reality: A Buddhist View of Physics and the Mind*, Ithaca, NY: Snow Lion Publications, 1996

Wallace, B. Alan, *Embracing Mind: The Common Ground of Science and Spirituality*, Boston and London: Shambhala, 2008

Walsch, Neale Donald, *Conversations with God: Book One*, London: Hodder and Stoughton, 1995

Walsh, John (ed.), *Bill Viola: the Passions*, Los Angeles: The J. Paul Getty Museum in association with The National Gallery, London, 2003

Ward, Keith, *Is Religion Dangerous?*, Oxford: Lion, 2006

Watson, Peter, *A Terrible Beauty: The People and Ideas that Shaped the Modern Mind*, London: Phoenix, 2000

Weiss, Peg, *Kandinsky and Old Russia: The Artist as Ethnographer and Shaman*, New Haven, CT and London: Yale University Press, 1995

White, Michael, *Isaac Newton: The Last Sorcerer*, London: Fourth Estate, 1998

Wilber, Ken, *Eye of Spirit: An Integral Vision for a World Gone Slightly Mad*, Boston and London: Shambhala, 1998

Wilber, Ken, *Quantum Questions: Mystical Writings of the World's Great Physicists*, Boston and London: Shambhala, 1985

Wilber, Ken, *Sex, Ecology, Spirituality: The Spirit of Evolution*, Boston and London: Shambhala, 2000

Wilber, Ken, *The Marriage of Sense and Soul*, Dublin: Gateway, 1998

Wilber, Ken, *The Spectrum of Consciousness* (2nd Ed.), Wheaton, IL, Madras and London: Quest Books (The Theosophical Publishing House), 1993

Wolpert, Lewis, *The Unnatural Nature of Science*, London: Faber, 1992

Zohar, Danah, *The Quantum Self*, London: Flamingo, 1991

Zukav, Gary, *The Dancing Wu Li Masters*, London: Fontana, 1979

Index

Printed in the United Kingdom by
Lightning Source UK Ltd., Milton Keynes
141173UK00001B/140/P